W.H. MURRAY
UNDISCOVERED
SCOTLAND

W.H. Murray was born in Liverpool in 1913, but two years later his father was killed at Gallipoli. The family moved back to Glasgow where Murray spent his childhood, school and college years before beginning a career in banking. He made his first climbs in 1934 and later joined a talented group of climbers in the Junior Mountaineering Club of Scotland. This instigated his lifelong love of Scottish winter climbing, and it was with this set of young innovators that Murray began to undertake the adventures that he eventually transcribed on Red Cross toilet paper as a prisoner of war.

After returning to Britain from the camps, Murray once more began to climb with undamaged fervency, and later took part on key Himalayan expeditions of the 1950s. In 1951 Murray was on the critical reconnaissance that established a route up Everest via the Khumbu Icefall by which the summit of Mount Everest would eventually be reached. Marrying happily, Murray built a career as a writer and conservationist, writing *Highland Landscape* a counsel of protection for the National Trust of Scotland. Murray died in 1996, and his autobiography, *The Evidence of Things Not Seen* was published posthumously.

W.H. MURRAY
UNDISCOVERED
SCOTLAND

CLIMBS ON ROCK, SNOW AND ICE

Vertebrate Publishing, Sheffield
www.v-publishing.co.uk

W.H. MURRAY
UNDISCOVERED
SCOTLAND

First published by Dent, London, in 1951.
This edition first published in 2022 by Vertebrate Publishing.

Vertebrate Publishing
Omega Court, 352 Cemetery Road, Sheffield S11 8FT.
www.v-publishing.co.uk

A CIP catalogue record for this book is available from the British Library.

9781839811692 (Paperback)
9781910240298 (Ebook)

10 9 8 7 6 5 4 3 2 1

Produced by Vertebrate Publishing.

Contents

1

The Undiscovered Country

The exploratory urge moves every man who loves hills. The quest of the mountaineer is knowledge. He is drawing close to one truth about mountains when at last he becomes aware that he never *will* know them fully – not in all their aspects – nor ever fully know his craft. Like the true philosopher, the true mountaineer can look forward with rejoicing to an eternity of endeavour: to realization without end. I have climbed for fifteen years and have hopes of another forty, but I know that my position at the close of my span will be the same as it is now, and the same as it was on that happy day when I first set foot on a hill – the Scottish highlands will spread out before me, an unknown land.

The yearning to explore hills was born in myself in 1934, when I, a confirmed pavement-dweller, overheard a mountaineer describe a weekend visit to An Teallach in Ross-shire. He spoke of a long thin ridge, three thousand feet up, with towers and pinnacles and tall cliffs on either flank, which fell to deep corries. And from these comes clouds would boil up like steam from a cauldron, and from time to time shafts would open through them to reveal vistas of low valleys and seas and distant islands.

That was all he said, but the effect on myself was profound, because for the first time in my life my exploratory instincts began to stir. Here was a strange new world of which I had never even dreamed, waiting for exploration. And unlike so many other dreams, this was one that could be realized in action. At the first opportunity, then, I went to one of the few mountains I knew by name – the Cobbler at Arrochar. It was a fine April day, with plenty of snow on the tops. When I stood by the road at Arrochar and looked up at my first mountain, the summit seemed alarmingly craggy and blinding white against blue sky. How I should ever get up I could not imagine. I picked out a route by the line of a burn, which vanished towards a huge corrie under the summit rocks. And what then? I felt a nervous hesitation about my fate in these upper regions. Had I been entering the sanctuary of Nanda Devi I could have felt no more of the sheer thrill of adventure than I did when I stepped off that road on to the bare hillside.

Later in the day, when I entered the Cobbler corrie, I recognized that I *had* entered what was, for me, true sanctuary – a world of rock and snow and glossy ice, shining in the spring sun and, for the moment at least, laughing in the glint and gleam of the world's joy. I too laughed in my sudden awareness of freedom. Had I thought at all I should have said: 'Here is a field of free action in which nothing is organized, or made safe or easy or uniform by regulation; a kingdom where no laws run and no useful ends fetter the heart.' I did not have to think that out in full. I knew it instantaneously, in one all-comprehending glance.

And, of course, this intoxicated me. For it was a great day in my life. And at once I proceeded to do all those wicked things so rightly denounced by grey-bearded gentlemen sitting at office desks in remote cities. I climbed steep snow-slopes by myself. Without an ice-axe or nailed boots, without map, compass, or warm and windproof clothing, and, what is worse, without a companion, I kicked steps up hard snow, going quite fast and gaily, until near the top I stopped and looked down. The corrie floor was now far below me, and black boulders projected out of the snow. If I slid off nothing would stop me until I hit something. I went on with exaggerated caution until I breasted the ridge between the centre and south peaks.

At that first success a wave of elation carried me up high walls of sun-washed rock to the south peak. That rock had beauty in it. Always before I had thought of rock as a dull mass. But this rock was the living rock, pale grey and clean as the air itself, with streaks of shiny mica and white crystals of quartzite. It was joy to handle such rock and to feel the coarse grain under the fingers.

Near the top the strangeness of the new environment overawed me a little – nothing but bare rock and boundless space, and a bright cloud sailing. Nothing here but myself and the elements

– and a knowledge of my utter surrender to and trust in God's providence, and gladness in that knowledge.

On the flat rocks on top I sat down, and for an hour digested all that had happened to me. In being there at all I had, of course, sinned greatly against all the canons of mountaineering. But I did not know that. This was my Garden of Eden stage of purest innocence. It was not till later, when I plucked my apple in search of knowledge, that I read in text-books 'Man must not go alone on mountains' – not when he is a bootless novice. Meantime I looked out upon the mountains circling me in a white-topped throng, and receding to horizons that rippled against the sky like a wash of foam. Not one of these hills did I know by name, and every one was probably as worth exploring as the Cobbler. The shortness of life was brought home to me with a sudden pang. However, what I lacked in time might in part be offset by unflagging activity.

From that day I became a mountaineer.

Upon returning home and consulting books I learned that there are five hundred and forty-three mountain-tops in Scotland above three thousand feet. They cannot all be climbed in one's first year. This thought did make me feel frustrated. I once received a book after waiting long and eagerly for its publication. Like a wolf coming down starving from the mountains I gulped the courses in any order, reading the end first, snatching bits in the middle, running here and there through the pages in uncontrolled excitement. I wanted to know it all immediately. In the end I was sufficiently exhausted to sit back and read whole chapters at a time. That was exactly how I felt about mountains.

In my first year I sped all over Scotland – going alone because I knew no one else who climbed – snatching mountains here, there, and everywhere. As it happened I could not have made a better approach. The best and natural way of dealing with mountains is the way I luckily followed: before starting any rock-climbing I spent a summer and winter on hill-walking only. Rock-climbing, as a means of penetrating the inmost recesses and as sport, should not come until later. Thus I made a wide reconnaissance by climbing several peaks in each of the main mountain districts.

This preliminary survey gave me a good idea of their differences in character, which are surprisingly wide, and showed what each had to offer.

When I went from the rolling plateaux and snow-domes of the Cairngorms, mounted among broad forests and straths, to the sharp spiky ridges of Wester Ross, set between winding sea-lochs, I had the sensation peculiar to entering a foreign country; a sense not to be accounted for by any material changes in scenery, but one that is none the less shared by all men. I can travel from Inverness to Sussex and feel only that I have moved from one part of Britain to another. But Wester Ross is another (and better) land. Again, when I came from the Cuillin pinnacles and the stark isles of the west to the heathery swell of the southern highlands I returned from vertical desert to grassland, although still hungering like a camel after its dear desert.

Between such different areas Glencoe and Lochaber held a fair balance. They had everything: peak, plateau, precipice, the thinnest of ridges, and green valley, all set between the widest of wild moors and a narrow sea-loch – they were Baghdad and Samarkand, at once home and goal of the pilgrim.

Then I joined a mountaineering club. For the course of that first year's wanderings showed plainly that no man can have the freedom of mountains unless he can climb on rock and snow. The mountains are under snow for several months of the year. Indeed, they excel in winter, offering a sport and beauty quite different from those of summer, a sport harder and tougher, and a more simple and pure beauty. The plateaux and the summit ridges, the great cliffs and the snow-slopes, these are four facets of the Scottish mountains none of which can be avoided, except the cliffs, and these only if a man is content to walk on mainland tops.

In the Cuillin of Skye the rocks are not a facet, they are the mountains. Cliffs must not be thought of as blank cliffs. They are cathedral cities with many a spire, tower, turret, pinnacle, and bastion, amongst which a man may wander at will, and explore and adventure, upon which he may test qualities of character and skill, and by aid of which conquer nothing except himself.

In succeeding years the wider my experience grew the more clearly did I see that however much I might explore this unknown country called the Scottish highlands, I should never plumb the Unknown. To know mountains we must know them at the four seasons, on the four facets, at the four quarters of the day. The permutations are infinite. For the variations in snow and ice and weather conditions are inexhaustible. No winter climb, say on the north face of Nevis, is ever the same twice running. Its North-East Buttress, for example, is on each visit like a first ascent. If we go to the Comb of Arran in autumn frost, on a day of still, crisp air when distant moors flame red through a sparkle of hoar, we shall not recognize it as the mountain we knew when clouds were scudding among the crags and the hail drove level. I have been a hundred times to the top of Buachaille Etive Mor in Glencoe. In unwise and sentimental moments I am apt to think of it as an old friend. But I know full well that the next time I go there the Buachaille will surprise me for the hundred and first time – my climb will be unlike any that I've had before.

Treasures of reality yet unknown await discovery among inaccessible peaks at the ends of the earth, still more on the old and familiar hills at our very doorstep, most of all within each mountaineer. The truth is that in getting to know mountains he gets to know himself. That is why men truly live when they climb.

That heightened quality of life on mountains naturally enough came foremost to my mind in war. In 1942 I made an after-dinner speech in the middle of the Libyan Desert. The toast of 'Mountains' had been put to me by a young German with whom I shared the meal. In my reply I managed to say all that I have to say about mountains in three sentences. But first of all let me explain how the situation arose.

Just one hour before I had been sitting in the bottom of a slit-trench. My battalion had been whittled down to fifty men, and we were waiting, with the rest of our brigade, for an attack at dusk by the 15th Panzer Division. My battalion commander, with the perfect frankness that such gentlemen have, had said to me: 'Murray, by tonight you'll be either dead meat or a prisoner.' Thus

I sat in the bottom of my slit-trench and went through my pockets with the purpose of destroying anything that might be of use to an enemy. I smashed a prismatic compass, tore up an identity card and my notes on battalion orders. Then I came upon an address book. I flicked over the pages and read the names. And suddenly I saw that every name in that book was the name of a mountaineer. Until then I had never realized how great a part mountains had played in my life. Most of the names belonged to men who are very much alive and active today. While I read over them I also realized, again for the first time, how much I had learned from these men, and been given by them, and how little I had been able to give in return. The same had to be said of mountains. And while I sat in the trench I had a clear perception of the two ways of mountaineering that mean most to me.

The first is the exploratory way, the way of adventure and battle with the elements. I could see storm winds and drift sweeping across the plateau; long hours of axe-work on ice, among sunless cliffs; the day-long suspense on rocks that have never before been scratched by nails. These show the harsh aspects of reality, of which a man should know – of which he must know if he'd know mountains and know himself. Rock, snow, and ice sometimes claim from a man all that he has to give. Sometimes the strain on body and nerve may be high, discomforts sharp. But the mountaineer gets all the joy of his craft; his mastery of it is, in reality, the mastery of himself. It is the foretaste of freedom.

I made no effort to think in that trench. Ideas came and went of their own accord in a matter of seconds. I saw the other aspect of mountaineering – for the sake of mountains and not for sport. I could see a great peak among fast-moving cloud, and the icy glint where its snows caught the morning sun. There were deep corries and tall crags. All of these were charged with a beauty that did not belong to *them*, but poured through them as light pours through the glass of a ruby and blue window, or as grace through a sacrament. These show an ideal aspect of reality, of which a man should know, of which he *must* know if he would arrive at any truth at all about mountains, or about men.

At dusk the German tanks came in. When the shambles had ended a German tank commander took charge of me. It was bright moonlight. He waved a machine pistol at me and asked, in good English, if I didn't feel cold. Now the desert at night is often exceedingly cold, and without thinking I said: 'It's as cold as a mountain-top.' And my German said: 'Good God! do you climb?'

He was a mountaineer. We exchanged brief notes about mountains we knew and liked in Scotland and the Alps. After that there was no end to what he would do for me. He gave me his overcoat, and asked when my last meal had been. I said: 'Thirty-six hours ago.' So he took me over to his tank and produced food. We shared a quick meal of British bully and biscuits and German chocolate. After that he fetched out a bottle of British beer and knocked off the top.

'Here's to mountains,' he said, 'and to mountaineers – to all of them everywhere.' He took a pull at the bottle and passed it to me. I drank too. I felt moved to reply.

I said: 'There are three good things you get out of mountains. You meet men and you meet battle and beauty. But the men are true, and the battle's the only kind that's *worth* fighting, and the beauty is Life.'

I smashed the bottle on the German tank.

2

The First Day on Buachaille

Three years in central European prison camps. Release, April 1945.

During the fine weather of May I was unable to climb. At first if I walked for more than ten minutes I felt faint, and so felt no desire of mountains. My love of them was platonic, requiring of the body no act of outer expression. Four weeks later a first instalment of accumulating energy began to clamour for employment. My last climb in 1941 had been the Buachaille Etive Mor, and my first now could be none other. That is, if I could get up, which was exceedingly doubtful. My thoughts flew at once to Mackenzie. He was back in Glasgow. If any man could get me up Buachaille he could. So to Glasgow I went on 2nd June 1945.

After six years of war I could see no change at all in the Mackenzie – still lean and upright, hawk-eyed and brusque. He too was keen to get back to Glencoe. He had spent the last year or two in the School of Mountain Warfare, but not once had he enjoyed a good rock-climb. I told him gently that he could not get one now if he went with *me*. We must go up by the easiest possible route, go very slow, and not seriously expect to get to the top.

We left Glasgow in my old pre-war Morris eight very early in the morning. And a well nigh perfect morning it was. As the sun spread over Rannoch the genuine golden air of the good old days spread over the miles of moor (I had begun to wonder if my memories of such days were simple feats of imagination), and the liveliness of all spring mornings again entered into me. I felt now as Mackenzie always used to feel when the first snow of October came on the hills – days when MacAlpine drove us north from Glasgow, usually under rain clouds that boded ill for the weekend, but which had no damping effect on a Mackenzie wild with enthusiasm. His first sight of the snow-capped hills in Glencoe would conjure forth song and piercing whistles. 'Bound along, Archie! – or the snow will be away before we get there!' and similar exhortations inspired the driver.

So I ventured to suggest to Mackenzie that we must aim after all at getting to the summit. No half measures would do on a day like this. I would get to the top or drop dead trying. We came round the famous bend from the Blackmount – and there was Buachaille.

The day was again 8th September 1935, when the final entry in my diary reads: 'I think that for me the most vivid experience was my first view of Buachaille Etive Mor. In the clear morning air every detail of the enormous, pointed cliffs stood out sharp. But the most striking moment was turning a corner of the road and seeing the great shape, black and intimidating, suddenly spring up in the moor. To me it was just unclimbable. I had never seen a hill like it before and my breath was taken away from me.'

Days of innocence! Maybe. But that was precisely how I felt now. As always before, we went straight to Coupall Bridge in Glen Etive, put on our boots, and started. It is the great advantage of this starting-point, as against that from Altnafeadh in Glencoe, that the long approach over the moor is lightened by the shape-liness of the peak, inspiring one from the front, drawing one on and up. Every crag and each long ridge points to the summit-cone. It is a symbolism not lost on the climber. What delight to the eye that was! To see again all the detail of the rocks, every crag of which I knew so well. The delight of recognition – a recognition of form, beauty, character, the lines of weakness and strength, every wrinkle, pit, and scar, on cliffs dove-grey and terracotta. From a distance only is the Buachaille black.

An avoidance of the cliffs, such as we contemplated, now see-med to me miserably inappropriate. Surely we might manage to get up an easy rock-climb? A very easy one – say Curved Ridge, if we roped? I made the suggestion somewhat timorously, for I feared to burden Mackenzie with a hundred and forty pounds of human baggage. He agreed and grinned. We changed direction slightly. The moor was drier underfoot than I ever remembered it – our very boots took on an unaccustomed bloom to the brush of old heather, and the swish, swish of the boots was a song of old, an heroic poetry and new live drama all rolled into one after the dead mud of the prison compounds. I reminded myself from time to time that I was free to go in any direction I wanted. I could turn right round and go right home. Glorious thought! So on I went, breathing in great draughts of moorland air, a free man with a free wind blowing on his right cheek, and sun smiting his left, the scent of the year's new thyme at his nostril, and the swish of dry heather round his boots. Rock in front. I stopped. 'Bill,' I said, 'maybe we could manage Central Buttress?'

'Ha! *now* you 're talking!' exclaimed Mackenzie. 'We could manage it if we kept to a V-diff.' We changed direction.

We scrambled upwards over heathery outcrops to the base of Central Buttress, and moved rightward to the north face. We roped. I hesitated for a moment over the bowline knot, but tied it first time. I was greatly relieved. It would have embarrassed the Mackenzie to have had to tie it for me. He started up the first pitch and ran out about sixty feet. Then he turned and was ready for me. Now was the test. I looked at the rock, light-grey, crystalline, very rough – and so very steep. I stood back and chose my holds. What would happen? Was the old skill lost? – rock-climbing a thing of the past? I gave myself, as it were, a prod, and climbed.

At the very instant my hands and feet came on the rock six years rolled away in a flash. The rock was not strange, but familiar. At each move I was taking the right holds at the right time – but no, I did not 'take' the holds – of their own accord they *came* to me. Hand, foot, and eye – nerve and muscle – they were co-ordinating, and my climbing was effortless. I reached the top feeling trust in rock and, what in the circumstances was far more wonderful, trust in myself. And also, I should add, gratitude for the Mackenzie, from whom ten years ago I had learned much of my rock-snow-ice climbing.

The lower part of the north face goes up by a series of rough walls to the Heather Ledge, which divides the buttress about three hundred feet up. The last wall on this lower part is split near its top by a short crack at a high angle. The crack was my next important test – the test for exposure. For although the holds are good the body is forced out of balance over a long drop. When I came to make the move it certainly scared me, but the point was that I could control myself. I got up. The true testing question, of course, for progress in rock-, snow-, or ice-craft is not 'Did you get up?' but rather 'Did you *enjoy* getting up?' – if not always just as the moves are made, then very shortly afterwards. I was able to answer 'Yes' to my test, with the appropriate qualification. This meant that we could safely deal with the steeper and more difficult upper buttress.

We had a choice of four routes and I left the decision to Mackenzie. He chose his own Slanting Ledge route, which starts right in the middle of the buttress. This would certainly be less exacting than a continuation by the north face climb, the difficulties being not less in standard or exposure, but shorter in length.

On Heather Ledge we lay back and rested a while. It is the great merit of Central Buttress that it faces south-east – the sunniest cliff in Glencoe and Glen Etive. And Heather Ledge is a balcony, wide of prospect and fit for philosopher kings, where the governments of the earth are measured against the government of the firmament, and fall into perspective, and are made humble. To me, on the Heather Ledge, the fruits of the first were pitiful masses of humanity still crowding the barbed-wire compounds of Europe, and of the other, the mountain world. Everything that is wide and boundless and free, and which is therefore dear to the heart of a mountaineer, is here exemplified; the skies seem vaster than elsewhere, stretching to horizons too far to be identified. The very winds blow more fresh and clean. They purify – give health and life and power to the souls of men imprisoned in flesh and bone and long walled-up in the concrete of the barrack cities. They are purifying winds of the free firmament. To their influence aspire multitudes of men, ringed by the red-rusted wire of mud compounds, beyond and below the rim of the horizon, where governments of the earth sow and harvest. To such men they are true symbols of the winds of the spirit.

All men do not like mountains. It may be that many hate them. But they all love the free adventure and beauty to be found on mountains – or should I say to be won?

'Time's up!' said Mackenzie. We walked to the highest point of Heather Ledge. On the nearly perpendicular face above, a ledge ran forty feet diagonally left. We climbed without much difficulty to its top end, where we turned a corner on to a face somewhat less steep. This wall had good holds, on which we climbed until the increasing angle forced Mackenzie to make a long right traverse on rocks little less than vertical, and most exposed (as much so as anything on Rannoch Wall). He halted; then climbed straight up, advancing slowly and obviously having trouble in getting suitable holds. I remembered that on the first ascent eight years ago Mackenzie had nailed the pitch twice. But that was during a rain-storm in the late afternoon, and the pitons had been removed. I watched him closely, saw him resist the temptation to hug the rock, and deliberately force his body away from it, so that he could go up in balance on holds that were not good enough for the grasping and wrestling technique so fatally comforting to the unpractised climber. His rope hung clear of the rock, swaying towards me in a white and rifled curve, beautiful in the sun. A rain-bleached rope – pre-1939, I reckoned, on which wartime moths had dined too well. However, it would hold a second man. The Mackenzie vanished – upwards.

My third test was at hand. A very difficult and exposed pitch at a high angle. I did not pass this one with flying colours.

When I made the right traverse and looked up I felt as weak as a kitten – the drop, the angle, the lack of holds – frightening! but healthily frightening, and not like lying flat in a midnight cellar listening to a bomb whistling down like a grand piano, nor like going into a bare room to chat with the Gestapo – here one had chosen the route, was free to act sharply amid sunny rock and air, to rely on oneself. I remember Mackenzie's studied self-mastery, and pushed myself out from the rock. The moment I committed this act of trust everything went well. Up I went, treading precisely, taking my press-holds for the hands in the right relation to feet and angle. But I confess that I had to do this at high tension with set teeth. I could no more have led that pitch than flown in the air.

What a reaction that was when I reached the top! I mean the

rejoicing and being able to give thanks for it all – the joys of coarse-grained rock sun-warmed to the hand and firm to the bite of the boot-nail, the elation of mastering nervous limbs and of flooding their muscles with energy, of using them in a practised craft, fighting, winning – and sharing such adventure with a friend.

'What did you think of that?' asked Mackenzie when I joined him.

'Not bad,' I said. 'Best climb for years.'

'Now, are you telling me!' exclaimed Mackenzie. 'Indeed – who would have thought that!'

'Best climb I've had too,' he added a minute later.

Our climbing was by no means done, however. A stretch of easier rocks led to the top of the buttress, whence we traversed north on to Curved Ridge. I suggested that we now descend a little and climb the Crowberry Ridge Direct, but Mackenzie employed his veto. He swore he was feeling too tired. It is not like my Herr Mackenzie to be so tactful! It is rather his appalling habit to speak the truth *always*. Yet on this occasion I wonder …

So up we went by the Curved Ridge, and then by the Crowberry Tower, at last to plod rhythmically over the last brow to the cairn. I knew well how every stone on the cairn should look, and for a moment was wrathful to see that a few had been rolled away. Still, it was just the same cairn, and I clapped my hand on its top, suddenly remembered the blank despair with which I had last made the same movement, and laughed to myself at the folly of such days; for despair is only for the very young or the very old, and either way it is still foolish. I looked out to Schichallion eastwards, and followed the north horizon round to Mull in the west. All was as it should be. I had returned. I knew these hills so very well that they startled me into no transports of ecstasy – not even after long absence – but they had the greater power to bestow a content that I cannot name, save in terms that must seem vague to any one without a practical knowledge of them – the Re-collection and the Quiet. Peace, one might call it? – but again, how many men do know what peace is, as against the sympathetic experience of dimly perceiving it outwith themselves? Not many,

I fear. It might then be asked whether I mean that mountains are necessary to happiness or to the true completion of any man. Quite to the contrary. So little are they necessary that one of the happiest years of my own life was one of three spent in a prison camp. It would seem that whether mountains contribute to happiness or its reverse depends entirely upon a man's own attitude of mind and heart. They contribute happiness in so far as they elicit a man's love, at first it may be only of themselves, but in the end of the All of which they are just a part.

However, it is fatal (and impossible) for a man to be philosophic about such love at the time of union. The heart and will leap out to it, his mind grasps. In a second it is done. That is all.

'The one thing that matters among mountains,' said Mackenzie, looking out to blue and receding hill-ranks in the north-west, 'is that we enjoy them.'

Simple words. Greatly overlooked. They embody the whole secret of successful mountaineering.

3

The Great Gully of Garbh Bheinn

Since the beginnings of mountaineering in Scotland Garbh Bheinn of Ardgour has presented a double challenge to climbers: hard access and virgin cliffs. Ardgour has always been relatively unknown country, lying far to the west across Loch Linnhe – one of the greatest sea-lochs in Scotland; thus hardly accessible at weekends. In addition, being one of the best rock-peaks in Scotland and yet so rarely visited, Garbh Bheinn has remained rich in unsolved problems for the rock-climber. In 1946 the most notorious of these problems was the Great Gully. Its earliest history had, in broad outline, been much like that of the Chasm and Clachaig Gully of Glencoe. It had repelled assault over a long term of years, been declared impossible by a past generation of climbers, and finally been once again declared impossible so late as 1946.

The first notable attempt was by Messrs. Hastings and Haskett-Smith in 1897. They were defeated before the halfway point by an eighty-foot cave-pitch, bristling with overhangs. Subsequent parties met the same fate, so that around this pitch there settled a magic halo of impregnability. At close quarters the halo might intimidate, but at long distance it flashed like a lure. While I entertained no foolish hope of having skill enough to climb that gully, still – it was unknown – a gully presenting a challenge. Response had to be made. On 8th June 1946 good weather and a strong party set me westward bound for Ardgour. My companions were Douglas Scott and R.G. Donaldson.

On passing Glencoe village we had our first view of our mountain across Loch Linnhe, from which it rose two thousand nine hundred feet. By virtue of form rather than height it dwarfed all the other hills of Ardgour. A splendid rock-buttress, twelve hundred feet high, gave a free and noble lift to the summit. That clean grey tower, standing between a silver tide-rip and a dappled sky, was our battleground for the morrow. When we looked closely we could see the dark score of the Great Gully directly under the summit, splitting the buttress from top to bottom.

We crossed Loch Leven by the Ballachulish ferry and Loch Linnhe by the Corran ferry, and then drove seven miles south to Garbh Bheinn. That evening we camped in the lower part of Coire an Iubhair, a trackless glen running for two and a half miles beneath the eastern face of our mountain. A quarter of a mile from the main road we found flat dry ground and plenty of firewood beside the burn; so that we had our supper that night before a log fire at the water's edge.

The site was ideal. The true mountain atmosphere was ours. We were ringed by hills; all around us their crests stood in relief against the clear night sky. The burn flashed and glowed to the leap of flame from the fire. And there was neither sight nor sound of civilization. There was no distraction. Thus we had true contact with the hills; not the mere physical contact of sight or touch, but an effortless sharing or mingling of their presence and ours. That is the direct communion, which we lose utterly amid the distractions of hotels, barely sense in the traffic of hut or hostel, and know truly in a camp or bivouac. When at last we fell asleep before the open door of our tent we did so with a feeling of intimate friendship with mountains, the product of which, being unsought for itself, was happiness.

The dawn broke from a clear sky. At nine o'clock, however, we walked two miles up Coire an Iubhair under locally gathering cloud. Showers and sunshafts struck us alternately, and long wreaths of mist curled and swayed around the summit of Garbh Bheinn. Behind this dark veil the rock of our buttress looked most forbidding and inaccessible. But after we had reached the upper corrie, from which the final peak springs in one great cliff, the clouds lifted and the sky turned blue. The party now split. Donaldson wanted to reconnoitre the only once climbed North Buttress a mile farther up Coire an Iubhair, reckoning the collection of data for a new route there to be more profitable than our visit to Great Gully; for Scott and I were not so audacious at this stage as to say that we were going to climb the Great Gully. We were only going to look at it. At 11.30 we moved into its foot.

The first two hundred and fifty feet were easy and featureless, and we preferred to scramble unroped up the rocks of the north flank, until a sudden deepening of the gully warned us to traverse in. We climbed a high but easy pitch, then the gully deepened, widened, and at last was divided by an almost vertical rib of a hundred feet. The right-hand branch was a mere cleft with wet walls, steep as the rib itself. So we tried the broader left branch; but this started with an overhang on which we both fought and failed. The preliminary skirmish and repulse had one good effect: it woke us up. We put on the rope and metaphorically spat on our hands. I tried to climb the rib. The rock was a coarse gneiss, and came clean to the finger-tips; but after thirty feet the already scanty holds became too few and far between, movements of body too difficult to calculate in advance, so that the chance to traverse into the right-hand cleft came as a providential relief – to be quickly regretted when I entered the damp and dim interior and looked around. The inner wall was green with loathsome growing things, and the side walls moistly sleek, clean enough, but perpendicular.

Scott joined me on a narrow grass ledge. The remaining seventy feet of the cleft looked ugly, but when put to the trial gave me holds nearly all the way; when they failed I bridged – back on one wall and feet braced hard against the other – and wriggled up. The cleft ended suddenly on a thin saddle attached to the central rib on our left. We scrambled over the rib info the left fork, which was now imposingly deep and broad and the true line of the gully. With that cleft in our rear we no longer thought of just looking at the gully. We were going to force a route to the limits of our ability.

A hundred feet of scrambling brought the most notorious pitch of Garbh Bheinn into sight. There was a long level approach, allowing time for its full, disconcerting effect on the mind, and allowing the gully to bite into the cliff, at last to rise up in one eighty-foot step – a step not merely vertical, but starting with a sixty-foot overhang. The flanking walls appeared to lean towards the centre. One would have sworn they were unclimbable. People had thought so for fifty years: they would think so for another fifty. That was our first verdict.

We walked to the foot of the pitch and adopted tactics that once had proved of high value to me in the Clachaig Gully: we did not look at the rock for several minutes – we had lunch. During the course of it we developed an awareness that the left wall was not truly overhanging; it was only vertical with a bulge in the middle. I at once abandoned lunch and climbed to the bulge on in-cut holds. Then the holds gave out, and I had to come down. We resumed our lunch.

There remained the right-hand wall, the lower half of which truly did overhang. We munched bread and cheese and looked at that wall contemplatively. If one started sixty feet out from the inmost cave, possibly one might climb the overhang by means of a projecting flake, then make an upward traverse above the line of the overhang to the top. Any such move would be very hard and exposed, and the rock was slabby. I took off my boots and started in stocking-soles.

Two strong arm-pulls on the flake took me up the first overhang, only to be faced with a second but lesser one. Again providence supplied a jug-handle hold on rock that would otherwise have been hopeless. Many a party capable of climbing that wall must have turned away in the past without a trial. The route selection became hard. One had to find a way through the local bulges by balancing delicately across slabs and pushing upwards by shallow grooves. When sixty feet up I became alarmed by the holdlessness of the rock, and halted on a tuft of grass. I had already climbed the height of a city building and the next forty feet looked worse than anything below; it might easily be too much for me, and my ability to climb down was becoming suspect. Such uncertainty of the issue makes a first ascent seem very much harder than any subsequent one. Knowing this, I refused to scare myself further by thinking about hazards ahead, and henceforth lived only from one move to the next. By making good each hand and foothold as it came to me, I duly found myself at the top of the pitch. I had run out a hundred feet of rope and was only two yards from the gully-bed. The climb had not been more than severe.

Scott climbed in boots, and I should lead in boots on a future occasion. Meantime we rested a while in one of those exhilarating situations in which the upper part of the Great Gully abounds. Wide rock walls framed the sunlit summits across Loch Linnhe – the high sweep of the Lochaber plateaux, the pointed Mamores, and the swell of Appin. The land was pure and fresh after the swift showers of the morning; its myriad hues were clear despite their delicacy; deep-toned in the shadows, bright in the sun. For this was the spring sun 'that strikes branch into leaf and bloom into the world.'

Body and mind, we had been wakened up by that rock climb, and its demand for a full vigour and alertness; and so now the beauty of scene awakened us in spirit. We relaxed and rested, with a much more joyful awareness than at any earlier time that day of our good fortune in treading this earth. Below us the supreme obstacle had been vanquished, but up above there remained all the promise of the unknown upper gully, and outwards the broad lands glowing in the paradisaic light. Here, one could have sworn, on a planet such as this there could hardly be sin or suffering, and certainly not disease. The light fell warm and glowing and the things of the earth shone in their full response. We as men, as beings one with that universal whole, and on no account making any choice for ourselves of separation, shared in the full health of its glory. Where there is union there cannot be disharmony, and where there is wholeness – there alone and to the full we have happiness.

The scene below was nothing but a sign, I fear, of things that may be, but as such it gave us cause enough to rejoice, and the faint foretaste of participation, which to beings as weak as ourselves, seemed strong in all excellencies. Men may live and die even in the distant recollection of such promise, and be of good cheer whatever befalls. For the Way is before them and the End assured, if that is their will.

Once again Scott and I turned to our rock climb. We could not guess what lay ahead; for although the gully continued several hundred feet, the alignment of the walls prevented our seeing into it. The day would go hard with us now if we met defeat. I could not help reflecting that our baseless and chronic optimism, so frequently justified on long climbs in the past, must one day draw to its term, and our bluff be called. Shortly after the resumption the gully narrowed to an open chimney, where the route went forty feet up the slabby left wall. For a few dreadful minutes I thought that our final check had come, simple as the pitch appeared, because Scott, now leading, failed to get up. And he is a climber from whom I have a great deal to learn. As one might imagine in the circumstances I took to these slabs in a most energetic and business-like manner, which was luckily what they required. The holds were small and delicate, but they had to be used determinedly. After a short struggle I reached the top. Scott had only been off form and followed with ease. I breathed again.

Thereafter a long stretch of scrambling brought us to the main fork, about two hundred feet from the top. The true continuation of the gully was the left branch, the last hundred feet of which sprang up in a vertical chimney, capped by an overhang. Our success here would necessitate a very special dispensation of good luck, in no way inferior in quality to that enjoyed by us at the Great Cave. That we should receive such a blessing twice in the same day, even in the same year, was not to be imagined. However, we summoned up our energies once more and tried again to look determined. The walls were sheer and three feet apart. I accounted for the first seventy feet by leaning my back upon one wall and using foothold on the other, until eventually I came under the overhang – a projecting rectangular block, tilting down. At this very point the walls had become too wide to allow me to jam myself back and foot. For nearly half an hour I experimented with ways and means for attempting a direct ascent over the front of the block, but the holds were just not there. The sheer drop underneath me forbade the chancy tactics of 'smash and grab.' One may sometimes force slabs and walls in a movement unaided by visible hold, employing a technique called 'balance-climbing'; but on overhangs the laws of gravity are inexorable. 'Find holds,' they say, 'or fall.' And their still small voice is persuasive. Had there been one good hold on that block I could have pulled myself over it, but alas, there was none. I eased myself cautiously down.

In the right-hand branch we could see no difficulties, indeed no climbing of any interest, but right beside us, in the centre of the fork, stood a tall buttress of pale and beautiful rock. The craggy frankness of its face captivated our hearts; so we stood back and selected a route up it. The cliff was a hundred and fifty feet high. Scott led. We went fifty feet up its right-hand side, until holdless rock forced us into a long left traverse, at the midway point of which the rounding of an awkward rib made us swing out over space on the strength of an under-cut hold – a delightful out-of-balance movement. Coarse and reliable rock beyond led us steeply to the top of the Great Gully. Our climb had taken four hours.

We had suffered two minor defeats during the day: at the left-hand wall of the Great Cave and again at the left fork. These defeats have merit; for although the first ascent of the gully has been made, any future climber who can open up the more direct route at the cave and the direct line at the fork will have virtually remade the climb, and transformed a very good gully into an altogether excellent one; the thought that someone may yet enjoy this triumph, that its very possibility is there, gives Scott and me delight.

At the summit of Garbh Bheinn we found Donaldson. If he had inadvertently lost a great climb, he had spent the last hour enjoying one of the great panoramas of Scotland. On the one hand ranged a vast array of the mainland mountains, stretching in line of storm from the farthest north to the south horizon; on the other the Atlantic Ocean and the small isles of the west. This truly is the combination to which the Scottish hills owe all worthiness – rock, water, and the subtle colours of the seaward atmosphere. The part played by heather is small. Our senses were engrossed and our minds won by the free spaciousness of this land – the wide skies and broad waters, a cloud-winged host of mountains, and brisk winds. Such was Ardgour – its freedom and ours.

4

Affric

In all this earth does there live one satisfied climber? It is not possible. If satisfied he would not climb. My winter season of 1945—6, for example, had been extraordinarily successful – every weekend good, without fail! My list of hard climbs done – a satisfying one. Yet I found myself a dissatisfied man in April. Too much time had been spent upon cliffs. Rocks are all very well, I grumbled, but unknown hill-country, where cliffs are admired from a respectful distance and thought of as obstacles to be turned one side or the other by lines of least resistance, *that* kind of country is true mountain-land; its exploration gives to many a man a satisfaction he needs – as deep as he will find on rock if not deeper.

Happily there is no dearth of unexplored hill-country; for it is only necessary that it should not be known to oneself. Now there was one particular bit of country of which I was ignorant, and which had weighed heavy on my conscience for years. I had never been to Glen Affric, never even seen a map of it, nor read as much as a chapter. Rumours reached me of its being the most beautiful of all Scottish glens, and I knew in a vague sort of way that Affric was one of the great hill-passes of north-west Scotland. I knew rather less about it than I knew of some of the Himalayan passes in eastern Tibet. (Although I had not been there either.)

I explained this sorry state of affairs to my friend Donald McIntyre, whom I met one morning in mid-April at Fort William. To my great delight his frame of mind was much like mine. Glen Affric? Yes, he'd love to go there. But did he know anything about it? Well, only that Gladstone had once been taken to the end of Loch Beneveian and there been so affected by the view that he'd raised his top-hat.

'Donald,' I said solemnly, 'how long have you got?'

'About ten days.'

'Well, let's go for seven. But we'll need a tent.'

The man most likely to part with a tent, we calculated, would be the minister of St. Andrew's Church. Our choice of benefactor was an excellent one, for not only did he part with a tent, but finding us also destitute of petrol gave us enough for the sixty-mile journey north. Unluckily no provisions could be bought in Fort William – it was one of the innumerable fast days for which this town is notorious. However, we sped gaily northwards with our tent in a general state of unpreparedness for which a boy scout might have been stripped of his badges. We had one primus stove but no paraffin oil, and although we had matches, this was not by forethought. However, the weather was perfect as only it can be when it has not been considered for one instant.

At Spean Bridge we bought in the oatmeal which was to be our staple diet for seven days (bread for that period is too bulky for a rucksack), also sausage and kipper. Our halt allowed us to look at our map with a planning eye. From Kintail, on the west coast, Glen Affric runs thirty miles north-east to merge with Strath Glass, which continues to the Beauly Firth. The glen and strath form one great pass running coast to coast across the breadth of Scotland. We decided to make for the eastern gateway, where glens Affric and Cannich join Strath Glass. There is a tiny village called Cannich at the junction, where we arrived that night.

We camped at the edge of the River Glass, near the house of Fasnakyle, at the very entrance to Glen Affric. Our curiosity fetched us up early next morning. A touch of frost during the night and cloudless skies at sunrise helped us to get moving quickly. Our unusual plan was to have no plan at all, save to walk fifteen miles up the glen and then see what we could see. As for the rest, we should accept what the gods offered, and do what seemed right in the circumstances. This readiness to receive whatever might befall was a wise policy in view of our lack of supplies and knowledge. In addition, it gave us so marked a sense of freedom as we marched through woods by the River Affric that we wondered whether such an attitude of mind might not be the best for all life. We resolved to sow no troubles for the future by too rigid planning and the setting of our wills against providence.

Our first half-hour's walking was uphill work on a narrow road. Our rucksacks being weighty with seven days' food we were open to any temptation to halt, so that sounds of a waterfall made us turn off the road to the river, which was hiding among trees. Thus our good fortune brought us to sloping rock at the edge of the famous Dog Fall. It is a very short fall. Its fame, we concluded, must lie either in the power and volume of congested water, which hurtles down the throat of a small gorge into a cauldron gouged out of solid rock, or else in its beauty. The power of the fall is indeed extraordinary but not so great as to bring fame of itself. What of its beauty then? So simple that it can scarcely be made intelligible. And therein is the Dog Fall's secret and abounding fascination in the eyes of men: a thick column of water, pulsing with a sort of fierce life; yet seemingly frozen, and white like ice. The fall's frozen curve, combined with that fierce vibration within the curve itself, gripped our minds. For opposite extremes of stillness and motion were made one form. Beauty is born of such a union.

After half an hour's admiration we continued our walk, while the river widened and the glen opened out. There was no leaf on the trees, which in the lower glen are deciduous, so that every branch was bright in the sun's flood and our Golden Road awash. However, no cause had been given us to think Glen Affric superior, say, to Glen Lyon in Perthshire, until a bend in the road brought us on to the shore of Loch Beneveian. Groups of well-grown Scots firs clustered on the banks. Through a clearing came the blaze of sun-struck hills reflected in utterly calm water. Its richness of varied colour gave it the likeness of an ancient stained-glass window, but no window ever glowed like that loch. I had no more doubts of Glen Affric. Its attributes were made manifest.

We continued three miles along the sill of the magic window, then beyond its west end to the broad river. Grassy banks and the sun's heat were there too much to be resisted. I stripped and plunged, swam, and with McIntyre sun-bathed on the grass. Later we pressed on by a second and smaller loch.

Less than a mile beyond, or eight miles from Fasnakyle, we came to the end of the roadway at a whitewashed cottage. I still think this house to be one of the most remarkable in Scotland. It is built on the low ridge dividing Loch Affric (as yet invisible to us) from the small eastern loch by whose banks we had come. White walls fit peculiarly well into the highland environment. They are appropriate. Perhaps the cottage had been newly washed? Because now, in the sun's striking, it shone; the emerald grass before it shone; and the loch shone blue. The house was a focusing point of a shining world. And far back from the open strath and its wide-stretching waters and far-spaced pines, mountains, snow-capped, shone in the blue of the sky. All were focused in the eye of the white cottage: a wholeness of mountain scene.

A house standing alone in wild country always appeals profoundly to McIntyre and me. It suggests to us peace, beauty, the perfect freedom from interruption that gives a chance of understanding the things we love. Reason prevents me from picturing a New Eden now, in terms of the concrete. Should I ever do so I should picture something like the stalker's cottage in Glen Affric. My unaided imagination could conceive no more delightful home.

However, such a picture of freedom from worldly concerns is a symbol, not to be mistaken for reality. I often meet people living amid scenes of peace and beauty whose hearts share neither attribute. At first I used to be puzzled, dismayed, and even made miserable at finding them not only dissatisfied with their lot and disgruntled with society, but worse still, given over to disparagement of their neighbours. The breeding of ill will had become a chosen task. But true peace, that blessed by-product of an integrated heart and mind and will, depends on no scenery. It can be had everywhere – when the means are known.

The Affric cottage, I thought, looked well outwardly. Did peace live within? In any event to pass it by without a friendly word would be too barbarous an act. I knocked at the door.

The stalker was out on the loch, but his sister welcomed us with a most charming kindliness. No trace of ill will in this house! She hailed us into a clean and spotless kitchen, and gave us hot buttered scones and tea, and thoughtful concern for our prospects out in the glen. We, in return, gave news of the outside world, which seemed not too choice an offering. The outside world might call the cottage in Affric 'far from civilization,' when, in fact, it is one of civilization's first fruits.

We went on our way by a rough track winding through stone, tree, and heather above the northern shore of Loch Affric. The hill scene had greatly changed: we were right in among high mountains. The snow-peaks of Sgurr na Lapaich, Mam Soul, and Cairn Eige rose close above us to the north-west. This change had been a gradual one, but a more abrupt change, affecting the whole character of the glen, occurred at the west end of Loch Affric. We had travelled fifteen miles to the mid-way point. That eastern half had been a perfect combination of mountain, wood, and loch; the western half was perfect deer-forest – treeless. Before us stretched bare grassy moorland and the thin thread of a river winding between snow-peaks.

We pitched our tent on a high bank by the river. We had arrived. On every hand were mountains that we had never seen before, and of which we knew nothing. They looked delightfully mysterious. That night was bitterly cold and starry, with a touch of ground frost. On the other hand, we had plenty of wood, and ate a piping-hot meal beside a good fire. Having no plates we ate straight out of the pot, keeping pace with each other in spoonfuls. In its detail this way of feeding gives illuminating glimpses into a man's character. A valuable essay could be written on the subject, with a long and learned title.

Our next day's plan was to get a bird's-eye view of the whole area, so that we might know better what we were about; to this end we climbed Mam Soul and Cairn Eige, which are both above three thousand eight hundred feet. Again the day was cloudless, and we looked down upon a dappled sea of mountains extending from the Cairngorms to the Cuillin. Close at hand, to the west, Sgurr nan Ceathreamhnan (pronounced *Kerranan*) looked a most alluring hill: a far-flung mountain of ten tops and five great corries, all spattered with snow. It dominates the whole of this part of Scotland through its strategic position on the watershed; for its rivers feed both the North Sea, by way of Affric and Cannich, and the Atlantic by the River Elchaig. The highest source of the Elchaig lies well up towards the summit of Ceathreamhnan, and this tributary flows straight down to the Hidden Falls of Glomach on the north-west foothills. The falls are famed as the longest in Britain, being three hundred and fifty feet. They and the mountain lie in the middle of an almost uninhabited part of Scotland, and are thus difficult to reach and unfrequented. Our plan, then, for the morrow should be to traverse the long crest of Ceathreamhnan, find this source of the Elchaig, and trace the stream down to the falls. That would give us a round of twenty miles.

We made our descent over Sgurr na Lapaich. On the following morning I rose at dawn and crawled out of our thin tent into a thick white ground mist. But so light was this bank in its upper fringe that the reddened snow-dome of Sgurr nan Ceathreamhnan towered through it to heights that human imagination would never have dared to raise it. That is a not unusual effect of mist; but the usual effects were exaggerated by the contrast of its shining whiteness against the crimson crown. The crown was stereoscoped against a saxe-blue sky, which gave to its impossible height an appearance of reality that overwhelmed me. If we or any other humans weighed down with the clumsiness of flesh and bone should ever walk over the crest of that red flame in the sky we should surely be shrivelled up like moths. Yet mid-day found us walking three miles along that crest, which had materialized as hard and stony ground with cold snow lying in pockets. Below us to the west were a maze of sea-lochs.

After we had crossed over the summit we had a most fascinating glimpse into the west corrie of Ben Attow, which splits Glen Affric with a six-mile wedge. The corrie was ringed by rock-buttresses, perhaps ten of them, and not one had been climbed.

We passed over the north-west top, and descended two miles beside the river until the valley floor fell away from our feet in a great cliff, at the left side of which the Falls of Glomach went roaring over. But what constituted their 'hiddenness'? We peered over the edge and caught a glimpse of a great gorge. The falls were indeed invisible. The cliff to the right of the falls was exceedingly steep, yet we thought it might be climbable, and lowered ourselves tentatively over the edge. After coming all this way we must see the waterfall! We had climbed down sixty feet when our position became dangerous. The rocks were loose and rotten, and the falls still invisible behind a projecting column. An attempt to round that column was needful, but invited disaster. We turned and climbed back to the top.

The right-hand side of the gorge was a precipitous slope crossed by tilted ledges. On these ledges we were able to traverse far out until the whole of the Hidden Fall was revealed. The water came over the cliff in one bound of a hundred feet, hit a crag, and split into two falls, which made the final bound of two hundred and fifty feet. At the bottom a dark, deep cauldron was clouded by grey spray soaring high. The two long leaps of water struck the rock with a roar and rebounded. A fearsome sight, it lacked the beauty of the tiny Dog Fall of Glen Affric. None the less one could watch it for hours; the beat, the roar, the long white flash, spray soaring – they hypnotize the mind: one slips into reverie and time wings on.

We bestirred ourselves after an hour and returned to the cliff top. On our ten-mile walk back to camp a flight of wild swans gave us escort, flying from loch to loch as we passed through the glen.

We rose early next morning, being now in excellent training. I think that on any other occasion we should have gone to explore the rocks in that western corrie of Ben Attow. Instead we felt a peculiarly strong desire to explore Glen Cannich. I wondered what awaited us there. Accordingly we crossed the high pass between Mam Soul and Sgurr nan Ceathreamhnan to the upper part of Glen Cannich, which turned out to be treeless like its Affric counterpart; and like Affric the scene completely changed by the time we had gone four miles down to Loch Mullardoch. We had re-entered woodland. Most surprising of all, countless lizards idled on the road or darted across. I had not imagined that lizards in quantity were to be found in Scotland.

Halfway down Loch Mullardoch, just before we came to Cozac Old Lodge, we began to look for a good camp site, and saw a broad, tree-grown point projecting into the loch. At the toe of the point we found a most wonderful site. A big carpet of grass lay between a wooded knoll and a shingly beach. The water was still, deep blue, splashed by white patches of reflected snow-mountain. We pitched the tent and found beside us unlimited supplies of dried bracken for kindling and sticks for fuel. Day and night we enjoyed a red and roaring fire for our meals.

The following day was again hot and cloudless. We stripped off our shirts and sun-bathed all morning on the soft grass by the tent. I swam in the loch occasionally, but for the most part we just looked. The loch being absolutely smooth, reflections were brilliant, the white of each peak sharp amidst the blue. The mountains started from the water, dazzling us like those of the sky. The sunlike beauty of the scene radiated through the eye and mind, evaporating mental lethargy. We felt alive and alert and at one with the whole environment.

After looking out to the hills and water for a whole morning I noticed that while their radiant power of beauty grew their outer form ceased to matter. What indeed did it matter if a hill-slope ran this way or that, or a copse stood here or there? The foreground, in fact, was conspicuous by its absence, and the farther shore cut the middle of the picture: much of aesthetics was shown to be a vain rationalizing after the event. From the mountain-land burst a power of beauty subject to no bond of reason. The material aspect or vehicle had performed its service, and now effaced itself. I saw and recognized an imageless beauty, of which material things are outward signs, receiving from it their being and manifesting it as their purpose.

Next day we struck camp, and withdrew ten miles to Strath Glass. Instead of narrowing the field for future exploration our days in the two glens had expanded that field immeasurably. So that I am still not a satisfied climber – and know that I never will be. Life is short, the mountain infinitely high, but the route goes.

5

Twisting Gully

It was a dark, wet night in December 1946. Douglas Scott and I peered through the wind-screen of our car to see the croft of Altnafeadh, at the east end of Glencoe, loom up through the drizzle. We parked the car under the lee of the byre, and started down the quarter-mile track to Lagangarbh Cottage, which belongs to the Scottish Mountaineering Club. I had a bad cold in the head, and should never have been there at all had we not agreed to meet Jim Cortlandt Simpson at Lagangarbh.

'And the trouble is,' I said, as we picked our way by torchlight, 'that Jim has come six hundred miles for a good climb – something hard and icy. God help us. He 'll be bursting with enthusiasm. He *always* is.'

'He'll just have to burst,' grunted Scott.

A lamplight emerged from the cottage and moved quickly towards us. It was Simpson, bursting with enthusiasm. We shook hands vigorously all round, and swore through the haze of rain that this was a joyful moment.

'What shall we climb tomorrow?' asked Simpson eagerly. 'Do you think Crowberry Gully would go? Perhaps the snow will be good high up. *Or* we might climb something new?'

'Crowberry Gully is out,' I said firmly, 'and new routes are *right* out, and I'm nearly out too. If we do anything at all we shall do something very gentle and soothing – something nice.'

Scott, I knew, was grinning through the darkness. But in a little while we were roasting before a great fire in the kitchen and drinking Simpson's hot soup. Mountains began to seem less forbidding. Simpson certainly *was* in good form. However detachedly I might regard his warmth of spirit the fact was that I could feel it thawing out the closed parts of my mind.

'The whole of Glencoe is smothered in a wet blanket,' I said. 'We won't get a good climb at this end of the glen – the climbs don't lie high enough. Snow will be just slush. But we might get a climb on Bidean nam Bian. After all, it's three thousand seven hundred feet, and Coire nan Lochan nearly three thousand. It often has good snow and ice when there's thaw everywhere else.'

'You get a big choice of climbs in Coire nan Lochan,' assented Scott. 'Everything from easy to impossible. We'd better go there.'

Simpson agreed.

We went early to bed. I prayed earnestly for a pouring wet morning so that we might lie long. But the weather turned dry in the morning and Simpson had us up at dawn. Before midday we reached the rim of Coire nan Lochan, the great north-east corrie of Bidean. The two lochans had vanished under a thick snow-quilt. The shapely peak of Stob Coire nan Lochan rose to our left side among lowering cloud. Its northward-running ridge faced us across the corrie with four buttresses and gullies, all about five hundred feet high. The rocks were heavily snowed up, and the glint of ice could be seen here and there. My own contribution to the day's decision was purely negative.

'Whatever we do,' I said, 'let's rule out everything difficult. I could never get up a hard pitch.'

We examined the cliffs in silence for a few minutes, then Scott drew our attention to a great unclimbed groove on the left flank of South Buttress. It was a narrow and shallow gully with a slight twist in the lower half. In neither winter nor summer had a route been made there. It did seem to be a line of weakness on an otherwise unpromising cliff. About one hundred feet up a small crag divided the gully. In the right fork was a monstrous pitch of white ice. The left fork was no more than a chimney of twenty feet petering out on the buttress. It looked vertical, but then we were looking at it *en face*, which would make the angle seem worse than it was. We could form no sure idea of its difficulty without closer examination. We accordingly crossed the corrie and moved up to its foot.

My head was still heavy with cold and I felt like death. Thus

I had no intention of climbing that gully: I went only to look at it. The old familiar phrase should have warned me. Meantime every advantage was to be gained by climbing as far as the fork, if no farther. We should at least garner information for future use. I refused the lead and tied myself to the rear end of the rope. Scott went first. From the start he found himself involved in step-cutting on a steep, hard slope. Solid chips began to bounce off my head and shoulders. The South Buttress rose sheer on our right and our eyes were led upwards along lines of shallow grooves, which might conceivably be climbed in summer. It was that faint suggestion of weakness, the invitation of it, that made them seem so unspeakably ugly. The rock had a vertical stratification, dull black but frosted; the snow was bleak and without sparkle, the ice lustreless. The buttress on our left was much more heavily snow-covered on the crest, being at a lesser angle, but all that we could see of it now was the bare wall of its flank, partly overhanging.

All our hopes thus flowed in the gully-bed, drawn by the moon of reason, by whose light angles seen *en face* are lessened. But the ebb-flow set in at the fork. The true line of the gully twisted rightward under a down-plunging crag of the left buttress. The twist took the form of a mammoth icicle, not snow-ice, but frozen water, opaque, glossy, and as far as we could see fifty feet high – there might be more above. At a guess I should say the angle was seventy-five degrees. The leader of any attempt on such severe ice would have to spend on it one and a half hours' one-handed cutting, and even the followers would have trouble. I have no doubt that my silent dissent crept up the rope and affected Scott. Strongly held feelings, although unexpressed, are conveyed unerringly round the party on a hard climb. Scott turned away from the ice-pitch and looked at the left fork.

We were now able to confirm that this left fork was not truly a fork. The buttress protruded a crag sideways, and the 'fork' was merely a short vertical chimney running up the angle towards the crest. The chimney was completely choked with soft snow, and its black walls were slightly ice-glazed. Simpson thrust his axe into the hard snow beneath and belayed the rope, while Scott tried to force the chimney. He very nearly reached the sloping slabs at the top. I could see his hand hurriedly groping for non-existent holds. Then the angle beat him and he came down. However, his work changed the whole course of the day, for his excavations in the chimney had revealed an unsuspected cave almost halfway up. It was small – no more than a hole, but a hole big enough for a man to stand in. That opened up fresh possibilities. For one thing it gave a perfect stance and belay for the second man. Simpson climbed up and disappeared head first into the cave. He managed to right himself somehow, and at last his enthusiastic face appeared at the window. He beamed and directed the battle. Whatever happened, the party as a whole was now secure, and Scott made a most determined assault on the upper chimney. He neared the top and was motionless there for a long time, while his fingers searched sensitively over every inch of reachable rock. But again hold was refused him; he had to come down before strength failed.

Simpson, meanwhile, had been staring out of his window on to the left wall of the gully, which overhung. He could see what I below could not see well – that an out-dipping ledge, steeply banked with soft snow, ran ten feet across the overhang to the outer face of the buttress. He drew my attention to this interesting fact. The question was: could a man edge his way along the soft snow of that ledge *despite* the out-thrust of the overhang above him? And then, what would the crest of the buttress be like? It was invisible. There could be no answer to these questions without a trial. I did at last begin to feel challenged by the climb. What lies beyond? It is a question a mountaineer cannot resist. My cold in the head would have to be nursed later in the day; meanwhile I began to feel like Epstein's *Adam*, arising mightily from thick bogs of flesh and the world, a man aspiring upwards. Scott must have sensed the change. He asked me to lead.

I grasped my axe and moved up. I still did not propose to myself that I should climb the pitch. I was going to try to traverse that ledge, just to see if it were possible, and to find out what lay beyond – all this for future use. Simpson encouraged me at the outset by making alternative suggestions each time I failed to climb on to the inner end of the ledge. The surrounding rocks lay at awkward angles. The mind had to be gripped and stirred to find ways and means to force on the body. But at last it was done. And yes, it was possible to edge along under the overhang! My only trouble now was whether the soft snow would hold on its out-tilt of rock. The point was doubtful, and only Simpson's perfect stance made me risk the trial. I was not yet above him, and he could hold me with ease if the snow peeled off. Step by step I crept cautiously to the outer edge. Then I stepped round the corner on to a good foothold on the face. The change from a narrow gully to open rocks was too sudden – I felt an unwelcome sense of exposure. The rocks held a shiny glaze of ice where they protruded from the snow of groove and ledge. The buttress plunged to the corrie. However, eyes and nerves quickly adjusted themselves. I studied the rocks in front but their riddle remained unsolved, the answer buried under sheetings of snow-ice. They looked unclimbable, but if I cut the snow away what might not be revealed underneath?

I set to work with the axe, cut a foothold, moved up a step, and made experimental clearings through the ice above me, exposing grey rock and a few glazed holds. They were arranged rather like the direct start to the Holly-tree Wall on Idwal Slabs in Wales. Whether it were possible to make the initial moves, which included raising the body by the down-thrust of a clenched fist on a pocket of rock, while the rocks were frost-bound, was another matter. I made the move, and once made it seemed to me highly desirable not to reverse it. Twisting Gully would have to be climbed today.

On that first ascent of the pitch every move was an unknown quantity. It was not possible to say if the rock were climbable until stripped of its frozen plating. After the first severe moves the rock went well. Sixty feet up I found anchorage in a snow-filled groove. Simpson and Scott joined me. It now seemed to our advantage that we should continue up the buttress for a couple of hundred feet rather than make a more difficult and immediate traverse into the gully. We accordingly cut our way up snowy channels and over short rock-outcrops, swinging first to the left and then back to the right on a long upslant to avoid impending crags, until at length our route converged with the gully, about a hundred and fifty feet from the top.

The gully had now steepened and narrowed to a long throat below the fan-shaped mouth. Snow-ice lay here at a high angle; none the less it was straightforward ice, requiring common skill but uncommonly hard work. A way was carved through it to the final fan. The snow deepened and softened. It lay so heavily in the fan, at so steep an inclination for its bulk, that I began to feel uneasy at thought of its avalanching. I made a track straight up it. At the halfway mark I saw a crack open noiselessly right across the slope. As fast as I could drive myself to move I climbed about fifteen feet above the split and drove in my axe to the head. But the snow seemed to be too well bound to start cascading down the throat of the gully. The shape of the fan served to hold it. In another year, if the snow lies in such bulk, but in bad condition – either too wet or too dry and powdery – the avalanche risk will be real.

Simpson and Scott joined me below the cornice. It overhung throughout its leftward curve, but the rightward half was only vertical. I traversed right and brought Simpson to the base of the snow-wall, where he belayed me and was in turn belayed by Scott. For the snow was soft enough to kick and the holds thus made might break. I moved cautiously up the wall until I could get my forearms over the top, then with a quick jab drove my pick into the tough snow beyond. One pull up – and the climb was done.

Simpson, on arriving, inquired courteously how my cold was keeping. All trace of it had gone, never to return. It had vanished in a matter of minutes while I was dealing with the crux. The concentration of all the nervous and bodily powers to one end had unified the personality and thrown the cold out. I have known the same phenomenon in war, when men would go into action with minor ailments – chills or sickness – and cast them off in a few minutes; also in religious mystics in prayer: and all for this same reason – an integration.

When Scott pulled himself over the edge I could see from his preoccupied eye that our new route was forgotten. He was making a swift all-round search for photographs. But conditions were poor. Loch Linnhe reflected glassily the layers of high grey cloud, the sunless cliffs of Bidean stared frostily across Coire nam Beith, the glens were lifeless, the snows flat, the mountains stripped of every material thing that adorns. They were stark. There was nothing to catch the eye save bare and essential mountain. Perhaps that explains why they looked so mountainously noble. But their undiminished beauty could be caught in no photograph.

Scott looked distressed for a minute, then his face brightened. 'Well,' said he, 'that was a good climb. Four hours up.'

6

Night and Morning on the Mountains

The most acutely difficult expedition to achieve on mountains in this country is a moonlight climb in winter. Not that the difficulties are technical. A full moon among snow-mountains will normally provide visibility of twenty-five miles – if the sky be clear. And that is the root of the problem: to combine leisure with a full moon, a hard frost, and a clear sky. Success needs patience, long and persistent patience.

I had been waiting seven years for a chance of traversing by moonlight the Aonach Eagach, which forms the north wall of Glencoe. Its name, which means the Notched Ridge, is especially given to the rocky crest extending one and a half miles from Am Bodach in the east to Stob Coire Leith in the west. This ridge is the narrowest on the Scottish mainland. Throughout its total length of nearly two miles there can be no escape in winter down its precipitous flank to Glencoe, except at one end or the other. Thus its traverse under a plaster of snow and ice is by day a memorable expedition. By moonlight I hoped for a double ration of mountaineering bliss.

I made my first abortive attempt with Douglas Laidlaw in 1940. The war intervened. But at last the record frost of February 1947 brought the long-sought opportunity. One Saturday evening I arrived at Altnafeadh in Glencoe with Donald McIntyre. We stopped at Lagangarbh cottage for a meal and awaited moonrise. It came up at last over Rannoch Moor, gigantic as a melon – dwarfing the earth. We waited for an hour until it rose well above ground haze, by which time it shrank to normal size and its light power doubled.

Then we set out, not yet for the Aonach Eagach, but for a two-hours' prowl of delight up and down Glencoe. We went first to look at the Buachaille Etive Mor, whose massive towers had a coarse-cut strength and crystal glint: they might have been hewn out of ice. At the other western end of the glen, hovering insubstantially in a crisp, clear sky, the snow-peaks of Bidean nam Bian burned whitely over the dark earth. At ten o'clock we repaired to Altnafeadh. The car's radiator was frozen so that we lost a priceless hour thawing it out. Then we drove to the base of Am Bodach, from the summit of which we might traverse the ridge from east to west and back again. A double traverse was essential, for we planned to be eastward bound at dawn.

We started uphill at 11.30 p.m. The cold was bitter and the wind keen, but we wore kapoc-filled flying-suits, which, although too warm on the way up, would allow us to spend more time to good profit on the crest of the ridge. We came to the summit at three thousand-odd feet about 1.30 a.m. Our eyes were drawn westward to the sharp and sinuous blade of our ridge, when suddenly a blaze of white light from the north made us turn. But we looked in vain. There was nothing there. Then we saw that although the sky was clear, stars were few; while the Lochaber hills to the north were remarkably dim. Everything seemed shrouded by a strange milkiness of atmosphere, for which no cause was seen. Southward of Glencoe, however, the hills were bright.

As we looked north the entire sky again lightened, but again turned dark so swiftly that we doubted our senses. Between us and the mountains of Mamore lay the Leven valley; its bottom invisible to us, its breadth nearly five miles. Across this great gap there suddenly travelled a broad wave of light, which seemed to break like a roller on the crest of our reef, and then stream in a wide, shimmering curtain across Glencoe. The wave was followed by another, and yet another. It was the aurora borealis. Henceforth its display continued all night, but with decreasing power.

We began to move west along the ridge. Slightly below us on the Glencoe side the craggy tower of the Chancellor seemed to be clothed in white light rather than frozen snow. It looked as savage as an Alpine *Aiguille*, and was linked to our ridge by a jagged snow-*arête*. Its final tower, which is the culminating point of a tall buttress, projects against the sky when seen from Glencoe, and the local people apply its name to the whole mountain, properly called Am Bodach.

We were now faced with a very sharp descent to the base of the next peak, Meall Dearg. We roped up, and cut steps in snow-ice down to the col. From the col to Meall Dearg, which is the highest point of the ridge, we had easy work in soft snow, and therefore more leisure to look at the mountains. Among snow-clad peaks under a good moon there is normally an icy shine and sparkle on the tops, most wonderful to behold. But tonight the moon's power and brilliancy were stolen by the light-waves from the north. They pulsed athwart the ridge with an almost mechanical rhythm, making our route as clear as in daylight. Our descent from Meall Dearg thus went easily until we came to a long steep slab encased in a double layer of brittle snow and ice. This passage, over which one scrambles thoughtlessly in summer, now caused us some anxiety.

When I tried axe-work on the slab I promptly found that if the snow and ice were completely removed the rock thus exposed was glazed and unsafe. If proper holds were cut, then the snow-ice was too brittle to endure any weight. An unpleasant compromise was our only course. I removed most of the snow and ice, but not all of it – I left a less doubtful substratum, by the use of which we disentangled ourselves from an unusual snare.

For a while we walked safely before one of the noblest sights in central Scotland – a direct view into the great north-east corrie of Bidean nam Bian. The icy triangle of Stob Coire nan Lochan, backed by the snow-dome of Bidean, threw outward to Glencoe two splendid ridges. Encircled by these rocky arms lay Coire nan Lochan, a broad snow-hollow, softly shining, gently shadowed, but austere. The closer one's approach to beauty the more pronounced grows that seeming austerity; on hills such true beauty would seem more evident in winter, just as it comes out in the character of men more in times of challenge than in days of ease.

We had arrived at the thinnest and most rocky section of the ridge. The glen below us lay deep in the grey shadow of frost, and a grey skin of ice covered Loch Achtriochtan. That men should choose to inhabit such frozen furrows of the earth's crust seemed mad and unnatural. But to balance on the silver wrinkles – ah! that was work for wise and enlightened men! When the ridge narrowed we expected trouble at two little pinnacles, which completely bar the crest and are frequently sheathed in thin ice. To our surprise we found them bare. We grasped them and swung round on the south side. We were even able to force a route directly up the vertical step in the ridge beyond. We were now on a long raised crest; one of the few places in Scotland where double cornices may torment the mountaineer. Tonight there was no cornice but plenty of good snow. Its dry featheriness was searched out by the moonbeams, and its muted crunch underfoot was the only sound in the universe.

From this part of the ridge we were better able to see Bidean, to see it as a whole mountain – shaped by deep corries, thrusting its strong ridges outward to eight sparkling peaks, down-curving to lesser tops, emerging from the lowly blackness of Glencoe to a crescendo of light at the summit. That was the Bidean nam Bian of our physical world, by its mere presence there calling our hearts to the world inhabited by beauty.

The light-pulse of the aurora was beginning to lose a measure of its strength. We thought that dawn might come earlier up here than we reckoned, so we decided not to go on to the top of Stob Coire Leith, but to turn at once and start back along the ridge. At all costs we must reach Meall Dearg before sunrise. We faced up to an hour of toil and quick climbing; we drove our bodies relentlessly along the crest, dropped to the pinnacles, swung past and onwards, and so without pause or rest came again to the summit of Meall Dearg.

A cold, blue band lined the eastern horizon, with just a suspicion of light behind it. The hills below were snow-grey and night-bound, unlit by the moon, which was now thinly veiled by fast-travelling cloud. Dawn was a full hour away, so we hollowed seats in firm snow and sat with our backs against the cairn. At this point we enjoyed the qualities of our padded flying-suits. Despite quite exceptional frost we sat in comfort, observed the mountain scene, and were yet freed from the distraction of paralysing cold.

We were facing east. After a short desultory conversation we fell still – not a word was spoken for an hour. We drove from our heads every thought of self and simply observed the scene detachedly, allowing it, and nothing else, to flow into us. We were absorbed by the display that followed, which, although a continuous event and a unity, seemed to occur in three clear movements.

It was a simple enough scene: below us, in the near foreground, a short snow-ridge to Am Bodach; beyond, a wide expanse of moorland, swelling in white hills and pasturing flocks of ground mist. The horizon circled incredibly far away; throughout the length of its eastern arc was a faint flush of colour, turning to blue and deepening to black as the eye travelled to the zenith. The moon and stars were again bright. A simple scene, and not spectacular; for that very reason bearing in upon the mind more strongly its peculiar values.

On the land, silence; in the stars, calm. The more one listened to the earth's silence the more deep and intense did it grow: deeper still, and still more intense; one's mind was absorbed into it and pervaded by it. Thus there was conveyed into the mind by the hills and stars themselves and through part agency of the senses this knowledge that the night hush of earth is expectant: as though our universe were a live being, not a dead thing. Its silence is not the silence of sleep or death, but of life – intense – aware.

Towards the close of an hour the darkness lessened perceptibly. The horizon belt of pale cold pink developed deepening pastel shades of varied colour. No crude or startling effect was seen, but again this fell to advantage. We saw the more clearly how, at the touch of dawn light, the earth seemed to draw breath and stir to its shining.

The sunrise opened the final movement. At the first gleam of its rim great beams radiated across the earth's surface and middle air. Then the hills stood clear and the moors lay fresh, and the sky unfurled broad banners of blue. The act of adoration had begun, for this was the sun's hour of morning song. In that we shared; for we could say to ourselves: 'We had stood as the sure stars stand, and moved as the moon moves, loving the world.'

We came down in the forenoon to a point about a thousand feet above the Glencoe road. We now felt very sleepy, yet had all day before us; so we found a patch of sun-bathed turf, on which we curled up side by side and slept. There kept running through my head, between waking and sleeping, a recently read verse:

Thou shouldst die as he dies,
For whom none sheddeth tears;
Filling thine eyes
And fulfilling thine ears
With the brilliance ... the bloom
and the beauty ...

7

Winter Days in Coire nan Lochan

The iciest winter that Scotland ever had in my own lifetime was the winter of 1947. For two whole months, mid-January to mid-March, the western highlands enjoyed continuous hard frost and clear sunny skies. There were only two bad days. Heretical mountaineers complained of too much ice in proportion to snow. On the other hand the gullies of Glencoe promised freak conditions and extreme severities. Early in January Donald McIntyre and I made a swift reconnaissance of Coire nan Lochan, and were startled to see that the South-Centre Gully, which is five hundred feet high, began with an unbroken ice-fall of two hundred and fifty feet. That lower half was all clear ice, not snow-ice. The upper half looked like hard-frozen snow with a cornice at the top. So far as we could discover only five ascents had ever been made, and not one in conditions so remarkable as the present. Indeed, was such a climb as this possible? At the end of January we returned to the corrie with Kenneth Dunn.

Success in Twisting Gully a month earlier had, I fear, given me optimistic notions of what we could attempt on our first ice-climb for the season. I had got up Twisting Gully despite a bad cold, but Twisting Gully had not been an ice-climb; rather was it a mixture of rock-snow-ice with the rock and snow predominating. One can get up very hard rocks when out of training if one strikes very good form. But good form is not enough on ice. The bodily strain is too high. First-class physical condition is essential. Our visit to the South-Centre Gully, therefore, was to be not so much a lesson in ice-climbing, as a discipline in humility.

There are mornings when it is ordained, no doubt for our benefit, that all things shall go wrong. And this was one. My car had starting trouble when we tried to leave Lagangarbh, so that we arrived late at the base of Bidean nam Bian. Our ascent to Coire nan Lochan had then to be made in soft snow, so that we spent three hours in reaching the corrie's bowl at three thousand feet. The time was a quarter to one. Otherwise conditions could not have been better. Nearly seven hundred feet above, our peak's white point stood against the sky. The lochans were invisible under a double sheet of snow and ice. A great stillness hung about the corrie, for the frost was hard. The cliffs facing us were no more than powdered with snow, but clad in drapings of ice, their most awesome feature being that deep split between the South and Centre Buttresses. We could detect no change in the lower half, except that a faint tinge of green had crept into the ice, like the green of a winter's sea, visible at a distance but not noticeable at close quarters.

We walked across the lochan and climbed snow-slopes to the foot of the gully. Its lower half held three ice-pitches of forty, thirty, and seventy feet respectively, linked by ice-slopes of lesser, but not much lesser, angle. The seventy-foot pitch, being high above us, seemed to be vertical, which we knew to be not true; while the lower one looked a more reasonable proposition, and that was equally untrue. The angle of an ice-pitch is always underestimated from close below. My own duty was to lead the long and exposed final pitch, and I accordingly asked McIntyre to deal with the first. We roped up.

He started cutting with his long axe, but the steepening angle at once forced him to carve handholds, and he then had recourse to a short ice-pick, which he could use one-handed with less effort. In twenty minutes' hard work he reached a bulge at the halfway mark, by which time he was so exhausted that he had to come down. On a second trial the bulge still over-taxed his strength. He then surrendered the lead. Watching him I had wrongly thought that he lacked only confidence, for he was a beginner on ice. But in this I was over-simplifying his troubles.

I soon discovered for myself what his primary trouble had been. The high angle imposed continuous strain on the arm and shoulder muscles – the left arm's strain of holding the body in, while the right took the still greater strain of cutting above the head – and our real handicap was a lack of training. The demands of severe ice-climbing are unrelenting. However, I cut over the bulge and neared the top of the pitch. But before going on we all consulted and faced facts. The ascent of forty feet had taken over an hour: a further two hundred feet of ice rose to the middle of the gully, and the time was 2 p.m. We abandoned the climb.

Here was one of the best ice-climbs in Scotland, and climbable – by a man fit enough to give it all that he had, plus hidden reserves if need were. We resolved to return next week. Meanwhile I trained by running hard each night for two miles and spending fifteen minutes every morning on exercises. At the end of a week I felt reinvigorated – at all levels the purgatorial process has its reward. We now wanted good weather and an early morning start. To be assured of the latter we planned to camp overnight in Coire nan Lochan. But the weather grew doubtful as the week drew to its close, for the frost slackened.

When McIntyre and I reached Glencoe by car on Saturday night, drizzle was falling. We halted at Altnafeadh, and looked out at the murk. It was a demoralizing sight. The night was surprisingly warm and convinced us that even at three thousand feet we should probably find thaw conditions with wet snow and ice. Glencoe offered us two dry roosts, the relative merits of which we now debated. One was Lagangarbh with a fire. The other was the summit of Bidean nam Bian. At three thousand seven hundred and sixty-six feet we could reckon on getting above the thaw-belt. With a swift resolution, which I have admired in him ever since that day, McIntyre urged that we pitch the tent on top of Bidean. Such was his enthusiasm that despite the dark and the drizzle I heard myself agreeing. Should the weather clear while we were on top we might descend into Coire nan Lochan in less than an hour. The summit was a good strategic position – barring storms.

At 9 p.m. we started uphill by way of Coire nam Beith. Almost at once the skies began to clear. Stars twinkled. Unhappily there was no wind in the corrie; we opened our shirts and rolled up our sleeves – and were still warm. For two and a half hours we climbed by torchlight, then reached the snows of the upper corrie which gave us light enough to see clearly. As we neared the foot of the Church Door Buttress, which lies directly under the summit, the snow and air suddenly froze. We had climbed above the thaw-belt. Indeed we might have camped after all in Coire nan Lochan, but were now on the wrong side of the mountain. We cut our way to the summit by crusted snow-slopes.

At 12.30 a.m. we pitched our tent on the snow-cap beside the cairn. An icy wind from the south-east swept over the top. The exposure of the site was made extreme by the character of the mountain. Bidean is the highest peak of Argyll and dominates Glencoe and Appin. But how small a summit for so large a mountain! The flanks drop sharply to the corries, so that we felt pushed up at the sky on the tip of a finger. Despite freezing wind we made supper in comfort, for the tent had a sewn-in groundsheet and circular sleeve-doors. We could seal it hermetically, and relax in a warm fug. Winter camping need not be 'tough' when properly ordered. Two or three layers of newspaper insulated us from ground cold, and the continuous patter of snowdrift on the cambric, reminding us every moment of the airy and arctic world around, increased our sense of warmth in sleeping bags.

After supper McIntyre went out to look at the weather. He at once called me to come, and the urgency in his voice made me hurry. At the moment of emerging I was conscious only of piercing cold.

'Look,' said McIntyre, 'above and below.'

A black sky, densely packed with electric-blue stars, winked and glittered frostily. The valleys likewise were black, but a grey sea-mist on Loch Linnhe thrust long tongues along the floors of Glencoe and the Leven valley, and licked around the base of Bidean. This tide of mist looked so much like cloud of the sky, yet flowed so distantly, that our peak by comparison pierced the firmament. We were poised in space at heights unlawful. After our first shock of wonder a wave of cold air broke over the peak and chilled us to the bone. We took a last quick look round and dived back to shelter.

It is idle to pretend that we slept well that night. We dozed. One sleeping bag each was not enough. Early in the morning we peeped through a ventilator. Thick mist had fallen around us. Each time a gust of wind seized and shook the canvas we heard a sharp crackle from all over the roof, which sounded like the blatter of icy spiculae, travelling fast. In such conditions the gully would be impossible, and even ridge-walking an especial hell. We therefore lay back in our bags all the more happily and listened, between gusts, to that peculiarly soothing sound – the whisper of snow along the walls of a tent.

After a slothful morning and late breakfast we struggled outside to strike camp. Too late we discovered our mistake about the weather. A skin of ice, perhaps one-eighth of an inch thick, had formed over the tent fabric, and this it was that crackled to the wind-shake. The snow was not drifting. Moreover, the mist was only a cloud-cap on the summit – the other eight tops were clear! We walked the length of the north ridge over Stob Coire nan Lochan to Aonach Dubh. Dusky clouds billowed over the cols and rolled around the peaks and tumbled down to the corries, but spacious gaps were always left for the brown and red of the moorland heather to flame up from below. It showed how wrong is the common belief that the winter scene is without colour. The truth is that the colours are richer and warmer than those of summer.

The frost was hard in Glencoe that night, and continued for the rest of the week. Our hopes for a third attempt on the gully were high. Dunn and McIntyre joined me in Glencoe on Saturday night. We went up to Coire nan Lochan and pitched the tent in the middle of the loch. The night was windless and still, but the sky was veiled by a thin film of cloud, the presence of which we might not even have suspected had it not been illuminated from time to time by a flickering of the aurora. Stars were dim and sparse, but visibility was good and the corrie shone gently. There was nothing gentle, however, in the beauty of its west wall, where five cliffs towered stark and spiky, knifing the sky with a cold glitter like steel. The wild austerity of these frozen crags made a startling counter to the flowing lines of the corrie's bowl. Together they put forth a double aspect of beauty, each drawing out the power of its opposite, but both integrated in the beauty of the whole, named Coire nan Lochan.

That night we slept well. Profiting by our last experience we wore our kapok-filled flying-suits inside our sleeping bags. We woke at daybreak feeling warm, but shuddered when we heard the wind. It was blowing hard from the south-east, battering the tent. We looked out at sheets of drift driving across the corrie floor, and storming up the cliffs, which only occasionally loomed high and menacing through the spume. The weather looked like building up to a blizzard, so we hurriedly breakfasted, snatched a good snow-climb between the North and Central Buttresses, and withdrew, in moderating wind, to Glencoe.

Throughout the remainder of February Glencoe was blessed with unfailing sun and frost. Our final attack was now timed for 2nd March, when we should be reinforced by H.W. Tilman. He and McIntyre arrived in Glencoe on 29th February, and enjoyed an icy traverse of the Aonach Eagach ridge – despite delay in the glen with a frozen car engine. Boiling water, they said, had frozen while they were pouring it into the empty radiator. When I arrived at night and heard this tale I could not altogether suppress feelings of satisfaction. It seemed to me a tale of good omen. Our gully ought to be in perfect condition. This time I could think of nothing that could stop us getting on to our climb. The sky was clear and starry, and the moon so bright that we preferred to walk up and down outside rather than sit indoors. We stopped down at Lagangarbh that night, for the elapse of one month gave us daylight enough to dispense with a high camp.

Tilman is an early riser and works like a beaver on hut chores, so that we had time on hand to deal with our once more frozen car. At 9 a.m. we drove to the foot of Bidean and reached the upper corrie in two hours. The gully remained in the same general condition as before, the lower half being pure ice, but if anything thicker and more substantial.

Tilman urged that we try to by-pass the first ice-pitch by a rock-rib to its left. The rib projected seventy feet and bore a plating of snow and ice. None the less it might go more quickly if it were climbable. To allow us a choice of alternatives, yet not waste time, I asked McIntyre to begin work on the ice-pitch while I started on the rib. The crest of the rib went well to the midway point – good holds lay under the snow-plaster. On the upper twenty feet, however, the coating was thin ice with poor and scanty holds underneath. My technique was to balance on a boot-nail on these nicks and watch my holds take shape through the gouts of ice-spray that sprang from the axe-blows, then force every upward move. I reached a snowy platform on top, and brought up the others.

There followed a hundred-foot run-out on a thick, steep slope of clear ice set between straight walls. It gave joyous and satisfying climbing. I could take a full swing with my axe and hit the slope as hard as I liked. At each blow the pick drove in with a dull *click*, and the shaft vibrated on the palm of the hand. The chips came out clean at the third or fourth blows, and whirred down the gully. I reached a small spike projecting from the gully-bed. It could not have appeared more opportunely; for the slope steepened into an overhang about fifty feet above, and it seemed that my best course was to make a hard right traverse on to a raised chute, which now filled the right-hand half of the gully. The chute was seventy feet high and well iced. I brought up Tilman, who tied himself to the spike and brought up McIntyre. I fetched out my short ice-pick.

Since the chute was a raised one, my first move was to traverse rightward across its vertical wall, and so on to its upper face. The ice-work on the next fifty feet was all one-handed cutting, but from good foothold, for the ice must have been nearly a foot thick. The crux came just below the top, where I ran into a five-foot bulge. Ice overhangs can't be climbed. They have to be cut away. I spent a full forty minutes on these five feet. The excessive angle permitted no weight behind the axe-blows and the two-hundred-foot ice-fall beneath forbade jerky movement. Tilman and McIntyre could see nothing of me, their only means of gauging hope for the future being the volume of icy shrapnel raining through space and the fitful movement of rope. Writing later of his own view of this passage McIntyre said:

'The gully-walls rose steeply to imprison us. Ice-chips raced in a steady stream down the ribbon of ice and disappeared over the lip of the pitch below. They made a pleasant, tinkling, swishing sound as they went. The mist opened. The sun shone on the white crest of the Aonach Eagach, the lower slopes of which were rich brown. Cloud shadows moved leisurely. How pleasing was the blue of the sky above the white pitch and the black rock-walls! A fleecy cloud rushed over the top and, watching it, I nearly over-balanced. The mist closed in again, and we were conscious only of the pitch. For a long time the ice-chips still sped downwards; intermittently the rope ran out a few more inches.'

Fighting the out-pull of gravity I cautiously eased myself up the ladder of notches. Then the angle fell back and I was up.

I climbed firm snow for twenty feet and brought up Tilman. This was his first ascent of a Scottish ice-pitch and I was most curious to know what he thought of it. At last his head appeared over the top. He stopped on his last hold and looked up at me from under his eyebrows. 'This climb is an eye-opener,' he said, and climbed up. Tilman is not a talker.

He now took the lead and cut steps up two hundred and fifty feet of hard snow to the cornice. Its overhang looked flimsy and unsafe, and was unusual in being complete: no merely vertical passage offered a highway to the summit. To McIntyre, being relatively guileless, we gave the nasty job of swarming up first.

Tilman and I gave a double belay; I thought it more than likely that the cornice would collapse.

It held.

We finished our climb, and the sixth ascent of South-Centre Gully, at 4 p.m. The first sight that met our eyes when we crested the ridge was Loch Linnhe, and I can remember nothing else. All the colours of the encircling hills were in it, rich and subtle, the most potent of mountain bouquets. Under its influence, and a strong influence it must have been, I pitied Tilman. He had to hasten south this night and prepare to leave for the Himalaya.

Right before our eyes was the true country.

8

The Leac Mhor

The sky was darkening with thunder-cloud and a high wind was blowing up Loch Linnhe. I turned my car off the Fort William road and drove on board the Corran ferry. Then we got out and looked anxiously at the weather. With Robert Anderson, the artist, and Douglas Scott, the photographer, I was crossing to Ardgour to attempt an unknown rock-climb on Garbh Bheinn, and to make a record of it for a guidebook by the Scottish Mountaineering Club. One last problem had to be solved at all costs: what was the line of the direct route up the North-East Buttress? The buttress was twelve hundred feet high; an ascent of very hard standard had been made in 1943, but the record was scanty, the line of the route doubtful, the difficulties undescribed. Less than one month before, in May 1947, two very good climbers had been defeated before they got halfway up. Therefore good weather for ourselves was a matter of some urgency.

I turned to the ferryman. 'The sky looks bad,' I said, shaking my head.

'Yess, indeed, it iss a bad sky,' he replied. 'And you are the lucky man to be getting across. Thiss run will be our last run to-night.'

The boat began to lurch as the waves heaved under it. Alarm at the risk of the car's shifting position stirred up my memory. 'Did the ferry not sink once before the war?' I asked.

'Once!' exclaimed the ferryman joyfully. 'Och, man, it sank several times! But you will be all right now,' said he, 'for the new turn-table will float if the boat sinks under it. Och, yess, you will be all right.'

I began to wish that I was safely lodged on the face of some tall cliff. However, we relished the salt tang of the wind and the boisterous force of it. Although the sea ran high it did make us feel, by the time we grounded, that we had had value for money. Ardgour is notoriously hard of access, and when it adds high wind to the defence of its frontiers, one lands, if one lands at all, with a sense of privilege.

We drove south to Garbh Bheinn. There are no hotels near the mountain nor any other accommodation. Therefore we proposed to pitch a tent in Coire an Iubhair (the corrie of the yew-tree), which curves below the east face. We walked a quarter of a mile up the glen to a stretch of soft flat turf beside the river. Before we could unload our gear the skies split open. There was a blinding flash and a peal of thunder. The rain rushed down. Our tent seemed to go up with the speed of an opening umbrella. The guys and pegs were not nicely aligned, but luckily there was no wind in the corrie. We made supper.

We ate our meal to the loudest storm music and our bedtime lullaby was the swish of rain on the tent-canvas. This had seemed daunting at first in view of our plans, but now cheered us the more the harder it came. Experience of west highland hills suggested that torrential downpours at night are often followed by a good morning. The weather truly to be dreaded is the windless drizzle.

We wakened next day to a blue sunny sky. At 9 a.m. we walked two miles up Coire an Iubhair to the foot of the North-East Buttress, where Anderson made an outline sketch and Scott took photographs. I endeavoured to trace out the line of the route. Although twelve hundred feet high, the cliff is crossed by three terraces, the middle one lying at a slant so that they form a reversed letter S, which divides the face into four tiers. The first tier looked of moderate difficulty; the second short and hard; but the third impossible. It is formed in one enormous slab, topped by an overhang. The last tier of all is a great tower.

It was obvious that the third tier was the point of supreme difficulty. The angle was excessively steep for a smooth slab, and I could hardly imagine how it might be possible to force a route through the overhang, which ran the full breadth of the slab and looked eighty feet high. There must surely be some breach invisible to us. Thus far the true size of the slab had not registered on my brain, for the scale of the buttress being so big, the slab fell into place as one normal-size tier among four. It was Anderson, the artist, with an eye trained to assess proportions, who first realized the import of what we saw.

'That slab,' said he, 'must be four hundred feet high at least and four hundred feet wide. One of the biggest in Scotland.'

I looked again. 'By heaven!' I exclaimed, 'you're right. But there is no other single slab anything like the size in Scotland. The Cioch Slab in the Cuillin is barely ninety feet. We must get a name for this.'

'Let's try and climb it first,' suggested Scott – 'if we can.'

We had spent nearly an hour lying back in the heather; so we resolved to economize time by cutting out the first tier. This we did by means of an easy gully to its left, which led us on to the first terrace. The second tier was the shortest one, perhaps two hundred feet, and our route started near the left-hand side. We tied on the rope, and asked Scott to lead. He climbed only a few feet, hovered in indecision, and then came down to think again. The rock was a mixture of rough gneiss and polished quartzite, and slabby. The quartzite was hard as marble and Scott found his boot-nails very apt to glance off it. The rock was much more suitable for rubbers, but unfortunately was wet in patches despite the sunshine; and rubbers on wet rock are of more danger than help. However, Scott reckoned that the dry patches were big enough to allow us to use them almost exclusively. We should surely find some way of avoiding the wet quartzite.

Scott and I changed into rubbers and left our boots on the terrace. We climbed fifty feet on small, outward-sloping holds to a long grass ledge, where we stopped to bring on Anderson, who, not having rubbers, was determined to climb in boots and to rely on the rope for security. But these fifty feet convinced him of the worst. He found the struggle too severe a strain to be enjoyable. Scott and I, moreover, finding that projecting rock-spikes were barely adequate for belaying the rope, urged him to take off his boots. He did so, and threw them down to the terrace; henceforth stocking-soles and wet feet were his portion.

A further hundred feet of very difficult climbing led us to the base of a long overhang which ran along the tier like the eaves of a roof. We were forced to start edging to the right directly below it, taking our footholds on a slabby shelf. The drop below was a big one, foothold hard to find, and the way of escape hidden; thus the passage became most exciting. We began to feel, increasingly from now onwards, the sense of exposure on a great mountain-wall, where mistakes in climbing craft are barred, on pain of swift penalty. Treading delicately along the shelf for fifty feet we rounded the overhang, and saw before us an almost vertical wall, which was none the less so well weathered that we enjoyed good holds. Easy climbing led to the second terrace.

The principal obstacle of the day was now before us – the great slab, four hundred feet square with its overhung top. The bottom of the slab was either undercut or vertical to a height of twenty or thirty feet throughout its length. Thus our very access to the slab seemed to be a problem. Our eyes were drawn to a little bay below the left half, from which a wide crack or groove split the slab nearly to the great overhang, but exhibited another very short overhang at the halfway point. That groove was our only hopeful line; the slab to either side of it was uncompromising, destitute of belays for the rope. We therefore committed ourselves to the groove, but with a most uneasy awareness that should we get so far as the great overhang, and be stopped by it, we should be defeated very late in the day, and faced with an anxious descent.

We started from the bay. On the first vertical section we were aided by fissured rock and ledges. One had to summon up energy determinedly and expend it on strong arm-pulls; then the angle eased and the technical difficulties increased. Our delight in the climbing increased commensurately; for the situation grew ever more exhilarating as the wide sweep of the unclimbable slab on our right opened up to the thread of our route. We felt alive in every vein and tissue. We were poised in space, muscle and nerve tense, amid acres of arching rock, smooth rock in the sense of offering little lodgement for hand or foot, but coarse and crystalline, studded with quartzite that gleamed white on its grey

setting. The beauty of it struck to the eye. Through the very un-
certainties of our climb my mind became unusually observant,
embracing many simple things that commonly pass unregarded.
While searching for a handhold the eye would alight on a blade of
grass peeping from a crack, and see the amazing grace of its fluting,
the fresh brightness of its green against the rock; and although the
joy was that of one second the memory lived on. We all know
leagues of hillside heather, but stand on the ledge of a tall cliff,
look at a single shoot sprouting from a joint in the wall, its perfect
leaf-design, the pureness of the bell, the harmony between the
rich green and the purple, and there, in that one branch, you see a
beauty matching the quality of a hill. Touch gently an uncurling
frond of fern or the new shoot of a juniper bush – watch it closely,
and the heart is suddenly filled with a love for all things young and
growing. There is in these a tenderness most simple and exquisite,
made doubly clear by contrast with the severity of rock-work.

We crept slowly up the great slab until we came to a huge
boulder that straddled the groove. It looked most unstable. Scott
tested it cautiously, while we watched with exceeding wariness.
It was proved to be safe and the party gathered behind it for rest
and lunch. Directly ahead of us loomed the short midway overhang. It looked much more fearsome at close quarters than it did
from the terrace, and is, in fact, the crux of the climb. Conversation
was desultory. Each of us felt much concerned to try conclusions
without delay. Scott and I moved up to a small stance at the base
of the overhang.

The groove was here broad and shallow, but abruptly narrowed
to a ten-foot chimney which leaned gently outward. Since the
groove continued above the chimney the obvious course was to
try a direct attack. Scott tried several times, but failed. He tried
again, standing on my shoulder, but in trying to make an awkward
up-stretch wrenched a muscle in his back. He was now temporarily
out of action, so I took over the lead.

I too failed on the overhang. One alternative remained. It was
possible to climb on to the face of the great slab to our left. The
angle was high, the rock exposed, the holds minute; but there was

no other route. While climbing on to the slab I found it essential to use a wet, grassy foothold. This meant that relying on finger-tip holds I had to stand on the next sketchy foothold and dry my rubbers against the stocking of the opposite leg, an operation that placed a great strain on the fingers. After two more moves I was faced by a belt of quartzite. To my horror I found that this quartzite too was wet, and wet quartzite is like wet ice to rubbers. The holds were still tiny. I came down at once. Nothing more could be done. We were beaten – beaten not so much by the rock as by the thunderstorm of the preceding night. Any attempt to force the route in its present condition would be a courting of disaster.

We withdrew to the unstable boulder. Anderson, and then Scott, climbed down out of sight. I paid out rope and looked down into the distant corrie. Far below me a small white speck was travelling fast up the glen, bright as a snowflake against the brown hill opposite. The gull turned towards us and wheeled in a great arc over the corrie. Such superb mastery of space and depth made a defeated rock-climber feel positively dizzy. The liveliness of its white caused me to look with sudden interest at the brown hill which had been its background. That was a plain and humble hill if ever there was one. A shapely hump without the distinction of great cliffs or tower-like summit. I examined it in detail and deta-chedly, allowing it to make its own impression on me. The result was quite unexpected. The mountains had hit hard and defeated us – I confess we were just a little despondent. Now they came like some adversary of goodwill and smiled into our eyes. They won an unreserved devotion.

The slant of the sun across the hill picked out and burnished a multitude of scattered crags. They were light grey and clean-washed, and I felt refreshed in mind just by looking at them. The hill was dimpled by shadow where the hollows lay, but the broad sun-struck flank was a quilt of many colours; the quiet green of young uncurling bracken, the rust of massed heather, dark against old pale-yellow turf through which sparse new grass was pushing, the flash of torrents, and far up to the summit a cloud intolerably bright.

From each feature, all part of one mountain, there came its own glow of beauty, an arresting power. It evoked awe and reverence. These feelings stirred the thought that only a little earlier I was warming myself at the flame of that same glow in a solitary blade of grass and fern-frond, in one shoot of heather and a stone of quartz. The sweep of hill in front of me contained these little material things by the million, not one of them visible in its own form or beauty, but uniting to clothe the mountain, building a new beauty of feature, in the glow of which the mountain shone, shone for miles across Argyll, a burning beacon of truth.

'My One Beauty is in all things.' By the light of the beacon read the word on the mountain-face. From the minutest body or the greatest concourse there shines out the one light of its underlying reality, plain for all men to love who will look – a light of innumerable rays, any one of which, if artificially separated by the mind, an aspect to be named material or spiritual or mental; but all in fact integrated, one light of truth. When glimpsed even most fleetingly its glory is too great to be given title. We separate a ray for study, and call our act the method of science or philosophy, but in the very act divorce it from reality. The light of truth is to be sought whole, or it will not be seen.

From somewhere below me there drifted up a call from Scott. I threw him the slack of the rope and climbed down, but have little recollection of that descent save a general one of steepness, difficulty, and a spacious void, until at last we reached the second terrace. An urgent time problem then pressed for an answer. If we were forced to descend the very difficult second tier we should arrive too late at Corran to catch the ferry. Therefore we followed the slanting terrace downward until we came to its end, where a rock-wall overlooked the gully on the flank of the buttress. We had no knowledge that a route could be found down that wall, but we tried. At one point we doubled a rope round a rock-spike and slid down for fifty feet; otherwise the rock was easy. We trundled down the scree-filled gully, made a detour to get our boots from the first terrace, and raced out to the middle of the corrie. We stopped there for a minute and looked back.

The buttress towered. The sun was now behind it, causing it to look starker and more noble than ever. The great slab was vast and bare.

'That slab is the eighth wonder of the world,' said Anderson. 'We must find a name worthy of it.' Then after a while, and triumphantly: 'I've got it – Leac Mhor...'

'Lek Vore.' I sounded the words and strongly approved. 'What does it mean, and how do you spell it?'

'It means the Great Slab, and you spell it ... '

We have not been back to climb the Leac Mhor since that day. In course of time we assuredly shall go back. But does it matter whether a man gets to the very top? If he penetrate to the heart of the Leac Mhor the mountain is his.

9

The Forgotten Cliff of Aonach Dubh

In the course of our numerous visits to Bidean nam Bian during the winter of 1946-7, Donald McIntyre and I passed half a dozen times below an unclimbed cliff on the flank of Aonach Dubh, which walls the long lower part of Coire nan Lochan.

Like scores of other climbers before us, we saw and admired – and passed thoughtlessly on. Between sight and reflection there seemed to come an occult barrier. Not until our sixth passing, in the company of Tilman, did we really *see* it, in the full sense. It was four hundred yards long and six hundred feet high on the south-east wall of Aonach Dubh – only one thousand feet above the Glencoe road, from which it is invisible. The angle looked remarkably high. And no one had climbed there! And this 1947! Truly it seemed incredible that in Glencoe – the most popular climbing-ground in Scotland – a virgin cliff of that size should pass unnoticed so long.

'What are we waiting for?' I asked McIntyre rhetorically.

'Spring – and the first good weekend.'

On one of these protracted May evenings, when the sun shines long and low up the fifteen miles of the glen, and the white foam on the River Coe takes an unaccustomed sparkle, McIntyre and I crossed the ford below Coire nan Lochan. This undertaking was no light one. We were heavily loaded, the river was high and twenty yards wide, and our route lay over the tops of spray-splashed boulders, irregularly dotting the water in a long, curved line down-stream. Of all boulder-hoppers McIntyre is *the* most expert. He learned the art in the Cairngorms at the age of sixteen. Accordingly, while I dallied on the brink, searching for my non-existent courage, McIntyre gave his amazing display of animal grace. From boulder to foam-washed boulder he leapt like an antelope, but with the speed of a gazelle, coming down always at the right angle to make his instantaneous spring for the staggered stone ahead. His rucksack seemed to serve all the better for its weight to steady and ballast him. The exhibition must have given him a tensely thrilling enjoyment, because on reaching the far side he strolled off with studied nonchalance, not looking back, to signify that all this was a mere nothing. I smiled delightedly at his high spirits. I was duly impressed. I was even inspired to follow, like the common goat.

An hour's climb up the corrie, which would be more accurately called a ravine, brought us to a black crag on the left side, directly facing the unclimbed cliff. A big overhang of the crag gave a sheltered bivouac, much improved by some person unknown, who had built a stone wall round the north end. We spread our groundsheets and sleeping bags. We cooked a meal. Later, while we lay in our sleeping bags, the sun set behind the cliff in front. The sun was thus invisible, but light reflected from a cloud stained the cliff's face dark oak.

The next morning was dry so we rose early. Our bivouac was on the shaded side of the glen, but the sun was already warming the uppermost rocks of the East Cliff, and every detail of its face was clear and precise in the hard morning light. We examined the rock intently.

The cliff was divided vertically by a bow-shaped chimney, shallow in its lower half. Beneath the face ran a wide grassy shelf, marked at its midway point under the Bow by a short crag, from the cracked top of which twin rowan-trees sprouted. The Bow and rowans made useful landmarks, for the cliffs to their right and left were of quite different aspect. The left-hand half was a blank face, unbroken by rake or terrace, but seamed by countless ledges. The right-hand half was divided horizontally by a broad terrace. Above the terrace a great basin scooped the cliff, topped by enormous overhangs. Below the terrace was a convex wall, slabby towards the right.

We were preoccupied over breakfast. We had not a notion where we should go first. Indeed, we had no clear idea as yet what the qualities of the rock might be. So that after breakfast we naturally gravitated towards the middle, thinking that were we able to make a route there, we might at the same time reconnoitre the cliffs on either side. Then, well to the left of the Bow, we saw the Bow-string – a long chimney starting about a hundred feet up the face. If we could reach it the route would go.

The leading of the Bow-string was to be McIntyre's work, his first essay on unclimbed rock, and so a great occasion. For the highest delight that rock-climbing offers is searching out one's own way on crags unknown to men – doubt of the issue, encounter with the unexpected, the sense of exploration. However, to economize our time, 'through leads' were desirable. The first pitch being easy I took that for myself. I climbed eighty feet to a tilting slab about the size of a hearthstone. The wall above being now vertical I surrendered the lead to McIntyre. He led through, crossing the slab rightwards to an awkward corner, up which he scrambled. I joined him later on a grass ledge. Thence we climbed into the chimney's foot. The interior presented no serious obstacle, and on either side the outer walls obviously offered the better route. By these we continued over clean and easy rocks to the top of the cliff.

That reconnaissance had been a quite remarkable climb. It is taken for granted in Glencoe that a new route of six hundred feet will provide the leader with extreme trouble. Instead, so good was the rock that difficulties had been small. However, we dared not generalize. The rock on the right-hand half of the cliff looked a very different proposition. On the left-hand side we had noted the rock to be so indefinite, so criss-crossed by ledges, that no doubts disturbed our peace of mind – we could find routes there when we wanted them, and so leave them for another day. Our task now was the exploration of the Terrace Face.

We descended grass slopes at the south end of the cliff and returned to the foot of the Bow. The most fascinating quarter of the whole cliff was that above the Terrace, on either side of the great Basin. We should do well if we could open up the rocks there. We accordingly climbed at speed, unroped, up the lower Bow, and came out on the Terrace at its left-hand end. From here the cliff above looked alarmingly steep. But we were warmed up and at last on the warpath. The hardest-looking climb we could see was an almost vertical face of three hundred and fifty feet just to the right of the Bow. It was beautiful rock, of the shade of silver birch-bark, quite unlike the brown rock nearer the Basin. I did not seriously expect the sheer cliff to go, but felt the invitation of the lower part, where a hundred-foot rib projected like the Bow's quiver. Could we reach the top of it, who knows but some as yet invisible fracture might allow us to scale the unscalable.

McIntyre led the first half of the Quiver and I the second half. The rock had become exposed by the time we hauled ourselves on to the big platform on top. I looked up and confess to a twinge of conscience at encouraging McIntyre to face as leader the dire troubles in front. But I need not have worried. He is a geologist – the Ideal Geologist made flesh. Rock in any shape or form, at whatever angle, is the delight of his heart. He loves rock, in all circumstances. If he were ever about to fall off an overhang he would, just before parting company with the rock, draw his tongue over the surface to bring out the colour. I have observed him do this at other times and feel quite confident he would do it then.

'Your lead, Donald,' I commiserated. ' Bad luck.'

Looking all the while keenly up at the cliff, he swung his waist-knot to the rear, and his mouth tightened. He was in good training, I reflected, watching the spare face and clear eye. That would help him much when his situation became hopeless, and he had to come down; for such seemed the likely end to his efforts. Both to our right and directly above, the crag was impossibly smooth. On our left, however, a ledge ran diagonally up the wall for several feet, then appeared to peter out at the sheer edge. To this edge he slowly scrambled, and vanished beyond. My heart bled for him, especially when the rope continued to run out for another score of feet. His position must be getting more and more precarious, and return correspondingly hazardous. I began to look around for a still better belay. But still the rope ran out, and at no funereal pace. I stared in wonder as the whole hundred feet passed through my hands.

'Come on!' came the distant shout. I picked my way to the edge, passed cautiously round, and found myself on a smooth precipice. Running diagonally up and across, an unbroken thread of superb holds curved all the way to the top. The extreme airiness of the staircase made me tread warily, but the climbing could hardly be called difficult; perhaps moderate would be the better description. But exhilarating! The groove is unique in Glencoe. Agag's Groove on Buachaille, for example, is a wide groove, not a slender line like this. If we met no difficulties neither did we feel disappointment. We were charmed.

Down again to the foot. We had time for one more complete ascent, and this time had the good fortune to pick out, as our introductory passage to the Terrace, a route of high educational value, teaching us much about the rock peculiar to this East Cliff of Aonach Dubh, and so helping us later. The route chosen went up the great wall about twenty paces to the right of the rowan-tree block. Fifteen feet up was a grassy ledge, where we built a cairn. McIntyre started. On this occasion it was probably his very knowledge of rock that contributed to his defeat. For the rock was rhyolite – the same rock as on Buachaille Etive Mor. And at that angle rock on Buachaille is not normally climbable over long stretches. He went up ten feet and found the rock pushing him almost out of balance; he could see the pitch continuing at that angle for another eighty feet; he could not feel confident of getting holds to serve him throughout all that height: accordingly, and rightly, down he came.

I tried instead. The rock did require to be forced at ten feet, but I thought that I might be safe in pushing the fight as far as twenty. Holds were small but good. They *had* to be good; that was why it was so astonishing that they should still be of the same quality at twenty feet, at thirty, forty – right on until ninety feet of rope dragged heavily at my waist. I had a good stance then. McIntyre joined me and the rest was easy. At two hundred and fifty feet we emerged on the Terrace.

Directly above us, and just to the right of the Quiver, a ridge stood straight as an archer's back. It was obvious, at the first glance, that if this stiffly upright ridge could be made to go it would give us the best climb on Terrace Face. The upper third of the ridge looked impossible, but after our Quiver experience we were not to be intimidated. I started up.

Brown, tough rock. Coarse and clean. No trace of loose stone. We climbed two long pitches on the crest and swore that no better rock could be found in Glencoe. Then the edge sprang up fearsomely, little overhangs thrusting out against the clouds. I tried to climb through them, weaving a way among a tangle of slabs and walls, and failed. The descent taxed my ingenuity to the limit. We were obliged after that to traverse a thin ledge on to the right-hand flank of the ridge, which overlooked the Basin and its mammoth overhangs. Our only hope of ascent was then to go ninety feet straight up the vertical flank to a little corner under the crest. The wall was not broken: in other words, not climbable had the rock been normal. I might have been persuaded to turn away, for the place was exposed, had it not been for our recent experience down at the wall near the rowan-trees. My mind was becoming accustomed, at last, to the idea that we could expect all rock hereabouts to be *ab*normal. So I made an attempt.

Tiny well-made holds came readily to hand and foot. By the time I had travelled fifty feet and saw that I had still as far to go, the strain on my credulity was again only supportable as an after-effect of Rowan-tree Wall. Otherwise my lot would have been defeat by doubt. Were all the excellent holds required by the angle really there? They were too small to be visible more than a few feet ahead. Always, when I looked beyond, the cupboard was bare – hope could draw from it no nourishment. Yet at every step I took the next well-formed hold materialized out of the blank wall. I seized it, moved, and there was the next hold: I seized, moved, and there it was! Never failing. Such exercise in unflinching faith is common in rock-climbing; but certainly it is uncommon for our faith to be so fully justified. Not that each move was easy. The climbing was hard.

I was overjoyed when I reached the corner, and so was McIntyre, judged by the sparkle in his eye as he lifted himself up out of space.

'A severe!' he exclaimed. 'On the first ascent,' I agreed, ' – less another time.' He took the lead and passed on to a second corner, fifteen feet up on the right, where he waited for me. His final move was an exit over the right wall, his body curved over thin air while he wrestled with awkward rock. I followed. Easy rocks led to the top.

We returned to our bivouac and supper. The cliffs across the ravine now wore a very different look to our appreciative eyes. The inscrutable visage of unknown crags in the morning had been transformed in a twinkling to a friendly and open face. 'Come back,' they said, 'often.' And there was need of return. Never before had any cliff presented to us four new routes in one day, and we could see for ourselves that another four awaited. We had still to penetrate the Basin, from which routes should go right and left. The huge wall to the left of the Bow should give a long route of no great difficulty. Below the right-hand end of the Terrace, splendidly arched slabs were marked, although dry, by the dark stain of a water-slide. This weeping wall seemed to promise the hardest climbing on the cliff. There were other possibilities.

So that we were very happy. Reason, being thus encouraged, suggested that our surest way of *not* enjoying the cliffs to the full was to keep them to ourselves until we had staked claims and worked them out. Before returning we must pass on the news to other climbers. The feast was spread … A second reflection was that new climbs of extreme severity are not hard to find in Glencoe, but the discovery of simple and modestly difficult routes is so hard that something like an intervention of Divine Providence is required for their revelation. It was our remarkable feat this day to have made on Aonach Dubh no route of real severity. That East Cliff was a humble and generous cliff, giving freely the sound climbs that are the daily bread of the rock-climber; therefore of more value than many airy severities that I had happened on in the past.

On the East Cliff all men may climb.

10

Rock-climbing in Rum

My day of return to the Cuillin of Skye after six years of war was not, it seemed, to be a day of rejoicing. Yellow clouds were billowing over Sgurr Alasdair when I scrambled alone up the last rocks to the cairn. The rain sheeted down. The month was September 1945, and the wind wintry.

Hardly a sign could be seen of the rock-peaks around me, save at moments when the clouds sank and resurged. I paused at the top for a few seconds only, but in these seconds a rift opened in the cloud and closed. Through the long shafts of that rift I caught a glimpse of a steel-like sheet of sea and one island. It lay ten miles out. There was a cluster of graceful peaks at the south end of it, but the north half was low. As I climbed down the south ridge the scene stayed vivid in mind: the Hebrides are enchanters of old, and I saw no other view.

A cluster of dark and secret peaks on a sheet of steel-grey sea. An unknown island – unknown at least to myself. It could be none other than Rum. I soon discovered that few of my mountaineering friends knew more of it than I. But throughout the following year I slowly gathered information.

'The whole trouble about Rum,' said a veteran mountaineer, 'is the trouble in landing. It's a private deer-forest. There's no pier and the owner discourages visitors – her ferry may refuse to lift you off the steamer. That means you've got to raid the island by motorboat from Mallaig, at a cost of £5 10s. And after that you've got to get *off* the island again. You can buy no food on it, you can get no roof over you, and gales may stop you leaving just when you have to. In fact, is it worth it?'

I confess that my desire of Rum waxed stronger than ever. I then examined a young rock climber on his return from a recent raid.

At once his eyes sparkled with enthusiasm. He was overflowing with praise.

'It's the best of *all* the western isles! Six big tops strung on a long thin ridge. It gives a scramble like the Comb of Arran. But what views! – they 're the best on the Scottish seaboard – look at the map – just look at it!'

'What about the cliffs? '

'Gabbro.' A pause implied that no greater praise could be given. 'None of them big ones – nothing like so big as Skye. But there's plenty of them, and no end to the new routes you could try. Go to the North-West Buttress of Askival – it may be the biggest on the island, and no one has ever climbed it. Then the whole coastline is ringed with sea-cliffs. But they're big – some a thousand feet high – and sheer. They're not for us. Though they *are* good to look at. '

These dark peaks on a wide sea were still with me after two years. However, their magnetic power gradually overcame inertia, and in April 1948 drew me to action. My luck held at the outset, for I enlisted Michael Ward. He is a magnificent rock-snow-ice climber with a passion for exploring unknown hill country; one who has mastered the art of travelling light. He carries as little unnecessary baggage on his back as he does flesh on his body. Ward is young and lean, and the commander of great reserves of energy. Nor does he spare himself in action. This meant that a fortnight with him might be somewhat in the nature of a toughening course. He dispenses the medicine of strenuousness, of which I feel in need from time to time.

My second stroke of luck was in getting permission to land from Lady Bullough. She gave it most kindly and warned us only about the need for taking good food supplies and a tent. We were now free to travel by the Outer Hebrides steamer, which carries passengers twice weekly from Mallaig to Rum – an eight-mile sail for the modest fare of 5s. 6d.

At midday on 3rd May we arrived at Mallaig. Ward had excelled himself. He turned up wearing the torn and patched jacket of an old lounge suit. The patches were of black cloth, probably cut out of wartime curtains, and they had been clumsily sewn on by himself. However, the jacket served to cover a navy-blue rugger jersey, which was all that he wore underneath (the weather was cold). The trousers were peculiarly shapeless, even for navy-blue serge, and most wonderfully frayed. He might have passed for a tramp, utterly down and out, were it not for that upright bearing – and a food-filled rucksack. He had brought no change of clothing from London.

'After all,' he argued, 'we 're only away for a fortnight – and quite apart from the clothing our own skins are waterproof: we're inside them and *can't* get wet!' He glanced at my fat and bulging rucksack, and looked swiftly away, as though embarrassed by an indecency, then allowed his deep-set brown eyes to wander over my face with a pained surprise. But he said nothing. I must admit that I had brought more spare clothing than was strictly necessary. Most of my food and fuel had to go into a second rucksack.

We sailed in the early afternoon. New snow had fallen that very morning on all Scottish hills. The skies were slate-grey, and the peaks of Rum white until noon, but the scene completely changed in the course of our three-hours' sail. The clouds evacuated the whole sea area in favour of the mainland, which blackened, leaving the seaward heavens a fresh and shining blue. The sun grew hot. Almost in the twinkling of an eye the snow-caps vanished. We steamed into Loch Scresort. The loch is a natural harbour on the east side of Rum and a motorboat put out from Kinloch to meet us. We stepped on board to be warmly welcomed by Duncan McNaughton, head-stalker and uncrowned king of Rum. His welcome was my undoing. Out of the corner of my eye I could see that our gear was being unloaded along with the mail-bags. I assumed too hastily that no mistakes could be made. Not until we arrived at the jetty did we discover the loss of my rucksack, now bound for the outer isles with my sleeping bag, change of clothing, cutlery, stove, and two cameras.

Ward was most kind and sympathetic. However, I can read his heart like an open book, and could see him reflect that my bad luck would do me good. Mercifully, my rucksack with the food was safe, so that from his point of view our situation had in no way worsened: he had a knife and matches. If the weather broke I should certainly have a bad time. Meantime it was good. Our immediate concern was a campsite, and Kinloch was attractive, too small to be called a village, despite a post office, and its situation sheltered. Indeed, the air was balmy and many kinds of blossom-bearing trees grew in the woods around Kinloch Castle. The castle is not a castle, but a rather beautiful palace of red sandstone, much too large for the barren isles of the west. We liked Kinloch, and we liked the people we met, and there is an excellent camp site on grass near the jetty. None the less we determined to carry our tent six miles south to Dibidil, a ruined cottage below Sgurr nan Gillean. There we should be close to the high tops and the rocks.

There is no road to Dibidil, but a track starts behind the woods fringing the castle. We wound slowly uphill for seven hundred feet. That is a rough track, sometimes barely perceptible, skirting along the top of great sea-cliffs. We were lured to the brink at one point and looked over the edge of an overhang. Several hundred feet below, Atlantic rollers crashed against the cliffs and roared white across reefs. They sucked back green and foaming from caves, and swirled black and smooth around blocks and pinnacles. On the south and west shores grey seals bask and bark, but not even seals could have lived near this fearsome cliff.

We continued our walk in high spirits. The sea was Mediterranean blue, and beyond was the long line of mainland hills, snow-capped and sparkling in a bright tumult down the full length of the eastern horizon. Far to the north, at a great height above the mainland, were towering white clouds. These pleased us more than anything. 'They're sure to mean good weather!' I exclaimed, and so fell headlong into error – a tempter of providence ...

Dibidil lies close to the shore, at the foot of a broad glen. We pitched our tent on short turf beside the burn. When we began to settle down inside, Ward, forgetful of his own comfort, at once offered me his sleeping bag, suggesting we share it night about. When I refused he gave me his only two sweaters. That first night was by no means so bad as I had expected. The soft and springy leather of climbing boots makes a not uncomfortable pillow, and although cold interfered with sleep I was able to doze.

We rose at five o'clock in the morning. If one lies hard there is no temptation to lie long. Moreover, we were eager to see the un-climbed North-West Buttress of Askival, and to make an attempt on it. Halfway through breakfast we heard a sudden patter of rain on the tent canvas. After such a clear night we were dumbfounded, yet when we looked out the tops were engulfed in mist, preci-pitating a steady, windless drizzle. It looked as though it would last forever, so there could be no point in waiting for it to stop. We started immediately after breakfast and climbed up Glen Dibidil to the pass on the south ridge of Askival. We were now in thick mist, but traversed hopefully on to and along the north-west face, until at last a dark blur could be seen above. Our buttress. It looked broad. When we drew closer we could see definite ridges separated from one another by shallow gullies. The ridge second from the right seemed to be the steeper. Its left-hand edge looked sharp as shrapnel, and the top part vanished into woolly mist, so that we had no idea of its shape or feasibility. Greatly daring, we built a cairn at the foot to mark our start. We roped up.

Ward started the climb by going ninety feet up a crack to the right of the edge. The rock was crystalline: although it was wet and numbing to the hands, we could climb it without distress. I joined Ward on a platform bitten out of the edge itself. Direct ascent was stopped by the vertical nose above, so Ward suggested that I look round its left flank. I looked. I saw a long sheer drop below, and above, a thin right-angled crack of seventy feet, its walls smooth and at one point bulging. An attempt on it would be a hard test of skill on a warm, dry day. I said so.

'But do try,' urged Ward. He spoke pleadingly and with studied innocence, for he loves to see me in difficulties. He gave me an encouraging smile, full of simulated confidence, and in a moment of weakness I was persuaded. I traversed a narrow ledge to the foot of the crack, and after strenuous effort climbed three feet up. But every time I tried to move farther I felt my body pushed out by the rock, until at last I knew that one more move would unbalance me backwards. My only comforting reflection was that if I *did* fall off the angle was so high and the drop so long that I'd hit nothing – the rope would stop me. However, my fingers were numb and my heart was no longer in the battle, so I came down and had my revenge on Ward.

'I'm sure you could do it, Michael,' I said. 'All it wants is a little forcing. Up you go!'

He tried hard. Again and again he reached the position where his body swayed out and his foot strained to the slipping point. The nervous strain of watching these efforts was much worse than that of making them, so my revenge was an unsatisfactory one. I began to urge him to wait for a dry day. He then gave up, and I turned my attention to the other side of the ridge.

A few yards to the right was a very steep wall of fifty feet. I climbed halfway up and the rock was so rough that I could balance on tiny holds without any sense of insecurity. But a mantelshelf at the halfway mark nearly defeated me. Every time I tried to raise myself on to that shelf, which was too narrow, an out-sway of the body was again evident. The wall behind it was bare of holds. A long pause ensued while I made tiny adjustments of body and feet. This was a fight fought out on millimetres of rock; to Ward below there was probably no sign of definite movement. When all was ready and the final attack took me over the top, I felt wild with delight – a much fuller and fiercer delight than in muscling up easy rock, however exhilarating its situation may be.

Ward joined me, and our route went directly up the crest of the ridge, which grew broader. The main difficulties were behind, for there was now a wide choice of route. We reckoned our climb to be three hundred and fifty feet when the buttress abruptly ended on the summit-ridge near the cairn. We were still in damp, dense mist, and invited each other with heavy irony to admire the finest view in the west highlands. We were not yet drenched quite to the skin, but the wind was cold and we hastened back to Dibidil.

A rainstorm blew up and continued all that afternoon and night. Our tent was not thoroughly waterproofed; it sprang several leaks and much of our time was spent bailing. I had to 'sleep' that night in my wet clothes, which is by no means so nasty as it sounds. It seemed to me that the very dampness of the cloth, perhaps by swelling the fabric, helped to exclude cold air and preserve body-heat. But in the early hours of the morning I had another tale to tell. The very worst kind of cold is a damp cold. I found that my best way to resist was to try to work up heat by regulated shivering. This was an art I had learned in central European prison camps in winter. One lies with a perfectly blank mind, midway between sleeping and waking, and lets the body shiver for five seconds in every half-minute. The process is reinforced at five-minute inter-vals by a few more strenuous wriggles. The result is a frequent boost to temperature, which helps to make the night a tolerable one. The process becomes automatic with practice.

What about risk? I wondered; and decided, very little. Only when health has been neglected is there cause to dread cold and wet. It is a good sign of a man's wholeness of mind and body if he can lie out and be numbed with cold, then thaw in the morning and be none the worse. He should be willing to run a risk now and then – health demands that sometimes he should forget his health, and expose his body to rain, wind, and extreme heat and cold.

The following morning was again wet, but cleared in the fore-noon. We decided that the quickest way of drying our clothes was not to hang them out, but to put them on and walk hard. We accordingly walked the coastal track south to the shooting lodge of Papadil. At the highest point of the track, which rises five hundred feet to the top of the sea-cliffs, we saw a herd of red deer, and one of these deer was white. We could hardly believe it was true. We had never thought a white deer possible. The herd was three hundred yards away, and I tried to convince myself that our white deer must in fact be a goat. For herds of black and white goats are common in Rum. They are not small and slender, like Alpine goats, but large, tough, and hairy. None the less our white deer when seen in outline was distinctly *not* a goat. It persisted in remaining a deer. We saved up this problem for McNaughton.

On our fourth day the weather cleared. We rose at 5 a.m. and decided that conditions were ideal for a traverse of the six main tops from Sgurr nan Gillean to Barkeval. That ridge-walk was the one thing I had looked forward to more than anything else. And at the end of it we could descend to Kinloch and collect my rucksack, which the steamer, we hoped, would this day return.

We started for Sgurr nan Gillean at 6.30 a.m. For the first time we felt the old-fashioned joy of an early morning in spring. An eagle was soaring between us and the summit. We climbed through cool air towards a blue sky, with sunlight washing over the wet ground. Sgurr nan Gillean is a shapely peak, but the ascent from Dibidil is a blank face of the steepest grass, the terrors of which were mitigated by banks of primroses on the lower half. On the hill-slopes around Dibidil primroses were thick on the ground, bare ground openly rejoicing in this bravery of woodland bloom. We gained the top in two hours, and started along the almost level ridge to Ashval. Cloud was forming round the Cuillin of Skye and the mainland hills, but the whole sea-view was clear to the west. The long low line of the Outer Hebrides ran from Barra Head to Lewis in the north, marking the edge of the world; beyond was a waste of seas like outer space made visible, apparently limitless. A great part of the fascination of the outer isles lies in that 'edge of the world' atmosphere: they are the last lands, the gateways – beyond them nothing is known (one feels). Thus they appear as the symbol of the frontier, those shores of the finite from which every man is one day launched upon the seas of the infinite, and makes voyage from life in time into life eternal.

We passed over the summit of Ashval, and began the steep descent to the bealach below Trallval. The ridge was very sharp halfway down, and not until we were past that point were we free to look round. It was then that we made a discovery of great interest to rock-climbers. We were looking into the south-west corrie of Trallval. Several hundred feet below the summit we saw a great gabbro cliff. There was certainly no record of a climb there, and the cliff would give the longest rock-climb in Rum if only a route could be found. We resolved to explore it next day.

At the top of Trallval the ridge turned sharply east to Askival. On the descent to our second bealach we were looking across the west corrie of Askival on to its North-West Buttress. We could see our ridge-climb of two days ago, now called the Atlantic Ridge, with a parallel and farther ridge that seemed equally good. It occurred to us then that we might fare better if we went up Askival by that parallel ridge instead of by the main ridge from the bealach. We traversed across the face to the buttress. At the foot of our proposed climb we came upon a cairn, and the lower rocks were nail-scarred. Like Robinson Crusoe on the sands, I stood like one thunderstruck. Someone had been up before us, and our own route farther to the right was not a first ascent of the buttress.

While uncoiling the rope we were puzzled to see several burrows in the turf ledges around us. There are no rabbits in Rum, and the holes were much too small for foxes. What other animal could have been responsible among cliffs two thousand feet up on a mountainside? We could think of no answer until Ward put his ear to one of them and swore that he heard a noise like chirping. I listened. The chirping of a bird was unmistakable. But we knew of no bird that dug burrows; it seemed a fit companion for the white deer of Papadil.

We then repeated the slightly older climb and enjoyed it. The standard was very difficult and the rock good. We arrived on top of Askival just as the clouds began lifting off the Cuillin. They were already clear of the mainland, which probed much farther north than we had imagined possible. From its dim and distant tip hundreds of hills stretched south to the lands of Argyll, and we were quite unable to name even one of them. The angle was new to us, and we felt as though looking out to unexplored country, wrapped in thick mystery of the unfamiliar, but full of promise – each valley and mountain-barrier secreting its untold tale, calling us to the quest. I had never seen Scotland looking quite like that since my first climb.

We had now begun the best part of the main ridge traverse. The ridge between Askival and Allival is a scramble on rock, the narrow crest being blocked halfway down by a 'gendarme.' There is no tight-rope walking in thin air, but something of the same exhilaration without the nervous trial. From the top of Allival we had an unobstructed view of the Cuillin. They were less spiky than

I had expected, but more gracefully proportioned. The peaks were well supported on broad rock-busts; they rose out of the sea in a blue-black cluster, massively. At their heart was the basin of Coir-Uisg, of all solitary corners of Britain surely one of the least accessible. Ward and I were smitten with desire to go and live there for a week. It should be next week, we decided – if I recovered my rucksack; and if not, well – we should still go there.

From Allival to Barkeval was a level walk, after which we repaired to Kinloch, and sought out Duncan McNaughton. We found him at home at four o'clock. The steamer had called, and he had gone on board and taken off my rucksack. But that service had by no means exhausted his kindness. He asked us into his cottage, and his wife gave us a meal of two boiled eggs, tea, toast, hot scones, and lemon-curd. It made a joyful change from our porridge and pemmican. I asked him about our wonderland animals – the white deer and the burrowing birds.

'On this island,' he said, 'I've got nine hundred deer, and one of them *is* white. From a distance it looks pure white, but when you get close up it is really pale fawn. I used to have a white stag too but a poacher killed it. I know of only one other white deer in Scotland – a stag in Ross-shire.'

'And the birds?' I asked.

'That's the Manx shearwater,' said McNaughton, 'a mid-ocean bird, the size of a small gull, only black. It comes here in the spring, makes a burrow up on the mountains, and lays one egg. It comes out only at night – if you want to see it look for it with a torch. After the egg is hatched the mother fattens up the chick, then goes out to sea and leaves it. By September the young bird has worked through its fat, but it still can't fly, so one night it starts off in search of food and waddles right down the mountainside to the shore, where it pushes off and feeds in shallow water. When it's strong enough it flies off to mid-ocean.'

'Have you any eagles?' I asked.

'Three eyries all told. One of them on the low crags at Dibidil. And if you stay on another week you'll see the sea-cliffs alive with puffins. They're due to begin arriving any day now.'

After more tea and discussion Ward and I returned to Dibidil. That evening I took my first lesson in Atlantic bathing. An enormous weight of water thundered up the beach. I had to learn to run in quickly and take a powerful dive into each wave before it broke, otherwise it bowled me over and broke my skin on the shingle. It was all highly exciting, but enjoyable, if one was willing to accept some punishment.

The next day was cloudy but dry. In the early morning we crossed the main ridge and descended to the south-west corrie of Trallval, overlooking Glen Harris. We walked northward beneath our buttress. It looked much more intimidating at close quarters. In fact, on that first survey of its three hundred yards' length we saw no route at all. The rock was gabbro, distinguished by its great number of overhangs, most of them wet and streaked black and brown. The right-hand half of the buttress looked about four hundred feet high, the left-hand half about four hundred and fifty feet in two tiers.

Facing us across the corrie, on the north side, there was a smaller, triangular-shaped buttress. We thought that this too was unclimbed, and felt disposed to deal with it first. It gave us three good climbs on peridotite, an exceptionally rough and tough gabbro. By that time we were warmed up and more confident. We returned to the South-west Buttress.

At the very centre of the cliff was an ill-defined rib. We tried it, only to be turned back after fifty feet by holdless rock. The shallow gullies on either side of the rib were of no use to us, for both ended high up in great overhangs. We went forty feet to the right and looked again. The rock was there split by a crack of two hundred and fifty feet, vertical throughout. Again we moved forty feet rightwards, and then at last our blank eyes and long faces were enlivened by hope. A shallow gully ran up fifty feet to the base of a short pinnacle. Above and to the right of the pinnacle a broad ledge ran rightwards round a corner into a wide, right-angled groove. Thence it seemed just possible that a way could be found up one of the two opposing walls. They looked airy and remote, and led into an upper wall of slabs crossed by a line of overhangs, the difficulties of which were quite incalculable from below. In short, every passage was doubtful, but therefore hopeful.

We roped up and our troubles began. Ward climbed the initial gully, but found the base of the pinnacle to be dangerously shattered. He dared not touch the rocks lest they fell on him. He came down. I then led up the gully's outer left wall to a platform on the pinnacle's left side. Our task was now to cross the pinnacle to the main wall behind.

'Is the pinnacle safe from here?' asked Ward a bit nervously. Just in time I choked back that very question which I was about to put to him. Apparently Ward had a blind confidence that I would *know*. And I hated to shatter that innocent thought. I calculated quickly. If the pinnacle fell it would heel over slowly, Ward would be only six feet up, and ought to have time to jump back to the platform. In any event my stance was secure, and I could fully safeguard him with the rope. 'I think it will hold,' I said. 'We ought to go on.'

He scrambled to the top of the pinnacle. For a few seconds he hesitated, then spread wings of faith, and took a short bold flight across the top of the gully into a chimney on its right-hand side. Above this chimney was a vertical crack of twenty feet, but the holds were good, judging by the speed of Ward's ascent. He reached the wide ledge where I joined him. The next passage would determine our fate.

We walked rightwards along the ledge and climbed round the corner into a small bay. The huge right-angled groove springing up from the back of it looked impregnable, but the crest of its left wall was a sharp ridge. It thrust at the clouds, arrow-like. If its back were well notched we might get up; our chances were small other-wise. Ward started by going twenty feet up the groove, then struck straight up the left wall on to the crest. I joined him on a clean-cut ledge, and took the lead. The ridge was certainly very steep and felt exposed, but at every step the right holds came to hand and foot. We went up three rope-lengths, leading alternately, until the ridge merged in the final slab wall. The lead was now Ward's, for which I was duly grateful. Running across the top of the upper slabs was the long line of overhangs, which had looked even worse from below than they really were. To my surprise he went hard left, straight for the most exposed part, where a fine edge projected vertically against the sky. He worked his way slowly up a rough brown slab to the right of this edge, and then finally up the edge itself. All space seemed to ache beneath him, but Ward in good form is a joy to watch. Every move is sure and deliberate, and the foot placed with a kind of inevitable rightness.

When I followed him up I thought the pitch the best we had done in Rum, although not the most difficult. We had reached the top of our climb, and each feature of it had been one of character and interest. Our only remaining task was to name the buttress, for by tradition that was our privilege. The cliff faced Glen Harris, so we christened it Harris Buttress. The line of our climb I named the Archangel Route, for it is the prerogative of angels to balance on needles, and their leader is Michael.

We sat on flat stones and coiled up the rope. Our visit to Rum had come to an end – a good end despite the bad start. The bad hours already seemed unreal – well nigh forgotten! 'It's a trick of the mind,' said Ward. 'It always works. You can put up with extreme discomfort because you know that it won't last forever and that you 're going to forget it anyhow. But what you don't forget is the sun-warmed rock on a good climb.' He looked down to the Atlantic. 'And things like that down there ... ' he added. Travelling across the grey-green sea was a track of light, wrinkled and flashing, where a shaft stole quietly out from the clouded sun. In long, wavering lines, Atlantic combers creamed on the Harris shore. At our feet – brown crags and space.

11

Coir-Uisg

After five days on Rum Michael Ward and I sailed for Skye, our destination Coir-Uisg. It is the fate of all mountaineers to see their plans sometimes capsize, canoe-like in wild water. But on this occasion their end was to be more sharp and shocking than usual; perhaps because we planned for ourselves, greedily after our rough, first days in Rum, an immoderate share of sensuous and spiritual delight. Coir-Uisg, ringed by its score of three-thousand-foot peaks, save for one narrow outlet to the Atlantic, appealed as the perfect campsite for lovers of solitude. Around the Black Cuillin and their great corrie, as we had seen them from Allival, hung an air of mystery as tangible as the blue haze of their atmosphere; for there is real mystery in all beautiful forms, and most especially in the quiet of remote mountains. In all the length and breadth of the kingdom where else could we find such seclusion, and on what other mountains such beauty? So we dreamed dreams about nicely balanced days of idleness and action, and planned to explore unclimbed cliffs from our haven.

At 7 p.m. we reached Sligachan. There was no chance of our reaching Coir-Uisg that same night, but at least we might camp well down Glen Sligachan, and so cross the ridge to Coir-Uisg next morning. Our week in Rum had disclosed how few of this world's goods are required on mountains, so we resolved to shed much gear and food. To this end we sought out Mr Campbell, the hotel-keeper. He most kindly allowed us free storage space in an old attic room above a stable. Entrance was gained by a flight of outside stairs. The room was wood-lined, had one bed with a mattress, and a window facing Loch Sligachan. A day was at hand when this room would become our goal of all hope. We dumped our surplus stores, but took with us an extra tent, which we proposed to pitch and to leave in Glen Sligachan. From this second base we might later make a traverse of the main ridge.

At nine o'clock we set off down Glen Sligachan. It is a big, bare, and level glen, a mile wide, and running seven miles to the sea, dividing the east from the west Cuillin. Our route lay down the right bank of the river across moorland flats like marsh country. Even at the end of two miles, which was all we made that night, the hills had not begun to close round us. The twilight deepened; a grey-blue haze thickened over the flats. Long banks of mist appeared on the low and open ground around us, but the hill-tops were clear and stars twinkled. We camped on a little island of dry ground.

Next morning was dry and sunny. We went a further two miles down the glen, and pitched our second tent midway between Sgurr nan Gillean and Blaven – a good strategic position, but exposed to storm. Accordingly we pitched a high-altitude tent, which would stand in any weather, and crossed the Druim Hain Ridge to Coir-Uisg with a light summer tent, which had no sewn-in groundsheet. Coir-Uisg, we thought, was too sheltered to be troubled by storm.

We came down to the shore of Loch Coruisk near the sea-end, and had to walk a mile and a half north to Coir-Uisg, which is the mountain corrie as distinct from the loch. Along the east bank there was just a vestige of a track, winding its way through shrubs and boulders, and dwarf trees and innumerable plants not yet in bloom. The smoke-blue peaks lay well back from the water, which stretched black and glistening like a seal's skin. At the north end was a shore-land of flat gabbro slabs, where we found a patch of turf for our tent.

Four days of fine weather ensued, yet our plans of action all went astray. The unclimbed cliffs of Sgurrs MhicCoinnich and Dearg still front Coir-Uisg with a thousand feet of virgin rock – but they no longer tempt us. We crossed the main ridge to the Taimeilear corrie of Sgurr a Mhadaidh, and in Deep-Gash Gully, which too was virgin and fully five hundred feet high, were again routed on wet rock. Still, we enjoyed ourselves, swimming in the ice-cold waters of Coruisk, sunbathing on ridges, and exploring the Coireachan Ruadha and Corrie of Solitude. On our fourth day we transferred our headquarters to the tent in Glen Sligachan, planning to return to Coir-Uisg by the traverse of the whole Cuillin Ridge.

Ward opened the final day by climbing Blaven and Clach Glas alone at three o'clock in the morning, starting from a bivouac on the ridge and rejoining me in the glen at 6.30 to climb Sgurr nan Gillean. We spent our next eleven hours on six miles of rock, scrambling in constant sunshine with a light breeze to fan our skins, and never a cloud in the sky. On the last quarter of the ridge we witnessed the brewing of a big weather change. The sky clouded from south-west to south-east, and the wind freshened. I speeded up the pace, and towards the end went very fast – severe work for Ward, who had now done fourteen thousand feet of rock-climbing. But the wind was blowing harder every hour, and at any moment we expected rain. On Garsbheinn, the last peak of all, the rain started.

Our descent to Coir-Uisg took a full two hours. We reached the tent at 10 p.m. wet and exhausted. That hard cold wind on the last ridges had caught us when our bodily powers were reduced. We pulled on our sleeping bags most thankfully, then looked round at the unholy chaos of tins, food, clothing, cutlery, rope, and gear of all kinds strewn about the floor of the tent. We wanted something to eat, but being more tired than hungry contented ourselves with a few spoonfuls of pea-flour and water. Even that simple meal was a trial of patience – every time we laid down a knife or spoon it disappeared. Long and industrious search is required to produce needles from haystacks. 'We'll have a good meal in the morning,' we reassured each other. 'Or perhaps in the late forenoon,' we added hastily.

We lay back to sleep. The rain drummed down on the roof. It drummed so hard that instead of sleeping we began to listen with some anxiety. If it continued like that the ground would be flooded. However, here we were and here we must stay, so we turned over to sleep again. Half an hour later great gusts of wind struck the tent. They must have struck very hard, for they wakened me. I piled all stores on the inside skirts to try to stop the wind blowing under the walls, but their weight was woefully insufficient. At 1 a.m. a gale sprang from the south-east – the only direction from which we had no protection. A guy-rope tore out on the windward side and flailed across the canvas, then another. I pulled off my bag and rushed outside to secure the tent. The wind nearly bowled me over when I stood up and carried blinding rain in my face. The night was so black that I could see nothing at all. I groped about for the guy-ropes, and found them, but the pegs had gone forever. That our tent might ever be uprooted by storm at midnight had occurred to us only as a nightmare idea, which we never imagined could really happen to *us*. Such things happened only to other people. It was going to happen to us now. I could see no way out. For the wind was right under the tent, which was blowing out like a balloon. I felt the main end-guy tear away, seized it as it whipped in the air, and threw myself on the ground to hold the tent down.

'Michael!' I shouted. 'Pack up!'

'Try to hang on,' he answered.

It was like trying to hold down an open parachute. I needed all the strength I possessed to hold that tent, and the ropes were cutting into my hands. Ward was ramming all the stores and gear into the rucksacks, no doubt as fast as he could, but he took a long, long time. I made no allowance for the wild disorder inside, the weakness of his dying torch-battery, or the need to look out clothing for me. I heartily cursed him while my body went numb. I was soaked to the skin and the wind was bitter. After that ten thousand feet of climbing with neither a good meal nor sleep to follow, the twenty minutes' exposure to gale and rain was more than my body would endure. It mutinied and threw up the defence. I could feel the barriers go down and the cold sweep in. I knew then that there was going to be trouble. Meanwhile more urgent trouble pressed.

'Hurry up!' I shouted. 'I can't hang on!'

'One second!' cried Ward. Then: 'Let it go!'

I collapsed the tent. We groped about on the open ground-sheet for wet stockings, sweaters, boots, and windproof jackets. Despite the fury of wind and rain lashing out of a total blackness, we somehow found them, or most of them, and pulled them on. We rolled up the tent and tied it to my rucksack.

'Sligachan?' asked Ward.

'Sligachan,' I said.

I tried to lift that rucksack and staggered under the weight. I could not swing it on to my back. I had to sit down to get it on, like a camel, and raise the weight on my legs. It seemed double the load I had carried to Coir-Uisg five days ago. 'Michael,' I swore to myself, 'has stuffed the heavy things into my rucksack and all the light ones into his own.' That was the kind of thought that began creeping into my mind, which was closed to the obvious facts that saturated cloth accounted for one-half of the weight increase and fatigue for the other. Ward for the moment was something to be endured, like the storm. I could have eaten him up.

In the darkness we could find no trace of the path down the loch side and had to go at a snail's pace. I wondered whether we could make that seven miles to Sligachan over the Druim Hain Ridge. We were not willing to lie down and shelter beside a boulder, for the wind and cold were far too great. Our only hope was to keep moving: any other course would have meant our collapse through exposure. The first grey light of dawn filtered through thick layers of racing cloud, adding a new gloom to the storm-murk of the corrie. A full gale was still blowing up on the tops. Down at Coir-Uisg the wind had dropped below gale strength, but raged on the white loch. The tempest showed an awful beauty, like a Flying Dutchman overture, but the beauty aroused in us neither awe nor any other emotion. We were too cold. That is why it is so important to note that we saw it.

When we turned east into the protection of the Druim Hain corrie our respite from wind was countered by the climb of a thousand feet to the ridge. We had to resort to the old device of making good each step as it came and refusing to think of the one ahead. After crossing the ridge we were exposed to the full wind-force, which swept up the funnel of Glen Sligachan with driving rain – driving straight, never flagging, obscuring the glen's farther wall in long bead-curtains of grey. Luckily our high-altitude tent had stood up to the storm. We opened the leeward door and crawled in, but rapidly decided not to linger. We had no dry clothing here, and the damp cold of that south-east wind would penetrate farther into us the longer we stopped. I felt very badly chilled. We ate an emergency ration of chocolate, then struck the tent, and packed up hurriedly. This extra load was Ward's. I remembered that he had now done fifteen thousand feet of climbing since the previous morning. In fact it occurred to me in this more benign mood that I was thrice blessed in having him as a companion: that he should ever crack up was unimaginable.

We started off on the last four miles with the wind at last battering us hard on the back. We had now a goal to draw us – the old attic room at Sligachan – wooden walls and a dry floor – even a spring bed and a mattress! It was too much! At the thought of it I felt a sentimental emotion flood through me, and at the same time a flush of heat spread over my body so that I felt able to speed along, floating airily over the stones and potholes of the path. But it was the head that floated and the rest of the body just hung on to it, as though flapping in the breeze. I had a high temperature and was light-headed. However, while the trouble was in the warm phase the body tingled and possessed a strange energy, but one mile from Sligachan the warm phase changed suddenly to the cold. My feet felt like lead, the rucksack like a hundredweight. The pace dropped to a crawl. A fit of shivering came over me, and I stopped several times to rest. Ward, as a man of medicine, was intrigued. I could see him turn a calculating eye on me and look puzzled, but through perverseness refused to give him the satisfaction of knowing what was wrong.

At 7.30 a.m. we arrived at Sligachan. There was a joint meet of the Scottish Mountaineering Club and the Alpine Club at the hotel, but we decided that such august company was not for us. We climbed to the old attic room and stripped off our dripping clothes. I had a dry change waiting for me, but Ward had none, and retired to his damp sleeping bag. In a few minutes he was asleep.

Even with Shetland wool pullovers next to the skin I felt too shivery to lie down. Something drastic had to be done. It would be no remedy, I thought, to crouch over a fire or to put on innumerable wrappings. To avoid slavery to cold one must master oneself and the cold by action. I put that idea into practice. I swallowed two big spoonfuls of sugar, took Ward's clothes to the hotel kitchen to be dried, then went out again into the rain, and ran hard until I sweated. When I came back Ward awakened. We cooked a large meal of sausages and eggs, plum pudding, and hot sweet tea, and then we slept. By nightfall my high temperature had gone.

Next morning we returned to the mainland and arrived home in a heat-wave. When I sat down in my study a sweet fresh scent of apple-blossom and lilac poured through the open windows along with the sunshine. Azaleas and poppies flamed among greening trees. Rosebuds were bursting, the bees busy, and birds singing. The earth was quickening with life. I thought of the treeless isles and naked peaks of the west, yet could not find it in my heart to say: 'This is better than that' – least of all when I thought of Coruisk, raging white in the dawn. Discomfort of body is real enough at the time, but recollection shows it to have no standing power in reality; not even its sharpest pangs last. But remembered beauty is recognition of a power that is real. And it does last. Even when first seen in misery and labour it lasts. It returns to exact due tribute and to give out of itself all that a man can receive. Until he can receive, it waits for him.

12

Tournament on Ice

When the statement is made by a mountaineer that he has done such and such a Scottish rock-climb in winter, the information he gives means next to nothing until one hears very precisely what the conditions were. If he talks of a gully it may mean that a route normally very difficult was found easy, or vice versa. If he talks of a long ridge or buttress under good snow, it means that however often that rock has been climbed before he has climbed a new route, engaged on difficulties the detail of which could not be foretold, and the exact likeness of which will not be seen again. One of the most sensationally radical of such changes known to me occurred on the Shelf of Crowberry Ridge. In December 1936 it was definitely a rock-climb, covered in loose snow, a long stepped trough running up the north wall of the ridge below and parallel to the crest. In March 1937 it was Scotland's biggest ice-climb – a ribbon of continuous ice five hundred and fifty feet long. Mackenzie and I had seen nothing like it before, nor have we since. It bulged seven times in distinctive pitches of blue, clear, and white ice, these being linked by runnels of snow-ice.

In the preceding December we had received on the Shelf the most resounding defeat of our lives. Loose snow and wind had caused unimaginable delays: *verglas* on the final slabs had forced us down after sunset: two hundred feet of rope had been left behind on the climb when we roped off the last pitches in a blizzard. We badly wanted to go and get that rope back. And we had wanted more ice on these upper slabs – ice that we could use – ice in which we could cut. Well, there was no question that now we should have it. The extraordinary conditions of March had been caused by three heavy snowfalls in January, February, and early March, each followed by heavy thaw and sudden frost, and latterly by days of blazing sun and by freezing nights. The Shelf had become a natural ice-trap.

Our decision to go on 28th March being made, I have never felt more nervous about consequences. We received great help from Miss Nancy Girvan of Inverarnan House, in Glen Falloch, where we stayed overnight on the 27th. She rose at 4.30 a.m., and made our breakfast. Years later I am still impressed by that act of generous toughness, which contributed more to the climb than a lead on one of its upper ice-pitches. The result was that we reached the head of Glen Erive in time to see the Buachaille, covered from peak to moor in thick snow, receive the first fire of the sunrise. For a few minutes only the tip crimsoned and faded. For a few minutes mellow sunshine flooded down the eastern face, creamily brilliant, turning to a dazzle of white as the light strengthened. The Bua-chaille, meanwhile, was giving birth to the day's first cloud. Around the base of the peak attenuated streamers of mist were forming. They joined and formed rolling banks, slowly drifting up the mountain's flank towards the blue sky.

The Crowberry Ridge was entirely snow-covered, even on its lower nose and on Rannoch Wall, where the angle is eighty degrees. Perhaps this 'snow' was mostly white ice. As a pre-cautionary measure we called at Kingshouse Inn to warn other climbers not to send stones or ice over the Crowberry Tower. It was more than likely that we should have the seven hundred and fifty feet of Crowberry Ridge to ourselves this day, but were disinclined to leave the matter to luck. We then repaired to Coupall Bridge and at 8 a.m. set off.

There was not a breath of wind, and even at this early hour the strength of the sun was so great that we moved over the moor in our shirt-sleeves. The ground was snow-quilted but not embarra-ssingly so, and the heather-tops projected bushily. On the other hand, clear ice spreading thickly over outcrops of rock on the first steep slopes engaged us at too frequent intervals in axe-work. At the first opportunity we traversed into the lower reaches of the Crowberry Gully, and there found good hard snow all the way to the foot of Crowberry Ridge. Our proposed route was in full view.

We looked at it – and could find nothing to say. All the usual adjectives used to extol a climb in superlative condition seemed too cheap or inadequate to find a way on to our tongues. Our admiration and eagerness were touched by dismay. Perhaps Mackenzie was immune from this unease, but certainly not I. Eventually he said 'Ice! Well, we *wanted* ice.' I answered: 'It's more than I thought possible in Scotland.' And even at that we did not realize just how much ice there was. A great and craggy north face, topped by a tower of wilder outline than any other I knew in Scotland, divided by a narrow chasm from the thousand-foot cliff of North Buttress on its right, the whole face of which was plated in snow and ice from foot to crown: that was the bare framework for the line of our route. The Shelf on the north wall was badly foreshortened. We could see continuous ice for three hundred feet, which in itself was so far outwith our experience that we never imagined that to be only half the tale.

Running along the base of the north wall a steeply shelving snow-ledge allowed us to traverse rightwards to the first big step or butt of the Shelf. The first thing we saw there was the one-hundred-and-twenty-foot rope left by us last December. It hung free of ice, but its lower ends were embedded in deep snow-banks, frozen so hard that our most strenuous efforts failed to free them. The salvaging of the rope would have needed an hour's cutting, which we could not afford. The time was ten o'clock. We were now completely out of the sun, and could feel the sting of the frost in our lungs and around our necks. We pulled on all available sweaters, then roped up on a hundred feet of line, which we doubled.

Mackenzie dealt with the first pitch, which is a very wide rampart split by three chimneys. The best route today lay up the rib to the right of the centre chimney. To get on to it we had firstly to climb ten feet out of the chimney by its nearly vertical wall, which was larded with thin grey ice, and which at this early stage of the day we fondly imagined to be excessively awkward. We were soon to learn by contrast how meek and mild it really was; meantime we were glad enough to save a few minutes by making free use of the fixed rope for handhold. We thus emerged on the rib's back, which is slabby, and therefore, I thought, more likely to give us hard climbing than its lower wall. But the slabs were heavily iced in exactly the right places; if the cuttings of holds took time, the placing of hand and foot was easy.

Beyond the top a low rectangular crag gave a good rock-belay. The Shelf then rose in a straightforward slope of the type of white snow-ice common in the Alps, much more readily cuttable than the frozen water armour-plating the pitches, but not so deep as it might have been. Steps had to be slashed out too small to justify our moving together, and no axe-belays could be used. We arrived below pitch two, a chimney notable for the clarity of its great ice bulges. Another relic of our December rout – an eighty-foot fixed rope – was visible as the core of a huge pillar fully two feet thick. The very strands of the rope could be seen if one peered. It was not of very much use to us! Moreover, it lay to the left of the correct route, which went up the chimney – or rather up what I should say had once been the chimney. Now it was filled with ice of the first water, crystal pure. The cutting of holds in such ice was no easy work. Mackenzie took his short axe to it and struck hard. It was like trying to cut solid glass. The pick jarred. Splinters flew, but not in quantity. As he worked his way up I was at least able to give him some moral support. For I was tied on to the big ice-pillar, as safe as it was uncomfortable. The more normal stance is the cave under the pitch, but this was blocked with frozen snow. However, I barely had half an hour to wait before Mackenzie was up. On such very difficult ice this was fast work: of all things needed today speed and pace ranked foremost. Accordingly, to relieve and rest Mackenzie, we changed the lead.

A shallow tongue of snow-ice gave us technically, but not muscularly, easy work to our third obstacle, which was a wide chimney, mercifully short. The route lay ten feet up its vertical iced wall – an abnormal angle and brittle ice. Only the great thickness of the ice made the ascent possible. The exit required tricks of contortion reasonable, perhaps, on ten-foot walls. As we thus gained in height the Shelf grew steeper and more heavily frost-bound, and we became aware of it as a mere shelf in relation to the great scale of the rock-snow-ice scene: the chill and gloomy depths of Crowberry Gully close on our right, and the hoary north wall of the Ridge rising in overhangs on our left, and just across the gully the face of North Buttress, as vast in breadth as in height, blinding white in the upper sunshine but grey below. Everywhere was the glint of ice thrusting through flaky snow. As quickly as I could I cut up the trough to a third chimney, this one unusually wide and square-cut. All three walls were vertical and of height twelve feet.

Mackenzie resumed the lead. Technically this pitch was severe, but not being exposed put no strain on the nerves. There was exasperatingly little ice on it. All around us was ice in mass, green bosses, blue bulges, white boiler-plates; but here, on this twelve feet of rock, a black and skimpy smear. We had to go up by wedging back and foot on opposing walls, and had to be extremely careful how we did so; for slippery rocks and awkward angles of pressure made the positions enforced on us unusual. This was the very type of pitch that one feels to be climbable in the conditions only because it is short, and therefore fairly safe except at the top. For the third successive time I said to myself: 'If this had been long or exposed we should never have got up' – words that I should have to eat (twice over – and I do not joke when I say so) within the next two and a half hours.

The Shelf arched its back, and seventy feet higher ended against the upper and icy wall of the north face, on which we had still to climb two hundred feet or more to reach the crest of Crowberry Ridge. The crux of the whole route was the sixty feet of rock immediately in front. The ice there was again miserably thin. Re-membering the trouble we had just had on twelve feet of thin ice, we did not relish the prospect of sixty. But an extraordinary climb is worth extraordinary effort: if only we could put this pitch behind us we should gain access to the final groove of a hundred and fifty feet which, in summer at least, presents no difficult way.

We stood in an up-curling corner in the angle between the flank of the ridge on our left and a broad wall on our right, the latter topped by a small pinnacle. In summer one climbs the initial corner by a crack in the angle, then may traverse left and upwards to the crest of the ridge – a route impossible now on account of *verglas* lying on slabs. Our alternative was to take the wall right-wards to a square recess thirty feet up, the back wall of which rose high above the other two in a square-cut pinnacle. The shape of the recess was thus like that of a high-backed throne with box-arms. The route would have to go on to the seat and then up over one of the arms, which were vertical walls of six or seven feet. We could see nothing beyond. Mackenzie started.

The first thin crack was filled with black, unusable ice, so instead he took to a steep corner more to the right which brought him on to very difficult and glazed rock. The delicacy of this passage can hardly be exaggerated, and I doubt if any man would have climbed it save in one of those fits of *elan* that come on occasion to all of us, as it came now to Mackenzie. Such rock could be climbed in no passive frame of mind; every move had to be forced, and took minutes to execute; for minute adjustments of body and balance had to be made and striven for before hand or foot could lift to its next hold. The axe was carried by wrist-sling, or between finger and thumb, ready for instant use in chipping at ice. He crept up until six feet below the right-hand corner of the recess. He could go no farther on that line, and I thought he was beaten, but he managed to make a turn and traverse hard left under the left-hand corner, there to make a second turn and shorter traverse up to the base line of the recess, into which he climbed over a low vertical wall. All this manoeuvring on the iced rocks was made on holds too small to accommodate more than the edge-nails of his boots. He had spent one hour in climbing that thirty feet on to the seat of the throne, and the difficulties of the second thirty feet were to be still greater.

The seat was outward sloping, so he edged his way up to the pinnacled back. An escape out of the recess had now to be forced over the right-hand wall, and that proved the crux of the whole day's climb. After making one step up on this wall he discovered the angle to be too high and the face too holdless for a direct exit. He was obliged then to take the outside route by stepping on to a small and outward sloping hold on the wall's outer corner. For that he had no handhold of any kind. It was a pure balance-move above crusted slabs down-plunging several hundred feet to Crowberry Gully. By something very like a miracle there was no ice on the foothold. There he was, then, balanced by friction-grip on his right foot, with the urgent need of speeding rightwards round the corner, but with further move impossible unless he could change feet. When I saw that he was determined to try, without handhold, I felt almost sick with apprehension. It is better to lead a movement of that kind than to watch another.

Mackenzie lent slightly forward so that his solar plexus rested against the wall's sloping top, and so gave him a slight friction-hold, enough to help him for that fraction of a second in which the lightning change must be made. It was impossible for him to see the foothold, and if he should miss it nothing could then save him. He balanced, arms outstretched and fingertips just touching the rock – then – one quick hop and the deed was done.

He rounded the corner and I saw no more of him for fifteen minutes. He would be in the long wide groove running up to the right-hand side of the pinnacle. At short intervals a bit of rope would scutter over the rocky arm and a few flakes float down through space. Later came a torrent of chips. Quite unexpectedly his head appeared from behind the top of the pinnacle. He looked not at all triumphant. The pitch had been too severe to allow indulgence in self-congratulations. He was just profoundly thankful. What had happened round the corner I could not know until twenty minutes later when I myself arrived there. After the feet-change my right foot came round into the groove and on to a very high and rounded hold, frost-hoared, but giving friction for an upward-propelling scrape of the boot-nails. Like the preceding move it was very severe, but brought good handhold within reach. Some ten feet of high-angle snow-ice led thereafter to a saddle at the rear of the pinnacle. The time was then 2 p.m.

Like Mackenzie I felt very thoughtful at the saddle. I was shaken. That was the hardest pitch I had ever climbed in my life, nor have I since been up another like it. I swore that I would never go back in similar conditions, which were too exacting for pleasure even in retrospect. Meanwhile we nibbled at food, looked about us, and with quite a start awakened to a bigger and wider world than the next two feet of ice-encrusted rock. In the foreground the walls of the North Buttress were dazzlingly sheeted, most emphatically crowned in glory, and in great contrast to the hills of the distant north, which were quietly beautiful. The sun spread evenly upon the broad flanks and penetrated the great snow-corries. Close at hand every crusted crag surged out dramatically white upon blue sky. But the background was wreathed in sun and sleep, and there the snows held fast the illusion of their everlastingness. Over all that land lay the sign of inner and hidden things, like the background to an old Italian painting, where no revelation is ever made but the promise of it always hinted.

Near and present realities pressed for attention. An ice-choked scoop on our right rushed up to the ridge, an unbroken ice-fall of a hundred and fifty feet, twice bulging in fifty-foot pitches. These latter were a great surprise to us. We had been prepared for an icy ribbon lining the groove, but not for the formation of big ice-walls.

It was my turn to lead. We had already climbed ten feet up the scoop before diverging left to our present saddle; so I began cutting nicks up the remaining twenty feet towards the first pitch. But I did not have very much cutting to do: the ribbon was only two inches thick; occasional patches of three inches were something to be welcomed. At the foot of the ice-wall I stopped to bring on Mackenzie, who took up position ten feet below me. I turned to examine the ice. It was the white and bubbly kind, as unreliably brittle as one could well find. Would it take my weight at *every* move on the fifty feet? The answer was certainly not known to me. Instinctively I looked down to see how Mackenzie was placed. He had been unable to find a rock-belay on either wall of the groove, so had belayed me instead to his axe-head, the pick of which had been stabbed two inches into the snow-ice. Well, it was a gesture – slightly better than absolutely nothing. Behind him the groove swept down a further twenty feet, to end at the edge of the wall dropping into the chasm of Crowberry Gully. The text-book answer to this predicament is simple: Unsafe ice, exposed position, no belay? – Turn back! But turn back with five pitches below us, one of which had taken two hours to ascend, and with neither rock-belay nor piton from which to rope off! The text-books have no answer to that, save to point a moral.

It seemed to me that we should have to go on and make the best of what the gods were giving us. I cut an experimental hold or two in the brittle ice and tried them. They held. Was the ice just 'leading me on'? I shall never forget that next five minutes' agony while I tried to make up my mind. If a hold collapsed I decided I should try to fall facing in, and brake with my pick the moment I landed on the ribbon. Mackenzie might then succeed in stopping me. I cut a few more holds, and eased myself on to each, trying to put as little weight as I could on my hands, and indeed attempting desperately not to put weight on anything, as though I were practising levitation. I began now to get the 'feel' of the ice and to judge its holding power. There was one harrowing patch near the halfway mark where the ice was replaced by frozen snow. The snow itself was good, but was it well frozen to the underlying ice? I cut at it above my head, using the gentlest of chip-strokes with the pick, not the blade, simply to minimize the jar of each blow. Thus I fashioned two handholds and two footholds. When I moved there was just the slightest subsidence of the handholds – an instant's alarm – but they held. On the last twenty feet the ice was so thick that security was ensured. At the top I had safe though shallow footing in frozen snow to bring on Mackenzie.

The second ice-pitch followed immediately. A narrow chimney of easy angle ended high up against a vertical face of white ice. The latter, we thought, could not be climbed direct, but trusted that some way of turning it might yet appear. I had trouble with the initial chimney despite the angle; for the too narrow walls prevented my cutting on the clear ice so thickly lining the interior. I had to go up by bridging. Near the vertical ice I managed to unravel a route over the left bounding wall, which gave me harder climbing than anything on the preceding pitch, but pleasanter.

Sound rock and the sunny air of our near approach to the ridge gave me the first truly carefree moments of the day. Beyond the left wall I arrived in a short gully filled with firm snow. Mackenzie came on and a few minutes later the shining crest of the Crowberry Ridge was level with our eyes – a knife-edged *arête* crested by fins of translucent ice two feet high, through which we looked for a moment as through glass towards the Blackmount. Most regretfully we smashed the fins with an axe and stepped on to the edge.

After five hours of shade and frost we suddenly came out into a world of brilliant, warm sunshine, but with sharp, crisp air to preserve the snow and ice, which glistened everywhere, beneath our feet and on the rims of the distant hills. A sombre haze in the valleys picked out the succeeding and receding ridges of the vast southern panorama, where peaks soared like an Alpine chain, their shining crests heightened by the shade-girt flanks and hollows.

We turned again to our ridge. The Crowberry Tower was ponderous with snow and ice-plastered. Its ascent would take an hour at the very least. But running leftwards around the base was a snow-ledge overlooking Easy Gully. To save time we chose to follow it: an uneasy proceeding on unstable snow, tilting steeply to the Rannoch Wall. This traverse brought us into the upper part of Waterslide Gully, in which we kicked steps to the summit.

At the cairn we sat in sunshine for two hours, until the twin horns of Cruachan turned black in the orange sky, and blood-red clouds hung motionless behind Bidean. Then we walked west towards the col half a mile away along the summit-ridge. A bright flash of light marked the Firth of Lorne, and all the peaks of Lorne and Appin emitted that dull, hard glint, which can come from ice alone at the first approach of dusk. The snow of our ridge was already beginning to freeze again, and the new, thin crust crunched under us all the way down to the col. There we halted to put on gloves and balaclavas. Across Loch Linnhe the low line of the Ardgour mountains stretched dark behind long streaks of the sinking sun.

We turned south to Glen Etive.

13

The Six Days Challenge

There is a solemn canon published from time to time by the Scottish climbing clubs, in which (among other listed sins) the innocent walker is advised to avoid alcohol, but this wise declaration is immediately followed by the cheering counsel that 'a flask may be carried for emergencies.' Every April, after repeating the solemn canon, MacAlpine proclaims that a state of emergency exists: his birthday. This event is of variable date, always coinciding with a good weekend on a mountain, and celebrated by a noggin of rum on the summit.

There was one especially fine day when we celebrated the rite on the summit of Cam Mor Dearg, and promptly thereafter enjoyed a two-thousand-foot glissade right down to the Allt a Mhuilinn glen. I have never known a glissade like it. Two thousand feet of firm snow! At the summit I had been a happy mountaineer, receiving the spirit of the canon from the ministering hands of MacAlpine, but down below there were no bounds to my benevolence. So it came about that I accepted MacAlpine's challenge. For *he* arrived down in argumentative mood. He lit his pipe and looked at me. 'I can make one serious criticism,' said he, 'about men who write about mountains. You expurgate your diaries. You misrepresent your friends – make them out to be better men than they are. And does beauty move climbers as much as their later writings suggest?'

'It's a question worth asking,' I acknowledged. 'On the whole I think diaries may often give *more* praise to men and mountains than later writing – diaries are written while enthusiasm is fresh.'

'I wonder! In fact, I doubt. Bring out your diaries – take three lucky dips – then publish the results if you dare! '

A few random recollections began to pass through my mind and the palms of my hands to sweat. 'A three-round contest might just be misleading,' I protested. 'But I'd take the challenge for six.'

'Done!' said MacAlpine quickly.

One evening after we returned home MacAlpine sat down in my chair as judge and I fetched out my diaries. 'Play fair,' he directed, 'no special selections – but ignore entries too short to give evidence.' I opened volume one.

ELEPHANT GULLY ON THE BRACK. October 1938.
Dr J. H.B. Bell, Dunn, MacAlpine, Alan Garrick, and myself.

A foul and dismal day. Elephant Gully lies across Glen Croe from the Cobbler and splits a great crag six hundred feet below the summit. A gully three hundred feet high with vegetation enough to feed all the elephants that ever were. Yet there is no water in it. I myself climbed unroped. The others roped – I cannot imagine why, when any one of them could have led it. A poor climb. Standard difficult. After reaching the summit I was so wet and the wind was so numbing that I persuaded Bell to climb with me down the gully again, where at least we had some shelter.

We finally left Bell in Glen Croe in torrential rain, and the last we saw of him he was dancing about on the main road naked, preparatory to a bathe in the river.

I shut the book hastily. MacAlpine was beaming.

'My round,' said he. '*Now* we're getting down to hard facts. To foul and dismal mountains! Poor climbs! Doctors of Science – but do go on.'

'Don't exult too soon,' I growled. 'Wait till we see a few more.'

BEN VORLICH.
January 1939.
Mackenzie, Dunn, and myself.

On Saturday Mackenzie came to me with a light of sudden and unusual virtue in his eye. Would I agree, he wondered, to a 4 a.m.

start tomorrow, so that we could reach Glencoe at dawn and get a hard ice-climb on Bidean? I did not demur. Ice-climbs are ice-climbs. 'But how shall we ever fetch Dunn out in time?' I asked. From long and painful experience we knew that upon calling for Dunn at any agreed hour of the morning we must devote the better part of an hour to hounding him out of bed and to getting him dressed, fed, and properly turned out complete with climbing boots. The boots were important. They were sometimes apt to get left behind in the mad scramble of departure – irate friends clamouring in his bedroom.

Mackenzie was equal to this difficulty. 'We'll tell him the starting hour's three. He should just be ready when we call an hour later.' I approved this plan. It was most judicious. And so it was done.

On arriving at his rooms at 4 a.m. we found Dunn actually out of bed and halfway through breakfast. There was something truly great in the audacity with which he at once accused us of lateness. Secretly he must have thought us strangely tolerant that morning.

We had reached the head of Loch Lomond and were halfway to Glencoe when a terrific rainstorm broke.

The car's headlamp could hardly reveal the roadway through the spray of rebounding rain. In Glencoe there was probably a full blizzard blowing, so there seemed no point in going farther. At 5.30 a.m. I drew the car to a standstill before Inverarnan Hotel. The bleak eyes of its many windows glared through the driving storm. Inverarnan is our winter headquarters, but at such an hour in the morning we had no more hope of rousing any one than of raising the devil.

'Pity we can't get back to bed!' I sighed.

Dunn started. There was no doubt where his heart was. His face shone with new hope. 'An ice-axe,' he barked. 'Take an ice-axe and prise open a window. We'll get an empty room and we will get back to bed! '

We carried out that job with a Sikes-like efficiency. Within ten minutes we had found a room with a bed big enough for three – the bridal suite, no doubt – and in no time our snores were a coronach to the death of our mountaineering hopes.

We remained undiscovered and slept happily until noon.
It even began to seem likely that we should miss a weekend's
climbing for the first time in eighteen months. This unendurable
thought roused me to action, and I prodded my wrathful friends
with an ice-axe. We threw on our clothes, walked boldly out by
the front door, and climbed Vorlich in improving weather.

MacAlpine was again happy.

OBSERVATORY BUTTRESS OF BEN NEVIS.
August 1936.
Variation of the Direct Route by Mackenzie, Dunn, MacAlpine, and myself.

We all foregathered at Fort William on Saturday evening and
bought in stores. Not till 8 p.m. did we leave the distillery. The
weather during the preceding week had been magnificent, but the
day's forecast spoke of Atlantic depressions moving in on the west
coast. They duly arrived. We climbed to the hut under a dark and
lowering sky, arriving 10 p.m. At eleven the conventional Nevis
drizzle had begun.

Next morning we delayed until 11 a.m. in hope of a clearance.
Mackenzie was in one of his abstracted, maddening moods.
He floated around the hut asking innumerable foolish questions.
To MacAlpine, who was busy frying bacon and eggs, he said:
'Are you making breakfast?' He looked into a pot of porridge
badly needing to be stirred, and asked: 'Are we having porridge?'
Then he glanced at an old magazine which had lain around for a
twelvemonth: 'Why did they bring this up?' And he wanted
answers. MacAlpine lost patience first.

'For God's sake go and do something,' he ordered.

'Do what?' asked Mackenzie defensively.

'Go and fetch a bucket of water,' said MacAlpine briskly.

Mackenzie looked at the large, empty bucket. 'Is this the
bucket?' he asked. That was the end. MacAlpine let fly a frightful
oath. 'It looks damned like a bucket to me!' he thundered.

*'All right, all right,' said Mackenzie hastily. I just wondered if
there was another.'*

He won. The hut exploded.

'Stop!' exclaimed MacAlpine. 'Is there any need to go on?'

'Well,' I laughed, 'you are doing well. But this entry is a long one.
If ever we have a good climb I always write it up in full and not as
a brief diary entry. I don't think you've won this round yet.'

MacAlpine subsided. I continued reading.

*At 11 a.m. we set off for Observatory Buttress. A long grind up the
screes of Observatory Gully brought us to the start of the direct
route – about the middle of the buttress and just to the left of a
bulging rib. The weather was wet, the mist thick and
penetratingly damp, and the rocks streaming.*

*Mackenzie led off on an easy upward traverse to the right, then
back towards the left on moderate rock. After that the climbing
changed, becoming distinctly harder and slabbier. We were all on
one rope of two hundred feet, and had just begun to deal with the
harder rock when a stone from far above hummed in among us.
It cut the rope between MacAlpine and me. We thankfully tied
the rope's ends and continued. Balance-climbing predominated,
for the rock was slabby throughout and definite holds seemed few
and far between. The further we thus advanced the more difficult
the climbing became, until at last it was obvious to us that this
could not possibly be the direct route, which is only very difficult.
Our way was obscured by the grey, clinging mist, and of course by
the high angle of the rock, which had no predominant feature to
guide us. But these worries were Mackenzie's, and to him we
confidently left them – save that we felt a sympathetic concern.*

*Progress suddenly became slower, and continued so. As third
man on the rope I had to wait a while before I could see and
understand the cause. The start of this long, new passage was a
pitch of very great difficulty, topped by a short fierce chimney,
which I am sure would be severe when dry and warm. The holds
were minute. The rain was pelting down and flowing over the top*

edge of the chimney. Each time I took a high handhold a cupful
of chill water poured up my sleeve and spread over my chest and
stomach. The rock was cold, and each of us, I think, finished this
exposed pitch with numbed fingers.

Our concern about the route was no longer just 'sympathetic.'
It was real and immediate. Where were we? The rock in itself
might have no terrors with Mackenzie in the lead, but we were
soaked to the skin and chilled, and that plus demoralizing
uncertainty could defeat us. I followed up for another fifty feet,
gaining by a hand-balance movement a small platform set in an
open corner. Above me a short chimney gave on to a blank face.
I was dealing somewhat gloomily with this face when suddenly
I heard a most joyful and infectious laugh from Mackenzie close
above me. I had not even seen him for an hour. To hear that
laugh come floating through wet mist on the face of a great cliff,
on which the route is lost and the rock severe, was one of the most
heartening experiences I had had in years. I forgot my chilled
body, and eventually landed at a good stance to the left side of
a long chimney.

Mackenzie and Dunn were there. But why the merriment?
For the chimney was absolutely unclimbable. It was right-angled
and well defined, but there was no route up it. None the less
Mackenzie grinned at me from ear to ear. 'You're doing a new
route, Bill,' he said. 'Hope you like it.'

'But where?' I asked.

'It's the belt of unclimbed slabs high up to the left of the direct
route.'

'We just strayed on to it like browsing goats,' murmured Dunn.

'But we're not going back,' added Mackenzie after a pause.
'We're beyond the rocks that beat Hargreaves and Macphee.
Main point is we know where we are.'

This comfortless knowledge seemed inexplicably to comfort
Mackenzie; for he turned to the chimney, saw it to be hopeless,
then without hesitation climbed up the open crest to its left, and
so reached a poor stance. However, it had a belay, so he called up
Dunn, who cursed but complied. All this manoeuvring on little or

no hold, in the midst of precipitating cloud, seemed at first sight a waste of time, because the wall they were on was no more climbable than the chimney. I reckoned they had nearly reached their limit, and I was right. However, Mackenzie had an ace up his sleeve.

He moved up a few feet farther to a slight overhang, and there indulged in what I still thought to be pointless gardening. 'Take cover!' he shouted once. I pressed myself as close as I could against the rock-face. A large stone came rocketing past, missing my right heel by six inches. His next move was to use the square hole thus created as a handhold, not to climb up as I thought he had intended, but to assist him in crossing the chimney from left to right. When I came to make this move myself I found it of great technical difficulty. The few holds are pressure holds awkwardly placed. When the crossing is made, however, one lands on a good ledge. While waiting there with my nose close to the cliff I suddenly saw the colours in the grain. Flecks of red, yellow, blue, crystal. Mouse-brown rock all flecked over. Beauty manifesting through the rock and as stirring as that of Mackenzie's lead. Each of its kind excellent.

Some way farther we reached a well-broken level area where we lunched. I imagined that our difficulties were over, but was disillusioned as soon as we reached the rocks beyond. They gave us good climbing for almost an hour.

More lunch in the Observatory ruins.

Thereafter we started down the North-East Buttress, and had trouble at first in hitting off the easy route. Dunn and MacAlpine, the rugged individualists, unroped and damned our eyes, then went back up the buttress to go down by the Carn Mor Dearg arête. Mackenzie and I persisted, almost at once found the easy slopes, and rattled down at breakneck speed to Coire Leis. We made the hut twenty minutes before the others, and thus honour was satisfied.

On our way back to Fort William the Herr Mackenzie sprained his ankle, and had to be supported all the rest of the way down by Dunn and MacAlpine.

A truly glorious night with a full moon. I travelled home in
Dunn's open Morris, enjoying unobstructed views of Glencoe, the
Blackmount, and Loch Tulla, all flooded with white light and
backed by the starred sky.

The true kingdom, it seems to me, is not in some far-off and
happier land. It's here and now. (But how to learn how to get it?)

I sat back and waited. MacAlpine stared reflectively through his
tobacco smoke for a minute, then said firmly: 'I give it to you, after
all, on points.'

DIRECT ROUTE ON EASTERN BUTTRESS, SRON NA CICHE, SKYE.
June 1937.
Dunn, Angus Smith, Marskell, and myself.

Showers in the early morning. We curled up in our sleeping bags
and listened with a good grace to the helter-skelter on the canvas.
Then a northerly wind drove the cloud off the Cuillin. We left
Glen Brittle in the afternoon and went up Coire Lagan. We
surveyed the precipice of Sron na Ciche. Debate. Four different
opinions about what should be done. To reintegrate the party
I tried for agreement on first principles, which was easy enough
– that our climb should be one that none of us had climbed
before. The party sat on its hunkers among the boulders and
smoked a pipe, choosing in the end the Eastern Buttress Direct.

We climbed on to the end of the Terrace, which we traversed a
short way towards Eastern Gully. The route now went up the face
of the buttress, but kept as much as possible to the edge over-
looking the gully. Our delight was intense on finding ourselves
launched upon the most charming route in Skye. None of us
knows a better. The standard is difficult, but not by such standards
should one judge the excellence of any rock-climb. The route goes
on brown gabbro, in great clean-cut steps over steep and exposed
rocks, round exhilarating corners, up an endless variety of slabs,
cracks, chimneys, and edges.

We found belays to be sound and plentiful, the rock unim-
peachable throughout, and open stances gave us wide views to
Loch Brittle, where the sea was bursting on the beaches, brilliantly
white in the new sun and the rain-cleansed air. The crux of the
route came just where it should – at the penultimate pitch. The
last two pitches were crack climbs on a steep wall. The first of
them was very hard – decidedly harder than the route's official
classification, although not exposed enough to be called severe.
I cannot remember enjoying a Cuillin climb more than this one.

At the top of Sron na Ciche, Dunn retired by the Sgumain
Stone Shoot, while the rest of us passed over Sgurr Sgumain and
the mauvais pas to Sgurr Alasdair. Came down the Alasdair
Stone Shoot in six minutes, without hurrying.

Every night just now is giving us wonderful skies of green, red,
and dark orange, barred with long horizon clouds, such as only
the Isles can show when the sun goes into the sea.

'A panegyric,' I said to MacAlpine. 'You must give me that one –
written in the first burst of enthusiasm. What do you make the
score now?'

'Call it three-two in your favour. Let's have something more
recent – skip ten years.'

I turned open volume two.

THE CENTRE GULLY OF BEINN LAOIGH. *February 1947.*
Norman Tennent, Trevor Ransley, and myself.

'It may be the best snow-climb in Central Scotland,' said my
companion grudgingly, 'but the man who sets foot on snow at
that angle must be mad! You'll never get me there! Never!'

Such were the words of no less a person than MacAlpine, on
Cruach Ardrain in October 1935, when he and I stared for the
first time in our lives across the intervening miles of Strath Fillan
to the Centre Gully of Laoigh. From here it seemed perpendicular,
as do all snow-gullies seen en face even when quite free of rock-
and ice-pitches – an elementary fact which we learned a month

later when the intrepid MacAlpine took me to the Centre Gully of Beinn Laoigh.

I had the good fortune to meet Trevor Ransley in February 1947. I found him at just that stage occupied by MacAlpine and me twelve years earlier. He had not yet done a good snow-climb. So I dearly wanted to go with him to the Centre Gully; for I reckoned, judging him by myself, that that would be to him one of the classic climbs. And he showed me that I was right. We had now had a full month's frost and snow conditions this season were never likely to be better. We fixed a date and were joined by Norman Tennent.

The three of us arrived at Tyndrum 9 a.m. and set off in a shrill and freezing east wind. The five-mile track running west to Laoigh was badly drifted. In one of the drifts we passed an abandoned car, obviously destined to remain there for another month – there were scores of drifts to either side. After three miles the great bend in the glen brought us to Coninish Farm, beyond which Laoigh raised that graceful peak for which it is famed, snow-draped and lustrous, deep into cloudless sky. Of its three thousand seven hundred feet the last seven hundred formed an icy wedge lifting up from the back of a great eastern corrie, which was flanked by sentinel spurs. The wedge had double summits placed close. Warning banners of drift flew from the twin tops, and between them the Centre Gully fell to the corrie.

Conditions, I could see, were going to be savage high up, but could hardly have been more pleasant for our present purposes – the long grind to the floor of the corrie at three thousand feet. When the climber has plenty of windproof clothing, and can work up warmth by hard work, there is sheer elation in facing high, bitter winds, and joy in the hard play of the muscles. We made a speedy ascent to the corrie. On my last visit there in the late spring I had seen a lizard basking on a warm boulder. I like lizards and wondered what had become of it now. Not a rock was visible. Every boulder was buried in soft snow and each crag plastered with ice.

We waded across the floor and started up the long, lower slope to the gully. The snow had fallen as dry powder; now it was well packed and fairly firm. One kick made a step. At two hundred feet we had a short halt while Ransley practised falling, and stopping by braking with his ice-axe. It is a very easy thing to do, but at first needs resolution. Ransley was somewhat frightened about letting himself go, but quickly grew bolder. I think it doubled his self-confidence – as indeed by the nature of things it always must. Confidence ensured that he avoided a crouched position and stood erect in his steps, and so had surer footing. It was valuable practice for later events.

The slope steepened to the foot of the gully. We roped-up – Tennent leading, myself last. Although it is shallow – little more than a groove up the face – the gully was well filled with snow. The rocky flanks were plated with white ice, but in the gully itself no cutting was required. We made steady progress at an angle of forty-five degrees until within a hundred and fifty feet of the top. There the angle steepened; the gully's walls fell away so that we were out on the open face and at the mercy of the wind, which at three thousand six hundred feet was vicious. The snow was wind-packed and the crust hard as a board. At this point I took the lead from Tennent who had so far done all the work.

We had been moving all together on a short rope until now, so my first order was to lengthen rope and move singly from axe-belays. I was in no doubt about the discomforts of the climbing ahead. The wind was already hitting us hard. We had to be vigilant about balance. Every move had to be firm. The cutting of steps is a part of mountain-craft in which I personally revel, but on this occasion I soon found that neither rhythm nor revel was to be my lot. The short route lay straight up to the ridge between the two tops, but this ridge being corniced I went direct for the true summit on the left – a steeper route, rising to fifty degrees. At every step we gained we were more and more delayed by the wind, which bombarded face and eyes with icy spiculae. Some-times I was unable to see the slope in front of me. It vanished in the flailing drift, and all I could do was drive in my axe-shaft to the head and hang on until the gusts slackened. But gradually, foot by foot, rope-length by rope-length, we fought our way on to the summit.

The wind at the cairn was so strong that we could not face into it. It fairly howled across the arctic world, heeled by hard sheets of drift that obscured the view and blinded us on impact. Directly overhead – no more than a few feet! – was the clear blue sky. That did madden us; for the mountain view that day must have been splendid beyond all telling – and there we stood in the main stream of the summit's plume. The cold was unendurable and we quickly agreed to make our descent by the north ridge.

Turning our backs to the wind we traversed the short ridge to the north top. Ransley belayed me with the rope while I crept – literally crept – to the edge of the north face and prospected. And there was the north ridge. It fell long and steeply. At a glance I could see it to be rocky and thoroughly glazed with snow-ice. Several hundred feet of downhill step-cutting was demanded, and that with speed. I let myself over the edge.

After cutting the first dozen steps I was overjoyed to find myself out of the wind. I was in perfect calm. The wind with its plume went streaming harmlessly over the north top. I rested for a minute, then thought of my companions freezing near to death just twenty-five feet above my head. I continued cutting until sixty feet of rope had run out, and waited for Ransley. When he joined me I had to move on, leaving Tennent still on top, for the footing was insufficiently good to support two of them during the delays of my own descent. At last I was ready. Tennent joined Ransley and Ransley came on. This was a moment that I awaited in mild anxiety. He could have no good belay from above, and the descent of hard-frozen snow on steep slopes is the beginner's most searching test. He amazed me. He stood up with his back as straight as an axe-shaft, his head poised, and every move a display of good balance. It was delightful to watch him – as it is to watch any man in complete control of himself, and working with skill and pace. The firm and easy sureness gratifies the eye: here is another fellow human fulfilling his powers! Probably he would not have moved one-half so well had the ground been easier and so less tonic to the nerves.

We were halfway down the ridge at sunset, and on the wrong side of our mountain, in the sense that our view was to the north-east. Yet if the sun were itself invisible the white-cowled community that filled the choir of Perthshire was growing every minute more glorious in reflected red, until the pure white by virtue of which they were able to receive the glow was transformed, utterly, into the full and holy fire of their sun. A vault of luminous blue arched them, and round their feet flowed the first dark tides of the night, the death that is the salt of the earth and life's brotherly shadow, flowing and rising, hazily and smokily blue along the glens.

Meanwhile I continued cutting. The air was very still now, and the axe rang sharp. Chips scuttered on the glazed surface. The rope rasped on frozen gloves. Gradually the angle of the ridge eased and soon allowed us to stop cutting, and to creep down on edge-nails, and at last to face out and stride. The last colour had gone from the north-eastern tops, to be replaced by a cold grey, too much honoured by the name of light. On reaching the sentinel spur, Tennent and I enjoyed the long fierce swoop of a standing glissade to the corrie floor, where we waited for Ransley, whose swoops were shorter. Then we hastened down to Coninish, and set out upon the last of our nine hours over the snow-blocked miles to Tyndrum.

Under the arctic silence of a still, starless sky the only sound to be heard was the crunch of nails on the freezing track, sounding through the lifeless waste and the enveloping gloom.

14

Gale Winds and Gabbro

One midwinter's night I opened the Scottish Mountaineering Club's *Guide to Skye*, hoping to find ideas for a summer rock-climb – a climb, I calmly decided, considerably more than difficult. There was indeed no fearsome severity I might not enjoy; for I sat in my old armchair and the fire was red. Almost at once I came upon a challenging passage framed by an editor who understood winter nights and old armchairs and young climbers, and the surge of the coming spring: 'Sgurr na h'Uamha is the beautifully shaped peak situated a mile south of Sgurr nan Gillean. It rises steeply from the Harta Corrie, and forms the true northern termination of the main Cuillin Ridge ... There is no record of an ascent of the steep south-westerly buttress facing Sgurr Dubh.'

My exploratory instinct awakened with a start. I referred at once to maps and long-distance photographs, and saw from these that the South-west Buttress must be anything between five hundred and a thousand feet high. No other buttress of that size (as distinct from a face) remained unclimbed in the Cuillin; that no one had ever been there promised some exceptional technical difficulty. I wondered what the intimidating factor could be. Surely not the 'steepness' mentioned in the guide – steep gabbro is the delight of the rock-climber's heart.

In order to arrive at a rational explanation I began to take soundings in the treacherous waters of my Cuillin geology. The Cuillin form a seven-mile horseshoe enclosing Coir-Uisg, and the rock strata dip always to the centre. For example, on the northward-running section between Sgurrs Alasdair and Ghreadaidh the dip is eastward, giving on the west (or Glen Brittle) side a succession of good outcropping holds and ledges, which on the east (or Coir-Uisg) side slope the wrong way for the climber. It is for this reason that no route has yet been found up the huge Coir-Uisg faces of Sgurr MhicCoinnich and Sgurr Dearg. On the parallel, northward-running section between Sgurr na h'Uamha (pronounced *Hooa*) and Sgurr nan Gillean the dip should be southward. Accordingly the South-west Buttress should cut across the dip at an angle. The image that formed in my mind was that of a great tower whose outer walls were in a state of chaos: overhangs, slabs, and ledges mingled disorderly. The buttress bristled. Climbers would not have been attracted, if I were right, because there would not be an obvious route – no outstanding rib piercing the difficulties, nor continuous fault inviting attack.

The more I speculated about the buttress during the following six months the more clear and firm did the image become. Like all such images it evoked thought, and thought action. For the dream became a plan – that next June I should go to Sgurr na h'Uamha with Kenneth Dunn and one hundred feet of rope, and try to climb that bristling buttress.

Six months later I arrived in Skye with Dunn. We camped in Glen Brittle and climbed for a fortnight on the South Cuillin. I regarded all our time thus spent as so much training for *der Tag*. I had thought about Sgurr na h'Uamha until I was rather in awe of its imaginary difficulties. Usually I feel less nervous apprehension before a new climb than before an old that is highly classified; for not knowing what to expect on the new, I hope for the best instead of fearing the worst. When trial is made and the worst materializes, then, of course, it tests the nerves higher than a known route already ascended by mortal men. So new climbs are encouraging in advance. But *not so* Sgurr na h'Uamha. We reserved it to the last, waiting like innocents for the Perfect Day.

The consequence was that we came near to losing all chance of trying the climb. At first the weather was mixed, good days and bad alternating, but latterly the rain grew squallier, and we had to be thankful for heavy winds, which kept the clouds moving briskly. The risk we were running was eventually brought home to me on 25th June when we went to the Bhasteir Tooth and tried a face-climb, of which Dunn had made the first ascent some years before.

The feature of the route is a 'stomach traverse ' of sixty feet, where a long, narrow ledge slants up and leftwards across the south face. There is a big drop below and the rock immediately above the ledge projects like an eave, forcing one to lie on one's stomach and wriggle. After sixty feet the ledge thins out and, fortunately, so does the overhang, so that one may first kneel and then stand, being now on vertical rock with good holds. That was where the wind caught me. We had to abandon the continuation by the exposed upper rocks of Naismith's Route. We then withdrew and took refuge in the North Chimney of the north face – a corkscrew tunnel twisting this way and that through total darkness in the very heart of the Tooth, at last turning right-about so violently that we had to squirm along a horizontal funnel, from which we popped out on the Tooth's crown like rabbits out of a burrow. We had not realized that rock could be intrinsically funny until we found ourselves sprawling on the top helpless with laughter. In that respect, at least, the route seems to be unique.

The wind was now blowing hard from the south-west. If we had been forced by it to abandon a climb classed as *difficult* then what of our hopes of climbing a new buttress on Sgurr na h'Uamha? They were already imperilled. That is, if the wind were maintained. It was raining by the time we got back to Glen Brittle. Only one week remained of our holidays. It was a question whether to hold off our attempt for a few days longer or to strike at once. That evening the clouds rolled aside; for several minutes a strange warm light spread over the glen; the field around the tent glowed a rich and unnatural green. I suspected then that a big change for the worse was coming over the weather. That decided us. Tomorrow's goal was Sgurr na h'Uamha.

Early next morning we drove the fourteen miles to Sligachan, and by 9 a.m. were walking down Glen Sligachan under layers of steel-grey clouds, hard at the edges and driving high, a dull, metallic glitter emanating from the under-layer. These were long-distance voyagers and carried no cargo for Skye. We had gone four miles south to the Bloody Stone at the entrance to Harta Corrie before we began to feel the kick of the wind, which was still blowing from the south-west; but so far we were protected from it in great measure by the long ridge of Druim nan Ramh. On the whole, conditions were good, provided that we were spared any increase in wind-force.

We walked a mile west up Harta Corrie, rounding the south face of Sgurr na h'Uamha. Its face was slabby, confirming my guess at the dip of the strata. But my intense curiosity about the South-west Buttress remained unsatisfied until the last moment. We struck uphill from the floor of the corrie and climbed several hundred feet up scree to the foot of the rocks, at a height of eighteen hundred feet. A short left traverse – and there was our buttress.

It was six hundred feet high. The lower half took the shape of a three-hundred-and-fifty-foot hump – and it bristled! It bristled with short overhangs and vertical walls, arranged in tiers, which were divided one from another by narrow, horizontal trap-ledges. I could hardly believe my eyes; for the rocks of imagination were realized in solid gabbro, correct in detail. Only one detail was incorrect. My imagination had created a tower for me, but the real rock was a broad-based pyramid. We built a cairn at the centre of its baseline, at the point where one may see into Lota Corrie on the left and Harta Corrie on the right. We roped up on a hundred feet of line.

Our problem was how to thread a route through that welter of wall and overhang. No line of weakness was visible – no continuous line to be picked out in advance and followed with hope. On the other hand, if the rock gave no promise, at least it made plain that only one tactical plan was possible: the overhangs of each tier must be turned on one flank or the other by means of traversing the horizontal ledges. Beyond that we could do nothing, save try; hope for nothing, save the best.

I climbed twenty feet up a wall of good rock to the first ledge below the first overhang. It was too narrow a ledge to accommodate Dunn also, at least not with advantage to either of us, so I traversed rightwards, blindly, with no idea what to expect. On the overhang's far side I found an inset corner. A steep groove in its back cut through the tier above, and up I went to the second ledge, where Dunn joined me. Like every true buttress ours was indefinite, and for that very reason we found the route selection of great interest. Every overhang we met henceforth we turned by a left or right traverse along ledges, until a corner, crack, or face gave a route to the next tier. Every unknown corner rounded was a doubt resolved, each overhang turned a tactical triumph. The pleasure of the exploration was cumulative. Our avoiding moves, however, were often exposed, and the wind, rising as we gained height, was beginning to buffet us nastily. Fortunately the gabbro was so coarse and tough that we felt fairly secure. Thus we climbed five tiers, the highest being eighty feet, and their total three hundred and fifty feet, to the top of the first hump.

The angle of the rock fell back for a hundred and fifty feet, then uprose in a further series of overhangs. This final rampart was obviously going to be the crux of the climb, for the wind had become ferocious. Lower down it had troubled us, but now it was rising to sudden long gusts of little less than gale-force. Every step we climbed over that next two hundred feet exposed us the more to its fury, which repeatedly staggered us. Perhaps it was strengthening at all levels.

High wind not accompanied by rain or wintry cold, and provided I can keep moving, intoxicates me. It goes to my head. I feel a redoubled energy. And so it was now. On top of that every muscle of my body was in well nigh perfect training. So that instead of being tempted by a long slant of slabs to the right of the serried overhangs, I felt an urge to go for the overhangs themselves. I was spoiling for a fight. Accordingly I climbed a great up-roll of slab to the foot of the first overhang, intending to repeat the tactics of the lower buttress. At the crease where this overhang rose out of the slab-wave a traverse had to be made right or left, but the crease was *only* a crease. Holds were small. Here it was not possible to climb, as I had hoped, relying simply on the effort of muscle and an overflowing energy to defeat the wind. The rock-holds were inadequate, and nothing less than big, well-cut holds would suffice, for the wind was beginning to wrench at my body, making suicidal any position that relied for security on balance rather than muscle. While I was descending the wind strengthened even further, and by the time I reached the foot of the slab-wave a full gale was blowing from the south-west.

It seemed to me probable that our retreat was now cut off, unless we could find natural spikes for roping down; the gale must now be playing on every part of the buttress. At all events we were still keen to go on rather than go down. A way of forcing the upper cliffs had to be found quickly, for I had forgotten my balaclava helmet and my body was beginning to lose heat more rapidly than I liked. Dunn, however, had all his winter climbing gear, barring an ice-axe, and already bulged like a brown bear in the autumn. I continued in the lead, none the less, because my hands were still preserved from numbness by fingerless woollen mittens.

We looked up and pondered the serried overhangs. It began to seem that our best route might be the one that at first sight, and in the particular conditions, had seemed uninviting. To the right-hand side of the overhangs were smoothly arching slabs one hundred feet high. Slabs have usually less definite holds than walls and cracks, and call more emphatically for the very kind of balance-climbing that we had now greatest cause to avoid. On the other hand, their angle was less high. It occurred to us that the gale, being south-west, would tend to blow us on to the slabs, to plaster us against them, rather than to blow us off. If the gabbro were the rougher kind, and technically simple, and were embellished by at least one midway stance, then we could go farther. For the moment we were sure of none of these things.

We made a right-hand traverse and I started up. At first I was scared to move, but quickly evolved the necessary technique. The first need was to have four good holds, then wait till the blow of the wind seemed steady, its jumpiness smoothed out, then make a quick, deliberate snatch of hand or foot at the next hold. The main consideration was always to have three points of attachment to the rock. The gabbro was luckily as coarse as only gabbro can be. I could feel the bite of my edge-nails right into the crystalline surface, the grasp of the whole palm on rounded ribs, or the tips of my fingers curl around square-cut edges. Never before had I felt such gratitude for the simple merits of weathered rock. I clung to it, not to wrestle as though with an enemy, but for succour against the real enemy – wind.

At fifty feet I found a stance. I turned to bring up Dunn. For one moment the wind threw my head back and stopped my breath. I could not exhale – my breath was forced back between my teeth. I had to tighten my neck muscles and bring my head down to my chest before I could breathe freely, and the pain of wind-blast on the eyes prevented my watching Dunn climbing. I took in the rope by feel.

As a result of confusion and trouble with the rope when Dunn arrived, I cannot recollect if he found a belay. I remember, however, dealing very slowly and cautiously with the upper passage. The slabs there were broad and splendidly arched, but the consequences of a fall would be worse for their greater height, and this thought was very much in my mind. I had a vivid recollection of a lesser gale on the Crowberry Ridge, at the September equinox, when I saw MacAlpine, on the rope below me, blown by one gust clean off the rock at the crux. He made an awe-inspiring sight – especially as I reflected, 'There, but for the grace of God, go I'. The way had thus to be forced in defiance of fear – the fear of treachery – a gust coming at an angle, or a violent whip of the rope. It was only the wind direction that justified us.

Consequently I continued to move in jerks – to hang on with all the strength of my body, every muscle of arm and leg continuously tensed – deliberately to pick out my next hold – to calculate the movement – to wait for the right moment, then – grab. I expended far more energy on this pitch than was strictly necessary, but the margin of safety had to be wide. Towards the end the climbing gave me sheer joy – the joy of free action over gale-swept rock.

The angle fell back. One hundred feet of scrambling followed on superb gabbro slabs. We were pushed in triumph and with great violence to the cairn. We paused there for one second, just to clap a thankful hand on top, and passed on. To the west and north the twenty black teeth of the Cuillin were sharp and clear in a sky fast changing in colour from steel to gun-metal. Everywhere was the heavy rush and thunder of wind. The terrific gusts, which had tormented us below the final slabs, had now merged into one continuously powerful blow, before which we fled to the col under Sgurr Beag, and thence down to Glen Sligachan.

Up on the tops the gale was mounting to a hurricane, which broke that night. From between its teeth we had snatched our buttress in the nick of time. Down in Glen Brittle our frail canvas roof was drummed and punched for three days by storms of rain. We had opportunity then to assess the merits of our route impartially. In fine weather the buttress would present little difficulty, its features reveal no remarkable character: it would not be what in Wales is called an elegant route. The weather had *made* our climb – given us a better and tougher frolic than a classic route in fair weather. To all humble buttresses called Difficult I give belated homage. And to all winds called Gale ––

But no, there is need of diplomacy. My days are not yet done.

15

Rosa Pinnacle

For a year on end, 1948 to 1949, my numerous efforts to reach Arran, in hope of climbing Cir Mhor by the Rosa Pinnacle, were foiled. Weather went bad, friends failed, work intervened. In a way these difficulties were right and proper, my ambition not being a humble one. By all reports – and these were few enough – the south ridge of Rosa Pinnacle was a tough climb, but almost unknown even to Scottish climbers.

Its first direct ascent had been made during the war by J. F. Hamilton; thereafter, little had been heard of it. For some years following a first ascent, such is the fate of many a great climb.

I knew next to nothing about the route until 1948. One evening at Inverarnan House in Glen Falloch (a headquarters of mountaineering in west Scotland), I asked Hamilton over a plate of eggs and bacon: 'Is Rosa Pinnacle any good?' He looked startled, as well he might, and fixed me with a bright black eye. 'Well, well!' said he, very gently. 'I'd say that climb was the best in Arran.' Then, with a sudden burst of enthusiasm: 'It's terrific! There's eight hundred feet of granite, but you 've never seen granite as rough – it's as rough as gabbro. It's terrific! It's absolutely––'

'How hard?' I ventured.

'Severe in rubbers. Two bad pitches, one in the lower third and the other near the centre. The first's a long crack like an S, and the second's a lay-back crack with a delicate traverse above. A bit exposed. No one has done them in boots. Take rubbers and pray for a dry day.'

Dry days came and went (at infrequent intervals), but rarely did they coincide with my own leisure, and never with that of my climbing friends. In consequence, Cir Mhor by the Rosa Pinnacle grew ever more desirable in my eyes, until it quite ousted every other mountain route in Scotland. Penance having thus been done, atonement made, I was given a reward far greater than I ever deserved. When I stepped on board the Arran steamer at Ardrossan in June 1949 I was able to heave a great sigh of relief – three sighs all rolled into one. The first because I had thought I was going to miss the boat; the second in gratitude for a heat-wave, now in its seventh day and destined to last for a month; the third because I had a substantial part of my reward already on board with me: my companions were Norman Tennent and his wife Mona.

Arran lies west of Ardrossan some eleven miles. No trace of it could be seen through the heat-haze. When we landed at Brodick an hour later we were thankful to see the long hill-ridges stretched out upon blue sky. It was now the mainland's turn to be lost in pearly fog, while Arran lay bright as Paradise. Our plan was to camp in upper Glen Rosa, which runs from Brodick Bay four and a half miles north-west to the south face of Cir Mhor. We had brought neither tent nor change of clothing; for in such weather we might safely lie out on the heather in sleeping bags. Should the weather miraculously break we need only call upon the boulder-lore of Norman Tennent. He knew the size and shape and relative merits of every stone in Arran big enough to shelter man or beast. He promised to find us a good cave near the foot of Cir Mhor if need were; or, if we preferred, individual boulders with overhangs. Tennent could stow away a whole mountaineering club on the bare slopes of an Arran hill, and have each man snug and happy. Our faith in him lightened our loads greatly. Fortunately the weather stayed dry.

When we had gone a little way into Glen Rosa I realized that I had never before been to Arran in June. The rich green of the trees and grass was astonishingly like that of the lower Alps. The path too was an Alpine path, a pleasure to tread (at least in daytime), for its rounded stones were firmly embedded in soil. The warm sweet scent of young plants mingled with the sharper tang of pine. We walked into the evening sun, which shone down the glen, not dazzlingly, for it was still well above the ridges, but slanting enough to flicker the air with the gleam of insects' wings.

In less than two miles the trees thinned and vanished. The path deteriorated. The glen broadened out to a moorland heath, where only thyme and bog-myrtle flourished, and sparse heather struggled through coarse grass. The glen turned sharply north. The rounding of that bend is a great moment among Arran hills. Deep pools of the Rosa Burn fill the hollowed foreground, from which the eye glances up long bare hillsides, which guide it straight to the spikes of Cir Mhor and the Castles. They do not so much dominate the glen as consummate all its beauties. The long approach exacts its proper sacrifice of energy and sweat, but never yet have I heard of the mountaineer who turned the bend of Glen Rosa and then grudged his offering to Cir Mhor.

The Rosa Pinnacle, I knew, must be facing us. I searched eagerly for it, but the detail of the south face was not yet distinct. There was a faint haze in the upper corrie, washed blue by a slant of the sun's rays. We stopped about a mile from the summit, ate supper beside the burn, then slid into our sleeping bags. Perhaps in contrast to the great heat of the day the night was cooler than we had expected. From time to time a sense of cold wakened us, when we gave a glance round at the hills and a swift wriggle, then dropped off to sleep again. Cloudless nights in the highlands at midsummer are no darker than twilight. Stars twinkled faintly, for though the sky was clear it retained in the north a pure and colourless light, which invaded the east and west, and permeated far southward. At any time through the night we might have climbed on rock.

Our full compensation for broken sleep came when the first sun-ray struck the highest crag of Cir Mhor, thus proving the summit. For the lighted rocks were not the summit as it appeared from Glen Rosa, but a seemingly lesser top to its right. A few minutes later the creamy fire touched the sharper tip of the mock summit, and flashed a short way down its east wall, which we clearly saw to be the Rosa Pinnacle. For a while I lay in my bag and tried to imagine our party of three climbing up that sunlit shaft – tried to persuade myself that in a few hours we should be there. The idea was too good to be true: a vision of the kind that goes through the gate of ivory – not to be realized. Until men take action good ideas seem like that.

We took action by breakfasting. While we ate, the sunshine crept down the Rosa Pinnacle until its whole eight hundred feet had been won from shadow. The Pinnacle, we could see, was built in two parts – a lower buttress of five hundred feet and a final tower of three hundred feet. From a distance that tower looked by far the worst part of the climb, its great east wall close to the vertical, its crest a fierce *arête*, to be turned on the left only by vast sheets of slab, each dipping to the south-west and overlapping. However, we knew the real difficulties to be concentrated on the lower buttress.

When the sun spread over our bivouac site we set off to the upper corrie, which we reached in half an hour. Its floor offered remarkably good camping ground – no scree, plenty of short turf, and several big boulders with commodious overhangs awaiting Tennents. We could see from here all the detail of Rosa Pinnacle. The lower buttress, broad below and near the base quite gently inclined, steepened rapidly to a hundred-foot wall topped by an overhang. In the middle of that wall was an elongated S crack, sixty feet high, wide, shallow, holdless – obviously the real crux of the climb. Above the wall the buttress tapered to a ridge of rounded slabs, promptly rising again to a sheer nose, then sweeping back to a terrace under the final tower.

We moved uphill to the lowest rocks, where I took off boots and put on rubbers. We roped up with myself in the lead and Tennent second. As usual before a hard climb I felt nervous – very nervous. For my own protection on such occasions my imagination has to be consciously damped down. Again as usual, all nervousness vanished when I set foot on the rock. I began to enjoy myself. When that preliminary concern is absent my climbing suffers.

We scrambled over easy rocks to start the climb proper at the centre of the buttress. Between the main face and a protruding mass on the left was an open corner. I stepped on to a tilted slab under this corner, but its walls were too steep to be climbable, so I traversed several feet to the right and found tumbling down the face a narrow cascade of good holds. These brought me in fifty feet to a nest-like ledge, to which Tennent followed. All this while I had to be most careful what movements I made with my hands; the rock was so coarsely crystalline that a careless knock, however light, rasped the skin off the knuckles. Hamilton had modestly called it 'rough as gabbro,' but in truth it is rough as peridotite.

One more run-out of fifty feet landed me on a long, narrow ledge directly under the S crack. While Tennent brought Mona to the stance below, I looked down and out to Glen Rosa's floor, where the speckles of bungalow boulders lay like clover on a lawn. Tennent joined me and anchored to a rock-spike. I turned to the crack. At my first glance I said: 'This is a different proposition.' It was a wide groove with a rounded crack inside. For the most part the crack was holdless, but extraordinarily rough. Yet the angle was so high that I had trouble persuading myself that rock-friction would avail me against gravity. At the very top the crack overhung. To Hamilton, who made the first ascent, I raised a figurative hat. After one tentative step up and return, I started.

All upward movement was made by the downpress of rubbers against the slabs of the groove. But while the feet were being raised, the body had to be held in balance and its weight supported. The only means of so doing was to thrust the right hand into the crack at chest-level and then try to jam it. The crack being a shallow one on the left side of the groove, only the right hand could be firmly wedged. I knew in advance that every wedge was going to lift off more skin, but never have I hesitated less over a sacrifice: I am not of the tigerish few, deaf and blind to the yawn of a drop. I gave all the energy and determination I had to each move up and jam – move up and jam – suffering no temptation to pause. I was surprised how soon I came to the halfway point. Sometimes a foot could be wedged, sometimes a handhold appeared; then I came under the 'overhang,' which was, after all, vertical. It would be impossible without a handhold or two, and I hardly dared believe that now they would appear after being denied to me so long. I edged up as high as I could, and stretched up the blank left wall with my left hand. The fingers gripped a perfect, cup-like hold.

The whole S crack is made remarkable by the gratitude that fills the mind at that moment. A noggin of rum would not have made me happier. I now enjoyed the exposure of the face for its own sake; enjoyed it again when more good holds came to hand beyond and above the crack. I swarmed over the top edge.

I arrived on a wide, out-dipping shelf slanting left. A detached pinnacle stood on it, ten feet high and triangular. It offered the only belay for the rope, which saddened me. No doubt it is really as safe and solid as all good pinnacles are in a happier, far-off land, but I have seen a bigger, better, and safer-looking crag collapse over a sheer precipice under one man's weight. The incident has conditioned my reflexes. I viewed the pinnacle with suspicion, pronounced it safe, and not without misgiving threw a loop of rope over the apex. Tennent began to take in Mona's rope.

The rock scene at the pinnacle-shelf is as bold as any I know in Scotland. On this granite there is no blemish of vegetation. To each side, walls, corners, edges, thrust cleanly up. The rock is an ashen grey, almost cream, its every face showing a sparkle of crystal-grain. The sweep and lift of the crags give to the very air an added airiness, and this it is that from start to finish of the day has impressed my memory.

Tennent began to climb. Like me, he moved quickly. I could see nothing, but could feel the pause when he came under the overhang, and hear his delight when his hand entered the cup. Perversely, I smiled to myself when his right hand floated over the edge bearing blood on its back. Mona in turn showed the same joy at the overhang, the same rasped hand above. Every party aspiring to Rosa Pinnacle must be prepared for that sacrifice of the flesh. They will give gladly enough when the call comes.

We had no idea how the route continued. At the low left end of the shelf there was no inviting way. Directly above us, by climbing over the detached pinnacle, we might reach an overhanging wall of thirty feet which girdled the buttress. It was split by a straight-edged chimney, possibly climbable. Hard to our right was a high and exposed corner. We could not see what lay beyond. One of the delights of rock-climbing is traversing round exposed and unknown corners. After an awkward descent of three feet from the pinnacle-shelf I balanced round the corner on a sloping slab. At first there seemed to be few handholds and these too far apart, but the traverse is simple when the drop below is ignored. Once round the corner I came on to a wide rectangular ledge, cut clean as a *route aux bicyclettes*. The others followed. On our right the ledge abruptly ended at another mysterious corner.

Standing at the end's lip we looked down a sheer face, and round the corner at an open chimney which split the face from top to bottom. I traversed into it, three feet across a perpendicular wall. The ascent of seventy feet, coming after the S crack, seemed not at all difficult. The party foregathered on easy slabs at the crest.

The buttress had narrowed, and might henceforth be more aptly called a ridge. Sixty feet above, it whipped up again. The edge overhung and looked unclimbable. Reconnaissance showed that we might turn it to the right or left by long traverses, although it was not clear by what means we should arrive back at the crest. If we went left I guessed that we might now arrive at the Lay-back Crack, which was, Hamilton had sworn, an experience not to be missed. Therefore we made the left traverse – a walk on rolling slabs for a hundred feet or more – while the ridge continued to rise on our right. Our soothing slabs at length upcurled in a great wave against a greater vertical wall, which barred the ridge. In the angle between this wall and the flank of the ridge we saw a long crack. It was the only breach, and lay on a tilt from left to right. Underneath the crack a similarly tilting slab gave Tennent and me footing. I would not call it a good stance. None the less it gave a flake-belay at knee-level. Tennent could tie on, lean back on the tight rope, and say honestly that he was safe, perjuriously that he *felt* safe.

Our climb back to the crest looked about sixty feet. I was alarmed at the prospect of having to make all that height by the lay-back technique: it is most exhausting. When a thin crack divides right-angled walls, which are holdless, one may grasp the edge of the crack (which must be sharp), place the flat of the feet against the opposing wall, then lean back on the hands and walk up. The pull of the hands against the push of the feet masters gravity. This difficult technique is made easier for a man short in the leg, but for a long-legged animal like me few things are more tiring. He is doubled up and straining all the time.

What the top part of the pitch was like I could not properly see on account of a sun-shaft streaming across the ridge straight into my eyes. So blinding was the stream that I was doubtful of seeing the holds even when I got to them. Although usually leader, Tennent is also the complete second. He produced a white sun-hat and clapped it on my head. I pulled down the brim and started. By lay-back technique I made no more height than two feet. I stepped down and looked again. It seemed that one did not start with a lay-back. I tried instead a rounded foothold on the left wall, and then took the lay-back position a foot higher than before. I moved up successfully, shifting the hands a few inches, then the feet a few inches, then the hands, until at ten feet I saw an excellent blunt spike ahead of me which I just managed to grasp with a quick movement. One heave up pulled me on to its top. That was the perfectly sited resting-place. I stopped for a while and panted. I was in good training, but lay-backs are not my forte. Whatever happened I swore that I would not continue up the crack, for its edge had become rounded. I looked rightwards. Across a wide expanse of wall and slab ran a chain of irregular knobs. I crept out on them for six feet to a point where the chain broke, but continued four feet higher, swinging sharply up. Obviously I had to use the knobs now as handholds instead of footholds. The point of real difficulty was that first step at the break. The right foot had to be planted on a steep slab, and trusted for friction-grip, while the body swung over and up to use the higher hand-rail.

I was still unaware whether all would now be well. At each move of the circling traverse I feared another break in the chain, feared it especially in the absence of definite foothold. However, the uncertainty was soon over, because there could be no loitering on that rock. I kept going at fair speed, and emerged once more on the sharp crest of the ridge. Just over its edge was a grassy hollow big enough for three bodies to stretch out in comfort – a sun-trap – the perfect, archetypal stance.

I fetched up Tennent. I expected Mona to have difficulty, for women are not muscularly so strong as men. The traverse being delicate, any leg-tremble or arm-shake due to muscular exhaustion at the crux would be fatal. But she arrived at the top more speedily than either of us, and by skill distinctly fresher than me. We resolved that this was lunchtime, less because we wanted lunch than because the hollow was made to be lunched on – it appealed to our hearts rather than our stomachs. The ridge above us overhung in a high nose. On all other sides we saw nothing but empty space, into which the crest of our ridge projected like the keel of an upturned boat. It was sunlit space, and sun-washed granite, and the sun's heat smote full upon us. A cool breeze made all that sun endurable. Looking back upon the scene I wonder that we ever prevailed upon ourselves to stir. There we should have lain, I think, until the hills crumbled into dust, satisfied in one part of our nature by sloth and ease, in another by the liveliness of beauty, had it not been for that third part, which brews energy and would always be stirring up trouble. In a quarter of an hour I was on my feet again.

The route goes to the left of the great overhang by triple chimneys spaced in vertical tiers. The total height may be a hundred feet. The first two gave plenty of muscular work and asked for little skill. The last was the type and epitome of all three. Under Chimney III Tennent belayed me in a right-angled corner between the ridge and an open wall to its left. On this left wall was the chimney. It was only ten feet high, exposed, and overhanging at the top where a big stone was jammed. The ascent was crude work at the top – a pull up on the stone – none the less giving unadulterated joy: it is so safe, yet the body swings free over thin air; the muscles tighten exhilaratingly; the climber within revels in what Tennent derisively reminded me was 'a glorious out-of-balance movement.'

Beyond the barrier the angle eased. We climbed together up gentle slabs to the Terrace below the final tower. The Terrace is a grassy scoop inclining obliquely right to left, by which one may walk off the buttress. Such a dismal detour would be taken by no man in his right senses. Straight ahead soars the rock of the pinnacle. From its sharp *arête* enormous slabs slope down to the left, overlapping each other in tiers. At each overlap is a vertical wall of ten to thirty feet.

We started our first slab at its lower left-hand edge. By a long ladder of tiny cobbles we came in a hundred feet to a vertical chimney splitting the first overlap. The holds were big. So, at each tier, the slabs yielded in the same way – a slender line, usually a crack, giving passage to the next wall. Towards the top we kept to the right-hand *arête*, where our way poised us on the edge of the great eastern cliff. The granite was rough as ever, and having been exposed to the sun since dawn, was hot to the hand. We climbed on ideal rock, on an ideal mountain, in ideal weather – the kind of mountain-day we dream about on raw nights in November – or at midsummer dawns in Glen Rosa. Our dream, after all, had passed not through the gate of ivory but through the gate of horn.

We came out on the topmost point of Rosa Pinnacle aware that something unique had happened to us: we had had the best summer rock-climb of our lives.

We descended into the Pinnacle Gap and climbed the last slope of Cir Mhor. Mona and I sat down on the west side of the cairn, but Tennent, thank heaven, corrected us. He hailed us on to the very tip. Only when we stepped on to that short thin ridge did we discover that a fresh wind was blowing on to the north-east wall, and striking vertically up: we had to stand on the brink to get the air-stream on face and chest. There was no distant view, and little colour from the sea and nearer hills filtered through the haze. But a good wine needs no bush and Cir Mhor no view. All height and depth, endless space, and the slender tips of all mountains – they were ours. We took deep breaths of the air shooting cool and fast out of the deeps of Glen Sannox and found it heady.

We also found it sobering. Rosa Pinnacle is a buttress. We had climbed Cir Mhor.

16

The Traverse of Liathach

On the afternoon of 7th January Edward Mortimer and I walked
down Glen Torridon in Wester Ross towards the west end of
Liathach. New snow blocked the road. The going was heavy, but
our way lightened by Mortimer's enthusiasm. He had never seen a
Torridon mountain before, and that first view of Liathach from
the Kinlochewe side certainly does fire the heart of a man too long
accustomed to rounded shapes and long slopes of grass. Here,
gaunt sharp peaks soar heavenward. Barely distinguishable at early
dusk against the palest of blue skies, the white cone of Liathach
floated like a cut feather – hovered in a cold remote region,
a stratosphere far removed from earth, or concern of man, or the
toil of a drifted highway in Torridon. It looked a mountain to be
watched from afar, I thought, but not one inviting so slight a thing
as flesh and blood to the summit.

'It's beautiful!' exclaimed Mortimer. 'Tomorrow we'll climb it.'

'In this north-east wind,' I reminded him, 'it's going to be the
very devil getting up the Northern Pinnacles, and after that a
tough battle along the ridge.'

'And I'm dying to explore that northern corrie,' added Mortimer
inattentively. 'The scent of the unknown creeps right down to the
roadway.'

At the shores of Loch Torridon we overtook an old stalker going
to Inver Alligin.

'Good evening,' I said as we drew level. 'It's been a bitter wind
today.'

'A good day to you,' said he. 'Yess, indeed, it hass been a cold
north wind. It will not be good for the hills,' he added, eyeing our
boots and axes, 'unless it iss that you are chust the hikers?'

'We like the look of Liathach,' I replied.

'Liathach!' exclaimed the old stalker enthusiastically. 'Man, but there iss no other mountain like her in the whole of Scotland! She iss machestic!'

He turned to us sharply. 'But you will not be thinking of climbing her? Not in the snowy weather?'

'We thought of climbing it tomorrow,' said Mortimer.

The old man was outraged. He shook his head. 'She iss not to be tampered with!' he warned. 'No indeed, she iss not.'

We said goodbye to him at Torridon House, where Glen Mhic Nobuil sweeps round from the back of Liathach to meet the loch. A camp there would place us favourably for a west to east traverse next day. We pitched the tent on a bleak snow-field. In the near background a black semicircle of pines gave us some protection from a biting wind, which rushed down Glen Mhic Nobuil and swept furiously through the branches. Long, grey skirts of hail trailed across Loch Torridon, which gloomed flatly. Inside the tent we were comfortable enough, and candlelight seems cheerful at night. Surrounded by the usual wild confusion of gear and food, we lay on our stomachs inside warm sleeping bags with a one-inch map between us.

Our problem was a calculation of time. The Northern Pinnacles Route, which was unknown ground to us, followed by the main ridge traverse, would give us the best winter ridge in Scotland, but might take us every bit of eight hours to the summit. In such heavy snow conditions we dared not reckon less. It was accordingly debatable whether we should get off the mountain in daylight. The ridge of Liathach is four miles long with six tops, running due east and west. The south flank drops in craggy slopes to Glen Torridon, but the north wall is a precipice, enclosing with its cirque of four great peaks the sanctuary of the Torridon Forest – the Coire na Caime. The summit lies at the far end of the cirque. At the near end is the second highest peak, Mullach an Rathain. Its north-easterly ridge, set at right-angles to the backbone, is a down-sweep of five pinnacles, known collectively as the Northern Pinnacles. Since their first discovery by Hinxman in 1891 they have not often been climbed – least of all in winter. Having no clue to their difficulties we felt unsure of our time allowance.

'Let's rise at five,' urged Mortimer.

I was horrified. 'Five's all right in a monastery,' I argued, 'where you enjoy the reward at once. But on a cold and squally mountain seven is the limit.'

We compromised at six, each gloating over the hour wrung from the other. At six o'clock next morning it was still night and sleeting. We breakfasted by candlelight on oatmeal, kippers, and brown bread. Big gobs of sleet sploshed and spurted on the canvas. Altogether I remember no other morning quite so discouraging. However, this was Mortimer's last day, so we rolled up our sleeping bags, lest we should fail to endure the temptation. By eight o'clock, when we set out, the sky had cleared.

Grey light helped us through the woods, where the line of an excellent path could still be traced under shallow snow. In the open valley beyond, the snow lay deep and the path vanished. The Mhic Nobuil glen swings in a great arc round Liathach from west to north. To reach the base of the Northern Pinnacles we had to walk four miles to two thousand feet. We were both in first-class training, and not inclined to spare ourselves, yet reckoned that we should need three hours to that four miles. At the halfway region thick cloud blew up and a wall of driving snow advanced down the glen. It hit us with heavy gusts, slowing us down still further, beating our eyes with snow-particles, forcing us to move crabwise, and to shield our faces with gloved hands. In half an hour it was all over. Broad fields of blue opened across the sky, and over them sunlit clouds galloped like white stallions, purposefully, as though 'going places.' The wind remained north-east. It was clear that our day's weather was to be alternate sunshine and squalls. But – which would predominate?

After going two and three-quarter miles up the broad and desolate glen, we could see the cliffs of the Northern Pinnacles a mile away on our right and a thousand feet above. We struck uphill but were still several hundred feet under the ridge when our second squall came over. It could not have chosen a worse time; hiding our objective in mist, it left us to guess where the best start might be. However, we soon came upon steep, rocky slopes, which could be nothing else, we thought, than the start of our ridge. At this higher angle the snow lay less thickly. The ground was free of technical difficulty and allowed us to climb unroped. We had made considerable height before the clouds began to thin out and lift. Then the whitened towers above slowly emerged, as though crystallizing out of the fog. They seemed rather too far to our left. With a moment's pang of dismay we realized that our ridge was not the pinnacle-ridge but a subsidiary one, separated from the other by a deep gully. However, we soon saw that a descent could be made into the top of this gully, whence we might climb a chimney to the lowest col or notch of the true ridge, thus arriving beneath its better half. For the lower ridge is a buttress, swelling gracefully in wall-and-terrace form to the first col, where a fundamental change occurs in its character. It becomes a rocky spur, pinnacled on its narrow crest and walled by red sandstone slabs.

We crossed the gully, kicked steps up the steep snow-chimney to the notch, and looked for the first time into Coire na Caime. Our straight-down glimpse to its floor showed a frozen lochan, pale green around the edges, lying below a ring of black cliffs. The cliffs rose high above us to buttress the main ridge. Their ebony was probably a contrast effect caused by the pure whiteness of new snow lining countless cracks and ledges, which ran up and down and across the face, dead straight as though drawn by ruler. Depths of blue space, and a chill, refreshing air, filled the corrie as spring-water fills a well, offering new vigour to men.

We were most grateful for the accident of this particular approach. It had brought us suddenly to the very essence of the mountainous scene, a true sanctuary at the inmost fastness, to which no man penetrates save the mountaineer. Our approach was also the quickest to the pinnacles. On the lower half of the ridge we might still have been wrestling up short walls – harder climbing no doubt, but disadvantageous. Time was our enemy. We moved up the crest to the first pinnacle. It faced us with thirty feet of vertical rock, which looked rotten and doubtfully cemented by frost. I traversed rightwards and climbed by a chimney to the top.

The second pinnacle was much longer and is no doubt easy in summer. On this occasion the rock-rib on which we started and then the long slope of high-angle scree above were filmed with thin ice. The rock was manageable but not so the scree. A dusting of powder on top made it worse. One put the foot down, allowed it to slither in all directions until at long last something seemed to hold it, then, calling loudly on one's Maker, one stepped up. The wearing of a rope would have given us no kind of protection. We took a leftward trend to avoid more iced rock ahead and entered a gully, which dropped down to the lochan. The snow was iron-hard. The blade of my axe stuck at every blow, forcing me to use the pick. From the top the third pinnacle, rising on the far side of a three-foot gap, looked most straight and formidable. Abrupt chutes flanked the gap, on each side of which was a short knife-edge of snow. At a first glance the gap excited the imagination, but its passage was easy. One kick flattened the knife-edge.

We had now a choice of ledges running left and right around the pinnacle. We tried to follow the right-hand ledge but soon thought better of it, for it girdled a crag to a cul-de-sac over all space. We turned and tried leftwards. This ledge wound upwards above the cliff overlooking the east gully – again an easy ledge in summer, but today piled to a high angle with floury snow lying on ice. The ice was the clear glossy kind, thin except at the lower edge, where icicles two yards long overhung the corrie. We cleared the powder and cut the ice, our picks ringing metallically on the rock below. Many of the steps had to be scratched out rather than cut. We edged up cautiously, until at last good rock on our right gave us a sense of real security. At the top we came out on a most graceful snow-saddle, an aerial perch between low corries and blue sky.

Our luck in getting so high between squalls had saved us much time and pain. Technically easy as it is, the ridge is undeniably narrow and in places steep; these plus treacherous ice and loose snow might have dealt hard with us in high wind. Meantime we gambolled in calm air – while our third squall was speeding up Glen Grudie from Loch Maree, and already breaking on Coire Mhic Fhearchair of Beinn Eighe. Our urgent task was to race it to the top of the fourth pinnacle. To get all possible speed out of ourselves we stripped off the rope and crammed it uncoiled into a rucksack, then climbed fast up a deep snow-slope to the pinnacle. All went well at first. One or two corners required careful footwork. Then we came to a sloping slab on the west face. Our next move had to be a horizontal traverse straight across the slab. A sheet of brittle white ice covered the rock – not frozen water, but melted and refrozen snow. Its stability being uncertain, we hesitated. The first cloud was around us and the wind was rushing among the crags. Plates of ice torn off the east wall went soaring high over the pinnacle. An occasional pellet of snow stung the cheek. Tentatively I cut a hold or two, decided that the first man across would be safe, and the second not, and proceeded alone. Mortimer fetched out the rope, coiled an end, threw it across. We tied on. Mortimer was halfway over when the skies opened and cascaded hail. It fairly bounced off the rocks. Un-happily he stopped for a minute to let the shower slacken, then, just as he reached the near side, one terrific gust knocked him off. His whole weight came on the rope, but I held him without trouble. After moving a few yards we continued unroped.

The fifth pinnacle was deeply snowed up but easy. With the wind behind us we went in leisurely manner to the top of Mullach an Rathain. There we turned east along the main ridge, and received the full blast on our left cheek. The time was shortly after two o'clock – seven hours since breakfast. We felt much in need of food, but the idea of stopping was not tolerable. For nearly three-quarters of a mile we had straightforward walking, rather slow walking because of low visibility and our intermittent fear of cornices, but rarely in deep snow, long stretches of which had been stripped off the crest. Rock and scree were exposed naked to the wind, and to a continuous stream of drift, speeding close to the ground and breaking over each stone in white spurt and gout.

The squall passed its climax. The wind slackened. Coire na Caime grew visible as a darker gulf. The mist above us became dry and shining, and from time to time windows opened through it to show bright clouds riding high. Below on our right a cloud-bank was surging and swaying, tunnelled by widening shafts, through which we glimpsed the pale gleam of the River Torridon, with a dark belt of trees by its shore. Broad grey flats at the head of the loch held a wet orange glow. On the blue-black loch itself were multitudes of white speckles, growing thicker and ever more like the silver scale on salmon the farther the eye travelled west, until they merged in a haze of gold air. Over the Atlantic hardly a trace could be seen of the storm clouds, which only half an hour earlier had overwhelmed the mountain world. Some had been whisked away into nothingness, others raised to lordly heights, where they puffed out white breasts, like fantailed pigeons, and strutted.

We lunched. A cloud was trapped in Coire na Caime and tried in vain to pour itself over the ridge. Great wisps boiled up out of the corrie. On to one of these wisps, when we rose to go, the sun threw our shadows tall as trees. Our Brocken Spectres paced us through the gossamer air. Bright halos crowned them. The symbols were flattering, too flattering to humbug mountaineers whose near future was stormy. We had reached the midway point, where the ridge changes direction north-east, when our fourth squall began darkening the hills around Loch Maree. At the same time a weak sunset flush spread over all the snow-peaks to the north and south, becoming wonderfully bright on the underside of high clouds. Above the sunset belt the sky paled, became green, was unsullied by one breath of vapour. The glow deepened on the mountains. The Sail Mhor of Beinn Eighe, pointing a leviathan fin out of the mist-sea beyond Coire na Caime, was touched by a fire like live coal.

We reached an eminence where the ridge fell away to the col below Am Fasarinen, whose triple pinnacles are Liathach's chief defence. The clouds approaching from Loch Maree were being held by the five-mile barrier of Beinn Eighe, but an outflanking attack had swept down Glen Torridon from Kinlochewe, and the first gauzy mists were flitting past the Fasarinen. The pinnacles are big and blunt. They had been well wind-swept, but grey hoar and a dull skin of ice encrusted the rocks, which, thrusting stonily through delicate mists, looked stark and stern, much larger than life as it were, more real than reality.

We dropped to the col, and moved unroped up the first pinnacle. Before we reached the top the clouds swept over and the wind struck. Throughout the day neither cloud nor wind ever arrived in advance of the other, but always together, with force and paralysing cold. We had to fight for our holds, luckily big enough to give us footing even when icy. The ascent of each pinnacle was relatively easy, for we climbed on the lee-side, but the descent to windward was a thrice-repeated nightmare. We climbed down blind. No route-selection was possible. Except for the six feet of frosted quartzite directly under our boots nothing could be seen through the veils of snow and hail, which throughout the passage of the pinnacles drove vertically upwards. On the ascent the sight of snow 'falling up,' and of whirlwinds at the top lifting the snow in tall, spinning columns, gave us great interest, but the actual passage of the tops and subsequent descents gave us hell. On the second or third descent we were astonished to find ourselves above a sheer drop. Mortimer went first. He lowered himself by the hands from a tiny ledge on one side of an overhang, and just managed to drop delicately on to a foothold, arms outstretched to preserve balance. Whether he was now some ten feet from the pinnacle's base or else poised on a north wall falling a thousand feet to Coire na Caime he could hardly tell short of jumping off. Yet he was seriously trying to get down farther. I leaned over my safe ledge and said mockingly: 'And the angels will bear thee up, lest at any time thou dash thy foot against a stone.' To Mortimer the hint was so broad that he turned at once. He had a struggle to get back. It is easy to drop down without an intermediate foothold but not to climb up. To save fetching out the rope I dropped him the end of my scarf. He took a twist round the forearm, we both pulled hard, and up he came.

We climbed right back, groping our way through the swirl of snow on top, and descended a gully on the pinnacle's south flank. It plunged into a seething white nothingness. 'This *must* be the route,' we said to each other reassuringly. We had to say it once or twice. But there could be no other. We kicked and cut our way down for fifty feet, then made an exploratory left traverse through hurtling fog.

Great was our delight when this move brought us to the ridge near the foot of Spidean a' Choire Leith, the shapely summit peak of four hundred feet. Unhappily it is also a stupendous scree-dump – loose, sharp, quartzite scree. We had rejoiced too soon. The ascent is purgatory on a good summer day, but when every stone is glazed and each hole masked by powder, cloud driving, and a north-easter shrilling across the face, it magnifies the name of Lucifer. At almost every step we had to stop and regain balance. It was half-past four and dusk when we passed over the summit.

We steered by compass for the north-west ridge. All our hopes of getting off the mountain before dark had gone. Our most pressing objective was to win clear of the northerly summit crags before light wholly failed, for we could not contrive such a clearance by torchlight in dirty weather. This last 'squall' had become a sore disappointment by proving itself to be no squall. It was on for the night, and worsening. There was no increase in wind-force, but snow came thicker. Having nothing to sight on, we took a dozen bearings on the first five hundred feet, ran into crags on the right and left, disengaged, and pressed on over broken ground. The lower we went, the deeper the snow – with this advantage, that we could see the way without torchlight; and this disadvantage, that sharp drops over low crags were invisible – all merged in apparently continuous grey slopes. I had two very narrow escapes from a crash. It became plain that a man could kill himself this way, on technically easy ground. We fetched out our torches.

The first misfortune of the day at last overtook us. Our intention had been to follow the north-west ridge right down to the Mhic Nobuil glen, but we must have borne too far left, for we fetched up in Coire na Caime. For a while we felt uncertain of our whereabouts. We seemed to be in a sunken bowl, and only discovered the lochan when snow and ice collapsed at the edge. We went in up to the knees and came out blaspheming. The summit had only been 'like' hell, but this *was* the ninth and inner circle. Three feet of the softest snow lay in this Nameless Pit, so that we could not distinguish the lochan's margin. We had to contour round, ploughing a furrow thigh-deep in search of an exit, while we repeatedly broke through into icy water. At last we came upon an issuing stream. 'No matter where we are,' I remarked, 'this stream will lead us down to Loch Torridon.' But I was reckoning without that three feet of snow. Although the stream was flowing level the banks rose and fell craggily. Some of the drifts exceeded three feet by far. The leg had to be raised so high for each step, and then sank so deep, that after we had gone a couple of hundred yards the muscles at the front of my thighs were red hot. One touch of cramp would have finished us completely: we were thankful now for the recent discipline of bad-weather training. We rested for ten minutes.

Upon starting again we both felt so utterly worn out that we toyed with the idea of a bivouac, and made tentative efforts to scoop out a snow-cave in a drift. But the snow seemed too soft, and I suspect that our efforts were not whole-hearted – we were wet from the waist down. Moreover, although we had each, secretly, given up hope of reaching camp that night, neither would openly admit the thought. Our exhaustion was just muscular. So 'Go slow,' urged Mortimer. 'Halt often,' said I. This counsel of conservation saved us. Mortimer, whom I admire as a man of spirit and untold energy, would never, I said to myself, admit failure. So neither would I, as yet. I had got to the clenched-jaw stage, consciously forcing each step, when at last our stream ran out on open, undulating hill-slopes. They were exposed to wind and the snow lay lighter – a mere twelve inches. Our uncertainty of the route cleared away when the River Mhic Nobuil appeared black and foaming in the torch-beam. As we followed the three-mile course down the glen the falling snow gave place to sleet, and sleet to pelting rain. We made camp at 9 p.m.

Our sopping clothes would have flooded the floor of the tent had we gone in. So we stripped to the skin in the wind and darkness, then dived inside to pull on dry sweaters and sleeping bags. We heard the music of a purring primus, watched pure snow change in the pot to grey slush, then to bubbling clarity ... we brewed up.

We were silent over our mugs, each preoccupied for a while with his own thoughts about that tough, thirteen-hour job on

Liathach. Our thoughts, it appeared, were short and simple.

'She iss machestic!' exclaimed Mortimer at last.

'But she iss not to be tampered with,' I added.

17

The Moor of Rannoch

The famous heatwave of June 1949 persisted into July. The drought afflicting the whole country became chronic. West highland villages had to get water brought in by carrier, and that was something I had not heard of before.

Conditions for rock-climbing had never been better: I could think of some new routes that I wanted to try. And yet – I thought also of the Moor of Rannoch. It is the greatest moor in Scotland, one of the most accessible too, yet curiously enough the least explored. It is vast and trackless. Perhaps that intimidates walkers? While mountaineers, who like deserts if they like anything, notoriously prefer their deserts vertical.

Too long had I been counted among the latter. At first, while my ignorance was darkest and heaviest, Rannoch Moor was damned just because it was flat – that was enough! Later, when cold reason was admitted to my counsels, it was damned because it was bleak, bare, featureless, and quite excessively extensive, therefore no fit place for a hill-lover, to whom a peak is paradise; and no whit short of hell in foul weather, when damp mists sink on to it, prospectless, and the bogs are full, or when snow-winds scourge it. So that in the end Rannoch Moor had to conquer me through my heart, and reason had to *follow* perception, not lead. Which is just. It was that eastern view from the Glencoe summits that won me – the sparkle of the numberless tarns at noon – the phosphorescent gleam of their night-eyes – the spike of Schichallion pushing up beyond blue haze at the farther rim, thirty miles away. I had been fascinated, too, by the distant sight of wild swans and great flights of smaller birds coming on to Loch Ba and Loch Laidon, which stretch in a linked waterway ten miles across the moor.

The scene from my watch-tower on the Buachaille showed me that the most interesting way of crossing the moor would be to keep close to the main chain of waterways, which rise in the Blackmount at Coire Ba of Stob Ghabhar, and run east through Lochan na Stainge, Loch Ba, and the five miles of Loch Laidon to Loch Rannoch – a distance of fifteen miles. Loch Rannoch continues beyond the moor fifteen miles to Schichallion, thence by the Tummel and Tay to the North Sea. The moor's northern boundary is the group of low hills called the Black Corries, the south boundary the high group of Achallader. Its entire area is said to be fifty-six square miles. My reason, now stripped of its old prejudice, informed me that from the centre of this unvisited moorland all the mountains circling round its rims would be seen anew, and charms not as yet known to me revealed. And of the moor's own secrets what did I really know? Not a thing.

On an evening of mid-July I arrived by road at the south-west side of the moor and camped between Lochan na Stainge and Loch Ba. I came alone. Let me confess at once that I prefer being alone among hills, provided that I am not climbing in the technical sense; prefer it also on moors, unless in dirty weather. But on this occasion I was not quite alone. I had as company a Golden Labra-dor bitch called Heather. She is a fine mountaineer with sufficient tops to her credit and ability enough on rock and snow to satisfy the Scrutinising Committee of the Scottish Mountaineering Club, from membership of which club she is disqualified only by sex. Her big black pads give her a grip on slabs and a quick, confident technique superior to that of her envious owner. Like me she is twice as much alive among hills as at sea level. And she doesn't talk. She just looks; which is quite enough.

We pitched the tent well to the east of Loch Ba because damp grey mist was rising off all the lochans. The day had been very hot. The fog, however, in appearance if not in temperature, was much like a mid-winter's ground mist. It cohered in banks, gently rolling sometimes this way and sometimes that, for no apparent reason – the night being windless. The sinuous sway of its forms would have been a perfect medium for the weird display of light had only the moon been full. But the stars were strong in a black sky and the mists greyly chill.

I had deliberately pitched the tent on top of thick heather and thus had a springy couch under me for my night's sleep. The other Heather curled up at my feet. After the experimental nibbles at my toes were over she made an excellent hot-water bottle.

We rose at sunrise. Not a trace of mist remained; nor was there any cloud in the sky. So striking was the latter fact that I realized how often in the past I must have talked about cloudless skies without ever having spoken strict truth, save in reference to a narrow view from close country. In the wider mountain skyscape, always, in some quarter of that mountain sky there has been cloud, perhaps a long bar of cumulus low down at the horizon, or a few puffs glimpsed through a pass. But today east, north, west, and south – clear sky, peculiarly and luminously empty like a heavenly vacuum. From behind the blue a colourless radiance shone, more than usually suggestive of infinite space and of the reality of that infinity. Provided that this were seen at all there could be engendered only one attitude of mind, that of a reverential awe.

After sharing the dog's breakfast I struck camp and left the tent at the roadside to be collected later by passing friends. By six we were away. The early start was necessary because I intended to make a double traverse – ten miles north-east to Rannoch station, then thirteen miles west back to Kingshouse, Glencoe – and because I had a strong suspicion that distances on Rannoch Moor were to be measured in time, not miles.

The first passage along the east side of Loch Ba gave us the heaviest going of the day; the heather was longer there and the ground broken by hummocky ridges and old water-courses. A short and twisting river linked Loch Ba to Loch Laidon. It was at these two ends of the two lochs that I had seen wild swans fly in and duck come down among the heather. In the breeding season black-and red-throated divers visit the lochs and behave like submarines when alarmed, slowly submerging until only the head and neck remain above water, like a periscope. The wide mosses farther away from the lochs harbour greenshanks. And that is the limit of my knowledge about Rannoch bird life, which is certain to be very much more extensive than I ever dream. These lochs would repay the bird-watcher. I should be most interested to know, for example, what birds find food or shelter on the wooded islands. They are small islands, well wooded with birch, yew, and pine – indicating that Rannoch Moor might yet revert to its Old Wood of Caledon days were it not for the hungry deer. I should like to be spared the wolves, the brown bear, the boar, and the outlawed brigands, but the natural forest that sheltered them I would have back if I could. New growth seems to flourish on the water-protected isles, which are inaccessible except to a man prepared to swim a hundred yards – and, if he wants to botanize or bird-watch, to push a raft with his clothing in front of him.

On reaching Loch Laidon I thought that the ground improved, although a certain amount of leaping from tuft to tuft was still part of the day's work. On the other hand there were surprisingly few peat-hags. I remember no more than one or two, still exposing the bare bones of the Old Wood, but I imagine that in other parts of the moor they must be abundant. On the line I chose, always close to the loch, the moor was well drained, and over its whole area I judge it to be equally well drained by the countless tarns. I met no bogs. One gets across in dry weather with dry feet.

Admittedly we had the moor in perfect condition. A west wind was blowing, of the kind we may truly call a zephyr, but the heat was semi-tropical, and away from the waterways must have been as consumingly fierce as the south Syrian desert. Unlike Loch Ba, Loch Laidon had a fairly straight margin: we could travel close to the shore, which we found indented by innumerable tiny bays. These were filled with a clean and gravelly sand, most tempting on a hot day. We had one bathe near the start, and ten minutes later, feeling as hot as ever, we had another. There were going to be more. Faced with the personal example of Heather's ever-readiness, I began to see my own repeated dressing and undressing as a pointless waste of time. There was little or no chance of meeting any one during the day. So I stripped once and for all and stuffed my clothes into my rucksack. The zephyr could now get at my skin, and the need for frequent dips became less urgent.

But for the bays our day would fast have become a sheer trial of endurance – worse by far for Heather than for me, her great handicap being fur and a lack of sweat-glands. During the first few hours' enthusiasm she covered three times as much ground as I, ranging out eastwards in wide circles. I let her do this to see what game she might start up. It astonished me that she drew a blank. Not one hare, not a rabbit or grouse, did she raise – absolutely nothing. The moor at this time of day seems to be bare of all animal life. Throughout our traverse I never once set eyes on a deer, although every winter great herds congregate by the roadside. I assumed that they would all be up in the corries of the Black-mount. The lack of other life is stranger.

We came to the north-east end of Loch Laidon where the River Gaur flowed out sharply right towards Loch Rannoch. The river must have been fifty yards wide. I hoped that it might be all the shallower on that account, and tried to get across by wading, my rucksack balanced on my head. Before I was a third of the way over the water had crept up to my chin, and by natural buoyancy my body was tending to float and capsize. Since the water looked much deeper and swifter in front, I came back and moved on a few hundred yards, then tried again with no more success. In the end we had to make a half-mile detour downstream to a ford, where a line of great boulders offered a dry route. After all my vain efforts to wade I was determined to wade at the last, and did so through chest-deep water. On the other hand Heather, who had already swum the river twice, and been forced each time to return in high dudgeon because I had failed to follow, was determined that since the ford was now found she would use it. She bounded clumsily on the polished boulders, not being able to get a good purchase on them with her wet paws, and landing each time in a splashing sprawl. But she was over long before I was.

We had now been going four hours. Cutting out the last few hundred yards to Rannoch station we rounded the head of Loch Laidon. There we struck an excellent track going half a mile back along the farther shore, *en route* to Kingshouse, then suddenly degenerating into a mere sheep-track. This northern shore was decidedly pleasanter than the southern shore. The sun was shining in front instead of behind, and there were wild flowers by the path. One little bay was full of water-lilies, and another, about a mile down the loch, had the best of all the sandy beaches. We turned aside on to the latter. It was backed by short granite crags, and covered deeply in coarse clean sand, on to which the sun had been beating several hours daily for a month. It was hot to lie on. There I lay, my back upon the warm granite, and lunched with Heather. On this side of the loch the shore shelved more steeply; one could dive in after a knee-deep wade. From time to time one or the other of us would rise and go down to the water for a plunge, then come back and sprawl. An hour passed away. We just luxuriated. Sometimes I would wonder whether to have one more swim in those blue waters or to go on towards the wide, sunlit corries of the Blackmount, or to the glens of Glencoe where the peaks were darkening against the sun. The walk to Kingshouse would certainly be the shorter, and even so was consuming me in a way that I had not believed possible. Twelve more miles, said the map? I had better allow six hours for it.

In due course we continued three miles up the loch-side, until at the ruined cottage called Tigh na Cruaiche the track swung away to the west, aiming straight for Glencoe. The so-called 'track' had long since become a purely imaginary line on the map, having no basis in a present reality. At the south wall of the ruin a barn still provides roof and shelter in foul weather. I could think of no better headquarters for a natural historian bent on adventure, or for bird-watchers or fishermen; for only a hundred feet below, a great bay of the loch contains seven islands, two of which are well wooded. No one will find comfort at Tigh na Cruaiche; only bare shelter and perfect solitude.

We had still to cover four and a half miles to reach the Black Corries Lodge. This part of the day we both found most exhausting. Heather was now following close to heel of her own free will. For my part I found the ground badly folded and the heather too thick.

Only now was the day-long breeze strengthening and beginning to feel rather too cool on my unprotected skin, so that when the lodge came into sight I was glad enough to put on clothing. The average height of the moor is a thousand feet; the lodge around twelve hundred: it thus commands a wondrously wide prospect across Loch Ba to the Blackmount. Had the tarns all been tiny the moor might have resembled a cratered battlefield; but the waters were broad and long enough to add beauty to desolation, both of their kind matchless. The circling hills of the east and west Blackmount, and the deep ranks of Glencoe, were in proper perspective, full in stature, clean-carved by corrie and glen, a deep and dusky blue in the hollows. I realized that not until this day had I ever seen the Glencoe hills as they really are. From the glen itself the mountains are sadly foreshortened, but this fact is never guessed, never realized, until one goes miles out on to Rannoch Moor.

I have no especial love for road-walking – a road is a tyrant, directing a man in ways planned for him, and most wearing on climbing-nails, which are costly. But I have a good word to say for the road from Black Corries Lodge to Kingshouse: it is only four miles and downhill all the way. I could appreciate that, in the circumstances. I was very tired. And a good dinner being only one hour away, I found myself still full of enthusiasm for the Moor of Rannoch; for its own sake as well as for its new revelation of old hills. At last I knew it – and at that checked myself. Moors, like mountains, are not known so easily as first visits tempt one to think. However, I had seen something of it in summer. What of winter? In winter I knew only the moor's western fringes. I had watched the sun shine low over wind-rippled snow-fields, and glance across frozen lochs, make of an ice-bound tree a flashing chandelier and strike fire from the frozen tower of Buachaille. A winter traverse of the whole moor would give a man these and other things, and an adventure into the bargain for which he would have to be as fit and as well clothed as for a mountain expedition. I had had enough experience of Rannoch blizzards to know that they rival Cairngorm blizzards in everything save wind velocity. In new, deep snow a crossing in one day would hardly be possible, but on old snow, in hard frost and fine weather, all should be more than well.

It may be that I exaggerate the worth of the day? It does seem to ask strenuous work and a sacrifice of either comfort or convenience. However, greater worth has always in my own experience asked greater effort, and the reward has borne proportion to effort, on one plane or another. Summer and winter there is a day for Rannoch.

18

Ben Nevis by the North-East Buttress

No man will ever know Ben Nevis. No man ever has known Ben Nevis – not even the famous Clement Wragge, who made a daily ascent for eight months; nor yet Dr Graham Macphee, who wrote the Nevis guide; certainly not I, who have climbed on it only thirty-seven times.

In winter the level of perpetual snow sinks below the summit, which lies right in the storm-track of the North Atlantic hurricanes, so that massive accumulations of snow and ice can build up on the northern cliffs in a few days' time. Routes like the North-East Buttress and Tower Ridge then give totally different climbs in successive weeks. The mood, temper, climate, and conditions of Nevis are inexhaustibly various; their changes swifter and more radical than on any other hill, and not predictable even one day in advance. No other mountain has been more roundly cursed by the disappointed climber, or so lavishly praised by the fortunate: because nothing he ever gets is expected.

The clearest insight I ever had into the wayward character of this best and worst of mountains was granted me one March. Douglas Laidlaw and I knew the North-East Buttress in summer as the biggest cliff on the mainland, eighteen hundred feet in height, presenting a ridge to the north-east and a vast face to the west. On the ridge we hoped to have one of the best winter climbs in Scotland – given good weather. I need hardly say that when we arrived below the mountain on Saturday night the weather was foul.

Our starting-point was the distillery under the north-west flank, which is a notable rendezvous on two counts. By its grounds access is gained to the track up the Allt a Mhuilinn glen; within its walls a whisky called Dew of Ben Nevis is distilled. It is thus an important crossroads where the Devil takes his opportunities.

He whispered to me now so loudly that I was sure Laidlaw must overhear: 'Outside, torrential sleet and thick darkness. Indoors the golden dew of bliss! What joy of the Nevis cliffs may not be found doubled in the Nevis bar? – and with what less effort! and what more ease!' I translated aloud into English. But my words were a mere casting of pearls – the far-away look that came instantly to Laidlaw's eyes showed that his heart had already climbed two thousand feet to the S.M.C. hut in the upper corrie. He trampled the pearliest of wisdom underfoot.

'In the Nevis bar,' said he, 'you get the uplift first and the head-ache after. On the Nevis cliffs the pains first and the joys after. If it were the other way round a blind drunk would be the good life and pubs temples. That,' he added after a moment's reflection, 'is morals summed up.'

I was astonished at his doctrine. I laughed. I even assented. And thus it came about that Laidlaw and I climbed Nevis. Our first move was to reach the hut. Before we were halfway up the night was pitch-black, blowing, and snowing hard. The rather faint track, which is never easy to find and follow at night, was drifted over. More than once we were forced into the frozen bed of the river, which gave us the only sure line to the hut. Time and again we stopped, swore that a hurricane raged on top, that to go on was madness, and to climb next day impossible. But I could never resist adding: 'And pubs is temples.' So that we always laughed and always went on. We reached the hut at midnight.

Our ascent of three and a half miles had taken four hours – double the normal time. We made a good fire and supper. At 1 a.m. I went out for my last look round. The hurricane had torn away the cloud in a rent as big as Nevis itself, and the moon shone full upon the two-mile range of cliffs close above me. Thinning mists still clung along its arctic wall and picked out great ridges and buttresses and many a spectral tower, all whitened with new snow. Within half a minute a cloud-mass broke over the summit, and with one mighty roll engulfed the cliffs. A second billow, charging over the col between Nevis and Carn Mor Dearg, choked Coire Leis and spilled down into the Allt a Mhuilinn glen. It began to snow hard.

I scrambled into my bunk. I lay back gratefully, watched the stove glow red hot through the darkness, and listened to the wind thunder on the walls and roof. 'We'll get a long lie tomorrow,' I thought, and sighed happily. 'Not a hope of any climbing.'

Imagine our astonishment, therefore, when we woke up in the morning to blue skies! The cold was extreme. After a hurried breakfast we walked up the corrie to the North-East Buttress. The wind was still blowing from the south-east. Puffs of powder raced down the corrie and stung our faces with flying spiculae. The spume hid the lower part of the cliffs, but the uppermost drift, twisting through crisp air, caught a sparkle of the sun. Beyond this battlefog of ice we could see blue sky, and that greatly encouraged us to go on – to suffer our measure of pain now in hope of the bliss to come. In a wind so violent and snow so heavy our prospects, none the less, remained poor. I knew of two parties forced to spend a night out near the top, one just below a famous rock-nose of ten feet called the Man Trap, the other slightly above it where an icy traverse had to be made round a corner and over slabs. We might suffer that fate if we failed to arrive at the crux before dark, but in truth our real concern was not that, but whether we should even get quarter-way up.

The noblest feature of Nevis that morning was undoubtedly the North-East Buttress. We looked straight on to its vast white face, which by an optical illusion seems always to be toppling over. Our day's route lay up the sharp left-hand ridge, which was silhouetted against the sky and from this angle looked unclimbable. It seemed far too sharp, steep, and icy. Worse still was the lower part, where a pyramid rises seven hundred feet to the First Platform. It loomed monstrously through the smoke and turmoil of drift.

We contoured below the base of the buttress to its east side and climbed laboriously a broad and broken runnel of powder-snow up to the crest at the First Platform. This so-called platform is a short, level part of the ridge, which steepens sharply again to a wide barrier-wall. Even from a hundred feet below the appearance of this wall gave a sure sign of the conditions we might meet higher. Its face was plastered, not with new snow, which is always bright, but with snow of a grey tinge, suspiciously like frost-hoarings, laid on in layers and basted by wind, which had ripped off the new snow as it fell. The entire ascent would thus take longer than we had bargained for: a great deal of cutting might have to be done. Had we not known something of the habits of Nevis we should probably have given up the climb and tried a more sheltered route elsewhere. Instead we said to ourselves: 'The day is too young to be judged – our proper course is to continue the climb meantime, and be prepared to smack it hard or to return.'

The wind was certainly blowing strong, but only in gusts. Moving slowly in soft deep snow we began to kick steps up a long scoop running obliquely right to left up to the base of the barrier wall. We were nearing the top of this scoop when Nevis performed two of its lightning changes. The snow froze and the wind died. Every rock and slope had a hard crust. But for that drop in the wind we should not have gone farther.

Our own mood changed as quickly as the mountain's. At once excitement mounted and our hearts rejoiced. We were going to get a climb – a hard climb! We set to work on the frost-bound wall with real enjoyment. It lies close to the vertical for sixty feet, but the holds are so big that our task of climbing with axes held ready to scrape snow-ice off each ledge as we came to it was fairly simple. When the angle eased above this wall the hard work of the day began. On every ledge and groove was hard-frozen snow, so that every step had to be cut. For this reason we kept as close as possible to the right or true crest of the buttress, where steeper rock meant lighter snow and quicker progress. Upon making this discovery we stuck to our straight and narrow path too religiously. Several hundred feet above the first barrier-wall we struck a second one. This, if anything, is steeper than the first, shorter but more difficult. Halfway up, a traverse must be made on rock that pushes out one's body awkwardly. Knowing that in summer the foothold is excellent I had no hesitation in going straight up until that midway traverse stopped me. It looked precarious. I brought up Laidlaw to give me a belay at close quarters, but did so with an uneasy feeling that we should not be there at all. When all was ready I edged out leftwards. The handholds I needed at the critical step were glazed, like the foothold. I had now no real intention of making that risky move, but for obscure reasons spent a few minutes as though trying to do so. Laidlaw broke the spell by telling me the time. We returned to the base of the pitch. 'And *that* is just a moderate wall in summer!' we reflected. Truly a Nevis ridge under heavy snow is transformed out of all recognition.

We traversed leftwards and turned the impasse by snow-scoops, then cut our way back to the crest, which had become much narrower than before – a true ridge rather than a buttress. The angle had slightly steepened, giving us delightful climbing free from all anxiety about route selection – but time consuming, for the snow was everywhere like iron. The ridge ran straight and true towards the plateau; its frosted edge, turned to a blazing cloud near the summit, gave a star-like glitter. On this crest we plied our axes for an hour or two until late in the afternoon it narrowed, again steepened, and confronted us with that ten-foot nose, called the Man Trap.

Although the ridge was so narrow at this point we had good footing below the crux – a little platform on which we could stand or sit in comfort, but not lie. We inspected the Man Trap apprehensively. Nevis had performed yet another quick change. We were only two or three hundred feet from the summit-plateau, and this whole upper part of the mountain was clad in a thick deposit of fog-crystals – even vertical and overhanging crags were covered. Some of the crystals grew out like fir-cones, two feet long, others were massed in overlapping banks, shaped like huge fig-leaves. They made our further ascent look a fearsome task, but in hard fact their presence was not in itself a serious matter. The trouble was that these crystals were only a top-dressing. I scraped them off the Man Trap with the blade of my axe and underneath disclosed thin, clear ice.

This ice was true *verglas*: it could not be chipped off the rock. We tried. However, the pitch was short. I climbed on to Laidlaw's shoulders, steadied myself, and reached to the top. But the ledge above bulged with ice – a boss of pale green ice, like candle-wax.

In this ice I cut a few handholds but found them of no use to me – between Laidlaw's head and the green bulge I still needed one foothold, and that I could not get. I came down again.

We looked round the flanks in search of some avoiding move. On the left flank the rock was quite clear of fog-crystals, which at this particular point had been wind-blasted. The rock fell away in smooth convex slabs, which rose to near verticality at the wall beside the Man Trap. The only semblance of weakness there was a shallow chimney, filled from side to side with a twist of thick black ice. Its ascent was not possible. For the first time we began to feel alarmed. The sun had long since dropped behind Nevis: the metal of my axe had become sticky to the touch of a bare hand, and the evening stillness noticeable.

We examined the right flank. There was here a much greater and more open expanse of rock, tumbling one thousand two hundred feet or more to the chasm between North-East Buttress and Observatory Ridge. Close under us the slabs were seamed by ledges, supporting much grey-green ice and snow which fell away at a high angle. On this face it might be possible to cut out a traverse and regain the ridge higher up – it *might* be possible.

Laidlaw gave me a very tight rope while I lowered myself from the platform and cut holds down a steep groove leading on to the face. I began to hew out a traverse. The falling chips scuttered on the crusted rocks with a hollow sound, took to the air in whirring hops, and then in long bounds as they vanished into the depths. Their noise seemed loud in the still air. With every step I took the more unpleasant my prospects grew. The rocks were slabby and offered no belays. However, it looked just possible to regain the crest by a forty-foot chimney choked with white ice – but again, no rock-belay, a twelve-hundred-foot cliff below, at least an hour of cutting – the mountain was asking too much of my nervous system. I turned and went back.

If we had reached the crux earlier in the day it is probable that we should not have pressed the attack further. But the horizon skies were green in the south, and the upper snows of Carn Mor Dearg red. There could be no thought now of climbing all the way down that rocky and frozen crest. We *had* to get up. I made one more attempt on the Man Trap, and although it failed I thought I saw a solution. I held my axe above my head, its point resting on a thick pad of scarf on my hip, its head against the glazed wall, while Laidlaw, the lighter man, climbed on to my shoulders and head, then stepped on the axe-head, and pulled himself up. I was not too happy about the soundness of the manoeuvre, but those extra few inches made all the difference. He disappeared above in search of a stance.

I looked rightwards across the cliffs on to vast accumulations of snow upon Observatory Ridge. It seemed incredible that only a few months before I had been climbing the buttress on its far side in sun so hot that we had stripped to the waist. Or there was that other day when we strayed in thick mist and rain on to unclimbed rocks. We had some long halts that day with rain streaming down the slabs and down our own skins. I remembered how the film of water drew out the most varied colour from the rocks – rocks that are just dull brown when dry – little flecks of red and yellow, and blue and crystal, gleaming with so unexpected a beauty that I remembered them now after all the discomfort had been forgotten.

I brought my mind back to the Man Trap. Laidlaw was still cutting. The red glow had vanished from the snow-peaks, which now were grey. The cliffs were as bleak as some long-deserted city. The stillness gripped the mountain-world, strongly persisting behind the occasional ring of Laidlaw's axe when the steel struck rock. The first faint stars emerged, brightening as the sky darkened to navy blue.

Laidlaw called me. I joined him with the aid of a strong pull on the rope. Immediately above us the ridge rose in another high step, and this one, I think, is unclimbable in summer. The only way of turning it is to traverse left round a corner and climb up a slab. We had just enough light left to us to make the traverse to the corner, which bristled with spears of fog-crystal, and to see the slab, which was sleeky with ice. The cutting of nicks up that slab looked like giving us most delicate climbing, for the coating was only half an inch thick. The situation looked most forbidding. The rocks beneath our feet were indistinct in thickening dusk, and swept away into a bottomless pit of dark. The possibility of taking a fall in such an exposed situation made my skin creep. Since the previous pitch, normally climbable in a few minutes, had taken more than one hour, I began to fear that this last obstacle of the ridge might have to wait until morning.

Balancing with my chest against the corner I swung off my rucksack and fetched out an electric torch. The moment I switched it on how different everything looked! The slab gleamed like a mirror, its numberless frost-cressets sparkled, the snow shone. They reflected light from so many different angles and textures that something of the beauty of a musical score in terms of light was presented whole to us – gay music: the music of the Dance. It enlivened my weary muscles. Moreover, the gloomy abyss had vanished away in the outer dark. For us it no longer existed. This short and beautiful slab was all that we need think about, and all that we need climb. I cut the nicks, and climbed, and cut again, lifting myself only on my edge-nails, but blissfully unconscious of anything precarious in our position, so that in ten minutes I had reached easy ground with a straightforward route opening ahead among huge and broken crags. Laidlaw followed. The way was clear to the plateau.

At first we had to climb little pitches, and cut an occasional step, but very quickly the snow became softer. We both remarked on the relative mildness of the air, and suddenly realized that Nevis was about to give us yet another and characteristic change – a temperature inversion. As soon as we stepped on to the plateau we saw that our guess was right. All southward valleys brimmed with cloud, from which the tips of high peaks projected like skerries. Eastwards the clouds were low down, spilling along the valley floors. From one of these cloud-lakes the moon was just swimming clear. Its upper half was yellow, like honey; its lower half blurred red. When it swam clear a mellow glow suddenly bloomed on the cloud surfaces; in a few minutes they flickered, as though with wild-fire, then changed to an even silver. On the broad snow-fields beneath our boots each crystal crumb threw its own shadow on to the gleaming crust. The whole frozen world was alive with the shining of light.

No man will ever know Ben Nevis.

On the other hand Nevis will always help him to know himself. There is no end to such knowledge. Likewise there is no end to the joy of getting it.

19

Benalder Forest

It is one of the unlisted privileges of belonging to a mountaineering club that one may meet men of the most adventurous instinct. They together possess a remarkable store of information about strange crannies in the high or remote parts of this earth's surface. This storehouse does not lie open, like a reference library, for all to draw upon at will. Rather it is like an orchard, where one waits for the fruits to ripen, until they may be plucked, or more likely fall from above and hit one on the head. In other words one must like one's fellows sufficiently well to learn by listening: truly it is wonderful what may be picked up from scraps of conversation. Many of the good days I've had on new climbs or in exploring new hill-country have been due less to my own initiative than to bright ideas given to me by unwitting mountaineers. For example, they gave me Benalder Forest.

Of all remote unget-at-able mountains in Scotland, Ben Alder ranks among the first. It lies in the heart of that roadless area of two hundred and fifty square miles between Loch Rannoch in the south, Loch Laggan in the north, Loch Garry in the east, and Loch Treig in the west. In the middle are the mountain ranges of Benalder and Corrour Forests, and hard on their east flank, under the east slopes of Ben Alder itself, is the fifteen-mile length of Loch Ericht, running south-west to north-east, its top end close to Dalwhinnie. A climber coming by road, say from Glasgow, must cover a hundred and twenty miles to get at Ben Alder, ten of which are on foot by the short hill-route from Loch Rannoch. Being thus too far for weekend climbing, and in summer holidays not far enough, the Benalder Forest is unknown country to all save a very few mountaineers. And it *is* troublesome to reach: the idea of investigating it never came to me until, little by little, scraps of information accumulated.

An alert interest was first roused in me when I was told that Ben Alder's north corrie was buttressed by crags which had not been explored; then that good pony tracks wound scores of miles among the hills and rivers between Lochs Laggan and Ericht; that these tracks could be followed forty-four miles from Dalwhinnie to Fort William by way of Loch Pattock, the bealach Dubh of Ben Alder, Loch Ossian, Lochtreighead, and at last by the Amhain Rath to Glen Nevis, with only one short break in the track from the bealach Dubh down to Loch Ossian. That drove me to the map, and by the map I was wholly fascinated. Even on coloured paper, all that country around Ben Alder bore the unmistakable stamp of the wild and the wilderness, recessed by corries great enough to have at their backs still wilder fastnesses, where secret things awaited inquiry. What *kind*, of things? you might ask. But, of course, I did not know.

Finally I heard of an unoccupied and open cottage at Alder Bay, on the south shore of the mountain. This was said to give comfortable shelter, but not necessarily a good night's sleep. The cottage was haunted. At first I did not take the tale of the haunting seriously. Its theory, however, was said to be backed by the fact that a previous tenant, a stalker named ---, had hanged himself on the back of the front door. It seemed to be a sound enough proposition that some undissipated energies thrown off from his dying body might persist for a while as poltergeists, and undirected by intelligence cause aimless dramatic effects and loud noises. What I did not credit was that such effects had in fact been observed. It is the usual weakness of these tales that one never meets the first-hand witness. So that I was drawn to Ben Alder not by poltergeists but by those unexplored cliffs of the north-east corrie and the hinted mysteries of a one-inch ordnance survey map.

My first attempt to reach the mountain was made in March from Loch Ossian. I stayed four days at the empty youth hostel on the edge of the frozen loch, listening to the hollow report and crackle of ice under the weight of wind rushing on to it from the hills, and to the endless drumming of drift on the wooden walls. On the rare occasions when I opened the door – to get fuel for my blazing fires inside – swirls of white powder eddied far within. The outside air was opaquely white. I could see my feet, none the less, therefore movement was possible and no excuse valid for idleness. Accordingly I did make two efforts to cross the watershed to Loch Ericht: the first by the bealach nan Sgor, the second by the bealach Cumhann. On neither attempt did I get far from Loch Ossian. It is intimidating to face a hill-blizzard without company. It has powers and a striking edge and a stark reality denied to a poltergeist. The labour it requires of a man is prodigious. Once or twice, just before I turned back on my second day, a momentary sweeping away of clouds revealed the broad and distant back of Ben Alder, luridly white against an inky pall of sky, hunched like a chalk Atlas supporting the heavens.

Ever after that glimpse I had a high respect for Ben Alder. Meantime I met my first-hand witness of the cottage hauntings in the person of Robert Grieve of the Scottish Mountaineering Club. He and a friend had spent a most disturbed night in the cottage. They were having an after-supper pipe in their sleeping bags when they heard footsteps entering the room next door and tramping noisily on the wooden floor. In a short while they rose and went next door to investigate but to their astonishment found no one there. They returned to bed. The footsteps recurred, not indoors this time, but outside on the cobbled causeway, which runs against the front wall. The noise was that of heavy, nailed boots on the stone, pacing back and forth, up and down the front of the cottage, and this was accompanied by brief pauses when Grieve and his companion strongly sensed that they were being watched from the window. They had the additional feeling of being regarded with hostility as intruders. That drove them into the open with electric torches, but as before nothing was to be seen. They inspected the outhouse and bam with the same result, and there was no other cover. Again they retired to bed. And again footsteps entered the room next door. After some aimless tramping there came a moment's pause, then the quite distinctive sound of heavy furniture being dragged over the floor, the kind of noise that would be made by the legs of a heavy table. Grieve and his friend were well aware that there was *no* furniture next door, so they once more went through to look, and found – a bare and empty room. They gave up then and retired for the night. Grieve freely affirms that he now felt frightened. But apart from continued noises no untoward event occurred.

That, of course, is by no means the only report of the hauntings, but is the only report I can trust. Grieve is a level-headed and practical man. He does not go around telling this story, for he feels that normally other men discredit abnormal experiences in which they themselves had no share, and their disbelief confounds the man who knows his experience to be true, yet not so important to the world as to be worth exposing to ridicule. Grieve, in short, convinced me as a reliable witness.

I made plans to go to Benalder cottage at the autumn holiday weekend in September 1949. Norman Tennent was the ideal type of youthful unbeliever to accompany me on this trip. He and his wife Mona and I agreed to spend two nights at the cottage, our main purpose being the exploration of the northern cliffs.

We arrived on a perfect evening at the west end of Loch Rannoch. The world was putting on its strongest colour – red and yellow on the open hills, smoke-blue on the loch; the air was still as in hard frost yet mild as the mellowing sun. That nine-mile walk to Loch Ericht was for once a delightful prospect. Our first four miles went by a surprisingly good track, which ended at the dam in the south bay of Loch Ericht. The dusk thickened. The way now went north-west over trackless moors in order to round the head of the loch and gain the woods of its west shore. Of this crossing I had been warned with many a blasphemous oath – rainstorm and low, dense mist, heavy going, boggy and featureless ground, endless compass bearings – my counsellor had not been lucky. But tonight our guiding marks were the bright Pole Star and the black arc of a bealach cutting the sky seven miles away. I think it says much for the ground that we could go with our heads often raised to that high sky-line yet stumble rarely enough to keep in good temper.

Flowing into the head of the loch is the River Chriochan, to the crossing of which I had looked forward with misgiving; it looked on the map a bad obstacle if full. Tonight it proved to be harmless, and an easy ford near the junction let us across to a well-made pony track heading north towards Alder Bay. The barren moorland soon gave place to richer ground, our way leading among fir-trees, between the wide gap of whose branches could be seen a great shining of stars, and through broad avenues among the trunks a dim glimmer from the velvety loch; leading through that most charming of all country, a natural wood, where each individual tree has living space, where there is no regimented crowding, but light and life and a healthful air, most gracious to the human soul lucky enough to be brought thither. The natural and unaffected response of the mind is to meditate – to receive the trees' symbol of life perfectly at one with Reality: then not just to dream or desire, but of free choice to *live* that life.

We had one more mile to go when our track petered out. Half a mile farther a thickly wooded hill persuaded us down to the water's edge for passage. We rounded a blunt point and arrived on the shore of Alder Bay. At the toe of the hill across the bay a bright light shone. Benalder cottage! I wondered if by some mischance it were filled with estate stalkers, for it was the height of the season. If so we should be refused entrance, indeed chased away in wrath. But I knew the cottage to be normally deserted in the stalking season – to be at all times one of the most desolate in Scotland. We sat down to think things over.

While we rested among the firs by the water's edge a light suddenly flashed at the far shore. That was fully a quarter of a mile away. Shooting stars were dropping frequently out of the crowded sky, but the flash was not that, nor yet the light from the cottage. The loch was black, the farther shore jet black. From the beach a light twinkled over the water and went out. A hundred yards to its left a second light flashed and went out – flashed again more openly at the loch, and went out. These flashings mystified us, for they were unaccompanied by movement in any particular direction; they seemed aimless. Something strange was happening around Benalder cottage. The time was now ten o'clock. Stalkers do not wander around like that on a cold September's night. They yarn round a good fire or else get to bed.

Another surprise was in store for us when we began to walk round the bay. Where the firs thinned out nearer the Alder Burn we saw an enormous fire like some coronation beacon, fed by a ring of four or five men who moved like demons among the towering columns of smoke and flame. We moved closer. They were young men, tough, but not more evil than we. We stepped into the firelight.

'Heading for the cottage?' they asked, and smiled doubtfully when we said 'Yes.' 'We're sleeping out here,' they added. Their voices showed that they had no doubts about which was the better 'howff' for the night. Otherwise they were not communicative. We pressed on to see for ourselves this source of all mystery. We had still to cross the Alder Burn which is notoriously fast and unfordable in spate, but the low water gave us an easy passage on boulders.

The cottage was then right before us – a two-room stone building with a porch in the middle, a sound slated roof, unbroken windows, and a big corrugated iron shed attached to its west gable. The rooms were candle-lit. We opened the front door. To either side of us then were two other doors, and straight in front a small, dark store-room. From behind the right-hand door came a noise like all the devils of hell let loose. Not *one* poltergeist – a whole legion of them – was in full occupation and hard at work. I turned the handle and swung the door quickly. There was sudden, dead silence. Ranged round the walls, fifteen pairs of eyes stared at mine. However, I held my ground and took a steady look at them. These fifteen poltergeists were, for the moment at least, clad in the flesh of male humans between the ages of eighteen and twenty-five. The eyes were bright and laughing, mouths still grinning through the sudden check of breath. On one side of a roaring fire sat a cross-legged youth, his lips still round a mouth-organ; while at the other side sat another, head tilted, fingers still hovering at the stops of a penny whistle.

At a quick glance I knew that these men were not climbers.

'Fishing?' I asked. 'No,' said someone. Then with a roar the whole chorus, whistle and mouth-organ, resumed the song at the very note on which they had halted four seconds before.

I stepped out laughing, and closed the door. Questions, it seemed, were not welcomed in this part of the world. I had never seen anything more like a band of robbers, and all in the tradition of Robin Hood, as indeed we were soon to find they were.

Next door were six humble fishermen. Theirs were the lights that had flashed along the shore, and the catch, we could see, had been good. They offered to make room for us on the floor. In both rooms the walls were wood-lined and the floors dry, but three more bodies would make for excessive heat and congestion. So we decided to look at the shed, and were thus introduced to the all too real ghost in the cupboard.

We went out and round to the shed door, gave it a push, and flashed on a torch. The first thing we saw was a bloody corpse hanging from a beam in the roof. This time we were startled in real earnest. A closer scrutiny revealed the victim to be less a corpse than a carcase. This was a gralloched stag. We began to understand the aims and objects of the Brotherhood indoors. Fortunately the shed was big and spared us the need to sleep under the dripping meat. There was room for a score of us and the floor was of dry wood-chips. We had no complaints.

Next morning we were up and away by nine o'clock, for there was a long day ahead: first of all a five-mile walk to the north corrie, then the exploration of the unclimbed cliffs, and finally a four-mile return over the summit. For three miles the path kept below the south flank of Ben Alder by the line of the Alder Burn. Like all the tracks in the neighbourhood this one was a relic of the golden age of stalking – broad, straight, and well drained. The sun fell bright on the loch behind us. Away to our left, moorland five miles wide swept up and westwards to the high corries under the peaks of Corrour and Rannoch. All of that country was far more spacious than the Middle East deserts as I remember them. Hill-distances make no less an impression of majesty on the mind than the most noble cliff scenery. It is well said of a Tchaikovsky symphony that it leads men to the edge of the Infinite and leaves them for minutes gazing into that. Something of the same could be experienced that morning in watching the swell of the far-away moors lifting into the grey screen of an autumn haze that lay thick in the distance, and beyond it lifting again to the clear mountains, up to the last hard curve of one peak, and there vanishing, at the edge of the Infinite. Too little of that beauty can ever break through the distractions of a path and company.

After climbing to two thousand two hundred feet the track swung north into the head of Glen Labhair, which fell four miles leftwards to Loch Ossian and rose rightwards to the bealach Dubh of Ben Alder. The glen below us was full of roaring stags and the shout of the hills' echo and re-echo. We took the uphill track and made the bealach. Culra Glen fell away five miles north to Loch Pattock. Mist banks forming at the lower end had risen to obscure the entire north flank of Ben Alder on which our cliffs lay. Until that mist cleared no profitable move could be made and we accordingly settled down for lunch. The time was shortly after midday.

A few minutes sufficed to establish that the cliffs were there, intermittently looming through rolling veils on a mile-long front. At the middle of the face a great ridge repeatedly appeared and vanished. Occasionally the mists would clear on its near side. It was directed away from us obliquely, so that all its upper half was silhouetted against the cloud as a knife-edge, set at no mean angle. Lower down the glen we could see the bottom quarters of three other ridges; these were slower in clearing. An hour's waiting brought the reward. They emerged, rock-crests picked out to great advantage by woolly wisps lingering in the gullies between. Tennent liked these farther ridges best and I the central ridge. However, the distance was too great for their real merits to be assessed. We walked half a mile down Coire Dubh.

We stopped directly under the Central Ridge and climbed a few hundred feet up grass to its base. It then seemed that the best name for it would be the Mythical Ridge. It had vanished. In its stead was a broad buttress of mingled grass and crag. There was no continuous rock-climb. Yet that ridge had looked imposing from a distance. However, there was a little corrie just to the left of the buttress and projecting over its lip were rock-columns, looking more attractive than the triple ridges lower down the glen. These latter, we were almost sure, were as broken up and as grassy as Mythical Ridge.

After struggling up scree to the corrie's lip our confusion was complete. The promising columns, the Mythical Ridge, the triple ridges farther north – not one was a full-bodied crag – all were mouldy, mica-schist skeletons, richly apparelled in blaeberries and a voluminous plant life. Had we only been botanists, with what unaffected pleasure might we not have flushed! Being rock-climbers we scowled ferociously. The day was lost – our so suddenly valuable time wasted. We cursed our luck.

And this was where our education began. For we scrambled up to the plateau by a zigzag line on the left flank of Mythical Ridge, and at last came out on to the top enjoying ourselves. And this was not simply due to the fact that our mouths were full of blaeberries. The plateau is a mile and a half wide. How very much like a Cairngorm, I thought; how open and lofty were the hill moors, all red and yellow and caverned by corries with lochs. In all the waters were as many shades of blue as there were lochans – a score of them – more no doubt than I ever saw – a country as bright as Spain. The root of its fascination was that all of it was unknown. We had never set eyes on it before. Here it was, in the middle of Scotland, and we, in our ignorance, might well have spent our energies searching out the corners of some far-off and less excellent land – had we not been lucky.

The maps had been encouraging enough. They had shown us that maze of right-angled valleys and high hill passes and tortuous waterways between Loch Ericht and Glen Nevis. They had enticed us with the emerald splash of woods, and crag-ringed hollows where unexplored corries lay, and lonely bays in blue lochs, great blanks of undetailed moor, ravines, peaks sharp and sweeping. The maps had promised us much. But the reality spread before our eyes was more moving still; for the scale was so much greater than we had appreciated, the land so much more colourful, and by Nature so very much better furnished. Exploring a tract of country like that was a worthy task for a man, besides which a short, severe climb up a small crag in one of those hundreds of corries was a triviality – something to engage a spare couple of hours before proceeding with the more enthralling pleasures of discovering the undiscovered country.

Our visit to Ben Alder had therefore turned out to be a reconnaissance. We arrived at the cairn, and each contemplated the scene in a manner suiting his own temperament. Mona sat on a boulder facing the northern panorama and pretended not to look at it in between bites at raw carrot. Tennent went a few yards to the edge of the eastern corrie and made a careful study of the depths. As for me, I lay on some flat stones and slept in the sunshine. I should have to come back soon, I decided, and make that walk from Dalwhinnie to Fort William. How long should be spent on it? Three days at least; preferably a week. I blessed the day that had introduced me to the Scottish highlands – a much better country than I had thought possible up to so late a date as the hour before. I felt an intolerable urge to know more of it; meantime there was nothing like enjoying what was at hand. I pillowed my shoulders on more comfortable boulders and let the sun soak in, and the wind brace, and the scentless air invigorate.

The wind became somewhat more than bracing after half an hour. We moved off southwards round the head of Choire Garbh. This is the eastern corrie, a mile long and a mile wide, its floor filled by a loch that is said to be alive with trout. Much rock was exposed on the corrie's walls – our hearts missed a beat, hopes jumped – but too short and discontinuous to interest a mountaineer. We descended south to Benalder cottage.

The sun was low but still shining over the tops of Corrour and Rannoch Forests when we got down, so we fetched out our food from the shed and dined in the open air. We were hugely interested to see the robber band set off, with a most business-like bearing, up the line of the Alder Burn. 'Where? ' we asked ourselves, 'and why?' Dusk was falling as we finished our meal, by which time the band reappeared in parties of four, dragging three stags, which they carried out of sight round the back of the cottage. These must have been shot during the day. Within an incredibly short time the leader of the band came to us with a stag's liver 'for tomorrow morning's breakfast.' The liver weighed pounds, but my real delight was in the man who delivered it. The full description he deserves is barred by our acceptance of the 'hush-money.' Like the rest of his brotherhood he was young, in hard and lean condition, simply overflowing with high spirits and enterprise. He had already spent two months hitch-hiking round Europe. I could not but feel an admiration for all of them. They had no money, but according to their lights made full use of their inheritance, hills and freedom. Stalking in Scotland is the privilege of the landowner; but the deer, in the end, are proving tougher than the dying lairds: they pay no death duties. Nonetheless, I hope that the semi-feudal system of the highlands will never die. Hunting another man's ground is one of the deep, dark joys of which we must never be deprived. The chance of it, at least, must always be there; life not made duller than it is. I wondered whether our poachers' energy, directed to such purpose in Benalder Forest, would have been directed at all in Glasgow – or just dissipated? If they are no better men than myself, then I fear the worst. For my own part I am no poacher because I love creating and loathe killing.

Next morning's weather was better than ever, with less haze and a hotter sun. After breakfast we sunned ourselves on the grass before the cottage. The robber band dispersed, some crossing the moors to Rannoch, a few making for the high passes to Corrour, each man carrying a rucksack weighted with a hundred pounds of venison.

When every one had gone the peace and quiet seemed so wonderful that we postponed our own departure. We lay in the quiet as one lies in an eiderdown quilt, luxuriating. I was sufficiently refreshed in half an hour to want a swim in the loch, whose waters were blurred with trembling autumn stains, stretching far out from the slopes of the far shore, but blue, icy blue at the near margin – as Mona and I found when we swam. Life and warmth in the body seemed doubled when we came out. Tennent painted, scoffed, and was lied to about the water's heat. At midday we set out for Loch Rannoch.

Although so much of our time had been spent on Ben Alder it was not till we were well down the loch that we saw it whole for the first time. An Alpinist, I suspect, would call it a shapeless lump – but what will astound and baffle him about those central highland lumps is how they contrive to be shapeless so gracefully. I watched Ben Alder now, an Empty Quarter of the skies, ash-pale in Arabian haze, wound around by the mirage of an everlasting river, and by the long blue flicker of the loch. From our feet to the desert's edge a green mile or more of broadly scattered firs stretched cool and erect in short single-files, or at ease in clumps, up to the ever-winding river. As it now was, so is the scene fixed forever in reality, changeless. I watched the lift of the trees' heads and the free sweep of a bird scouting high to Ben Alder. And I confess that I watched all this with a mind completely blank. I absorbed the beauty along with the sunshine, untroubled by desire to act or think. However, stray thoughts stepped forward from time to time and presented themselves for inspection. In the mountain scene around me the fittingness of everything most impressed me – the way in which so great a wealth of detail – diverse detail too – was integrated with the whole, a unity of order in which the good was manifested and beauty revealed. Man cannot live in that harmony with the good, as do the trees and birds and animals, blindly through the grace of nature: he has to do it of free will. And that seemed to be the purpose of man's life, as seen from Benalder Forest.

20

Castle Buttress

To give safe conduct to a mountaineer on the Scottish rocks in winter, all the wisdom of the owl, the cunning of the fox, and the guile of the serpent would seem to be of themselves insufficient. Desirable as they are as attributes, to them something else must be added.

I had long known that Castle Buttress of Nevis was a winter climb of which to be wary. Its upper slabs are smooth, and loose snow lying on them in quantity is notoriously apt to avalanche. Presumably it was for this reason that I could find no contemporaries of my own who had climbed the buttress in winter. Its history had been too discouraging. None the less I felt confident that by exercising a little foresight one should be able to outwit the elements. All that was asked of a visitor to the Castle was that prior to climbing he should acquire a knowledge of the snow conditions; then, if there were dry powder on the cliffs, or bulky snows in thaw condition, he could leave it for a day when the snow was firm. Theorizing in an armchair I believed that it might be as easy as that to judge a Nevis climb so inscrutable as the Castle. Not that I underrated the Castle: I underrated the difficulties of getting an exact and detailed knowledge of the snow.

During our day on North-East Buttress I told Laidlaw of the Castle problem. Would he go with me when the right weather came? I had climbed with him only two or three times so far, but had found him a born mountaineer, remarkably speedy and safe for a man of just less than eighteen years. Rather too promptly and unreflectingly he said sure, he'd love to come. He had still a blind faith in my infallible judgment only to be cured by repeated shatterings. So next January we carried a light tent up to the Allt a Mhuilinn glen and camped at the deer fence, about halfway to the hut. The hut was alleged to be full. We met a party of climbers descending and obtained from them a full report about weather conditions during the preceding week. Seven days ago there had been a snowfall of several inches – normal type snow, neither wet nor powdery, which had consolidated well. This had been followed by incessant south-easterly wind, perhaps more south than east. In other words the wind had been blowing along the line of the cliffs. There had been no further precipitation and no drift had been seen blowing about the plateau.

Had they climbed on the Castle area, I asked, or on the Carn Dearg half of the mountain? No, they had kept to the high half, left of Number Three Gully. My opinion after hearing them out was that Castle Buttress would be safe. Although the wind had been southerly the touch of east had put an edge to it, and there had been no trace of thaw. And no powder had fallen. It seemed to me that conditions must be very nearly ideal for our purpose. One clue to the contrary had been given to me, but so subtle a clue that I overlooked it.

Some fortunate premonition, however, made me declare for a 6 a.m. start, and Laidlaw's presence held me to it. He had been brought up in a stern school. His elder mountaineering brother (whom I now blessed) had trained him to rise in the early hours of a cold morning to waken his party and get the stoves going. He did this willingly, or at least uncomplainingly, being wild with enthusiasm for life in general and mountains in particular. He would keep waking up at every hour from midnight onwards to take a look at his watch and make sure that he was not sleeping in. The result was that at eight o'clock next morning we were plodding up towards the preliminary snow-slopes directly under the Castle.

The sky was cloudy grey but fairly clear as yet to eastwards. The first and last sun of the day was shining on to the Castle. Its wide upper turrets were heavy laden with snow, sparkling, almost dancing, against the leaden grey of the west and the massive, darker battlements just under them. All these top-most crags were ringed below and walled on their right-hand side by snow-sheeted slabs, and they projected heavily above the remaining four-fifths of the buttress, which depended from them like a down-thrust tongue. I guessed the total height to be eight hundred feet. The tongue tapered to a blunt and overhanging tip, and from top to bottom was encased in frozen snow. There were two bare patches where ice showed: the first of thirty feet, low down near the tip, probably caused by thinner snow melting by day and refreezing at night; the second an icy groove near the centre, probably scooped and scored by a snow slide from the upper slabs. The latter thought gave me pause for a minute. Then I rationalized, saying that if too much snow *had* come on to the slabs and so avalanched off, that very fact was our best guarantee of safety now, for I knew that no more snow had fallen since. We continued.

The shape of the Castle was determined on right and left by the clean deep clefts of the North and South Castle Gullies. They were snow-filled, so much so that no pitches showed, which surprised me at this early month of the season. They swept down either flank, dividing the Castle cliffs from the long pinnacle of Raeburn's Buttress on the left and the Castle Ridge on the right, and converging under the tip of the tongue. The whole form was a noble one. We approached the tip, for access to the buttress must be gained by a direct ascent of the overhang. In summer this overhang is twelve feet high, now shortened to six feet by a cone of snow, which had formed underneath. We stood on the cone's top and roped up on a hundred feet of line. Laidlaw had still to lead a big winter climb. I was determined that he should lead this one, at least as far as the slabs. After his initial modesty had subsided he agreed and started.

That first overhang is very difficult in summer, when good holds allow it to be climbed without a shoulder, and in winter I imagine it will often disappear altogether under the cone of avalanche debris. Today, with six feet projecting, it might have been a simple obstacle had the rocks not been so icy. After a few tentative efforts Laidlaw had failed to get over the upper lip. I could see perfectly well that he was self-conscious about style and not 'warmed up.' He stepped down and invited me to go ahead. Had I done anything of the sort his confidence in his own power to lead would have been spoiled for the rest of the day. My refusal on the grounds that it looked too hard for me bore much fruit a few hours later. Meantime I urged him to use my shoulder. He did so and began cutting foothold in the bulge at the lip. After a couple of blows his pick suddenly pierced the ice with a hollow *plop* and out flashed a spout of water. It came straight on to my face when I was least expecting it. The splash of the icy jet made me swing back involuntarily, and Laidlaw on top lost balance and capsized. We both rolled down to the foot of the cone. That was the most inglorious start I have ever made to a rock-climb.

We picked ourselves up and dusted ourselves down and tried again. To avoid the stream between the rock and the ice Laidlaw cut holds higher up to the left, but to get purchase to raise himself he had to step from my shoulders on to my head – his nails were tricounis, with sharp points. The rock above the overhang continued steeply and still thinly iced for twenty feet. Every hold cut filled immediately with water but the ice itself was surprisingly sound. Although it cut easily it held weight firmly. With thirty feet of rope out, Laidlaw reached a belt of rotten snow, a lower apron to the main mass of good snow, which he reached at fifty feet where the angle eased, and which became firmer and tougher at every step he took. We shortened rope after I joined him.

For a hundred feet at most we were able to kick steps in the snow, which thereafter gave Laidlaw constant cutting with the blade of his axe. The underlying rock is well broken up, with plentiful steps and ledges on which one may scramble in summer for a few hundred feet. For that same reason the rock is capable of holding snow in depth and piled at high angles. The whole back of the buttress was raised, polished, hard frozen, and felt distinctly exposed with its two gullies racing down to each side: an inspiriting position when things are going well as they were now. On this lower part of the buttress we climbed together without belays.

Three hundred feet of such climbing brought us at last to the icy scoop that we had seen in the centre, which at close quarters proved to be a short gully, a natural drainage line filled from side to side with pale green ice. A belay was needed here. For Laidlaw would have a long run-out. And who knows what may come down a drain-pipe? The snow-fan under the gully was so hard that an axe-shaft could not be driven in. I had to descend twenty feet and go left to get suitable snow. Looking up I wondered whether the rope would now be long enough to let the leader reach good snow above. I suspected too that he would take more time than we bargained for, so I put on spare sweaters and settled down for a long wait. The precaution was fortunate. He must have spent forty minutes cutting up the first fifty feet, losing time first on viscous snow-ice in which the pick stuck firmly at each blow, and then on the bare ice which had to be hit very hard. I enjoyed my leisure. The north face of Cam Dearg Buttress is worth studying in winter. On its near flank the long upper spire of Raeburn's Buttress, snow-covered on the slender crest, looked like the mast of a tall clipper iced up as it rounds the Cape. I had clambered up it in summer, but never yet had I risked it in winter – and I wondered … It would be a most spectacular climb. But the Castle was enough for the present. It was interesting to note how alarming the downward vista could look just because the surface had a glazed crust. Had the snow been soft it would have appeared much milder in angle.

Laidlaw took me up to a snow-patch at fifty feet and continued again on ice, which quickly gave place to snow. I was now right in his line of fire. As time wore on and his rope was running out he was *still* not getting snow to please him for a halt. He was beyond the gully but the snow was so hard frozen that he could not cut it with the blade of his axe – he had to use the pick. That is unusual on Scottish snow. The chips were beginning to shoot past with a horrid *whirr*, and when they hit they hurt. A larger fragment struck my head so violently that I was nearly stunned. I stopped him then and went up without a belay. The slope above the gully was at no great angle, and we moved together for a hundred feet to softer snow at the foot of the slabs.

Our first difficulty lay in dealing with a short corner caked with a kind of snow called *névé* – tough and tight-packed. It gave most reliable holds, but all movement was exposed and belayless. We then followed a line of least resistance leftwards to the foot of a long chimney, the first fifteen feet of which was choked with white snow-ice and the upper section with a light, almost feathery snow. As reward for previous sacrifice I now took the lead. I intended to enjoy myself, and to add to my comfort at the take-off cut a small platform and chipped out holds for seven feet up the chimney. I had moved up on these and was just clearing out some loose snow above with swipes of a gloved hand, when a minor avalanche of powder poured off the crags above and burst over the top of the chimney in successive waves, which apparently all found their way down my neck. When all was quiet again and the laughter from below stilled, I climbed another few feet, laboriously dusting the fresh snow off the rock. The difficulties were not inconsiderable, but whether I might eventually have overcome them was unfortunately never proved. For at this moment another torrent of powder-snow swept over my head and shoulders, and that was followed by a third. My whole face felt painfully iced. I was having no more for the moment and modestly resigned the lead. During all this time the tail-end of the rope had been convulsed with hysterical merriment. He then stepped forward, to confound my malicious expectations by climbing the chimney without further bombardment. He had trouble in plenty. Everything went well for fifty feet, but he had then to leave the chimney and cross a corner to snow-bound slabs on the right. The move greatly perplexed him. It was not skill he lacked but experience of unusual moves. At last it was done. The slabs were coated with an inch or two of *névé*. He cut rapidly and I soon followed in his tortuous tracks up the chimney and round a corner, and over twenty-five feet of slabs in two hairpin bends, this to avoid thin ice, and so to a snow-filled scoop. He had me belayed there, after a fashion, so I carried on past him, fifty feet up the scoop to a big and snow-piled ledge.

The route now lay to my right, over and up slanting slabs. These were bolstered with enormous snow-puffs, snow having a convex curve to its surface, and quite remarkably sleek. It was unlike any other snow we had seen this day, and much bulkier. The silken sleekness worried me. Against the wall to my left I saw a large detached stone and prised it loose with my spike. I pitched it on to the slabs. An instant after the strike I heard a rip, and a crack opened across the snow-sheet. Nothing more happened. The silken sheet was a wind-slab crust, which would avalanche off if disturbed further. I fetched up Laidlaw then and said that I should not like to risk going on. The wind-slab crust was not in itself particularly thick. Assuming that it would slide off when we stepped on to it I did not envisage the weight of the breaking slabs carrying us away – not if we had good footing below. But experimental soundings with an axe showed at once that under the wind-slab loose dry powder lay upon smooth, glazed rock-slabs. The powder seemed to be held together mainly by its wind-slab shell. We were astonished that it should ever have collected there, on such slabs in such bulk. If the shell went the underlying snow would go too, and it would be not the shell but the powder that would carry us off. We should then fall over the cliff on the right-hand half of the buttress.

'Not another yard!' said I. 'We have other climbs to do besides this.'

Laidlaw looked aghast at the prospect of descent. Our balcony did seem exposed when one looked out and down. I thought he was thinking of the icy slabs and the traverse into the chimney. 'I'll go down last,' I reassured him. 'Even if it does take hours we'll manage it.'

'Oh, I wasn't thinking of that,' he said. 'There's just one tiling you've forgotten.' He pointed his axe at the split wind-slab.

For one moment I looked blank, then realized what he meant. From now onwards the split wind-slab was liable to come away and the powder with it, and gather to itself any snow of a similar kind that might lie on the cliff below, and any loose boulders lying on ledges. This avalanche, if it ever occurred, would sweep the line of our descent. Our first stage of retreat by the chimney would be protected, for that lay to the right (looking down) of the avalanche track, but all the rest would be exposed. The extraordinary speed with which all the circumstances attending our climb had changed appalled us, and made us feel peculiarly helpless. We had climbed for four and a half hours in apparent safety, and now, in a few seconds, objective dangers threatened no matter how we might turn. No rats, confidently sprucing their whiskers, had ever walked more briskly into a trap than we.

'Let's have lunch,' I growled. 'It's past one o'clock.' Lunch, I thought, always remedies depression. But today our squashed jam sandwiches seemed even more squashed and dismally jamless than usual. We munched in silence and looked aimlessly around. A cloud, which had lain all day on the summit of Nevis as far north as Number Three Gully, had now spread still farther north to cover the top of Cam Dearg, and its first long tongues were licking around the crest of the Castle, close above our heads. The air was gloomy. 'It will be dark soon today,' I said. ' We had better not wait too long.' Silence. I could remember getting caught in only one other trap as nasty as the present one – the day when Mackenzie and I encountered brittle ice above the crux of Shelf Route. We had climbed out of *that* one in half an hour, but in this one half an hour would just see us farther into it, and every hour after that our position would get worse, with no hope of relief until the last low overhang was above us.

'Where *could* all that powder and wind-slab have come from?' asked Laidlaw. 'There wasn't any lower down.' We held a five-minute *post mortem*. I could think of only one answer: the south-east wind blowing across the plateau must have been a cold and humid wind and therefore an erosive wind. In that event drift eroded from the crust of the plateau would be swept along the surface by that south-south-east wind and a day-long trickle deposited gently over the northerly edge of the Castle. No drifting had been seen by climbers – but that only confirmed the theory of erosion. A mere trickle of drift continuing hour after hour for days on end would soon amount to the bulk we now saw on the slabs, and any surplus spilling off would be carried into North Castle Gully by eddies of south-easterly wind, which in turn would account for the absence of loose powder on the middle and lower buttress and for the well-packed gullies.

We were pleased with this theory. 'If anything happens to us,' said Laidlaw with a suddenly cheerful grin, 'it's good to know why.'

The cloud had thickened over the Castle, completely obscuring the upper turrets, and in a few more minutes sank right over us. That was a remarkably cold cloud; it drove us to quick action. Snow began to fall while we were climbing down the scoop – only a few, floating flakes soon verging towards sleet. At the bottom of the scoop I had a long wait while Laidlaw edge-nailed down the slabs, then worried his way round the traverse and eased himself into the chimney. He must have spent half an hour on them, but encouraged me by never coming on the rope. Nonetheless, he was sufficiently agitated when he reached the bottom to shout up, urging me to drive in a piton, and come down on a doubled rope. It is true that I had in my rucksack one piton and a spare hundred feet of line, but I wanted to keep that piton for later emergencies. It had occurred to me that if the slabs avalanched while we were down on the lower third of the buttress, who knows but there might be some little crag beside us into which we might just have time to drive the piton – clip on the rope – and pray briefly. Such was the pass to which we had come. Perhaps my idea was a mad one. Meantime I preferred to climb down.

The long wait in sleet-chilled mist had numbed my hands, and I felt sluggish with cold when I came to the awkward traverse. While in trouble there I remembered that Laidlaw had almost certainly no belay. I called down to him: 'Take off the rope. You couldn't hold me anyhow.'

'I'm *on* your rope,' he called back. 'I'm going to stay on.'

The only thing I could do was just not to fall off. A difficult end to achieve. The greatest difficulty, after I reached the chimney, was trying to see the footholds below; everything was whitened with the powder cascade of midday and the lower part of my body blocked the view. However, I managed it somehow, and over the last five feet revenged myself on Laidlaw by stepping heavily on to his shoulder.

The whole upper crag of the Castle had now vanished into purpureal gloom. The mist clung more thickly around us, although the lower vista was clear all the way down to the desolation of the Allt a Mhuilinn, save for a scattering of wisps in the middle air.

Suddenly there came a smart shower of hail, immediately followed by a hissing noise from our axe-heads. The cloud was charged with electricity. We could feel the tingle of it on our eyebrows and the fringe of the hair above the forehead. I had clipped my piton on to my waist-loop with a karabiner (a steel clip-ring), and these too began to sing complainingly. We scrambled hastily down thirty feet of easy rock and the caked corner at the foot. There was all the while a very strong antiseptic smell in the air, probably caused by ozone.

We began descending the very hard snow leading to the centre ice-scoop. *En route* we reaped an advantage from the too big steps Laidlaw had cut on the way up, more than cancelled out by the too big space between. Intermediate steps had now to be cut to preserve our balance; a slip on this frozen sheet would have been hard to stop, and sometimes impossible. Yet speed was a prime necessity. We were now right in line of fire from the upper slabs. There was one thing of which I was becoming more scared than of anything else – a lightning flash and thunder on the crest of the Castle, because the tremendous vibrations there would almost certainly start the avalanche. While a thunder-cloud is actually resting on a Scottish summit, I remembered (from Observatory records) that discharge rarely occurs. The dangerous moments are while the cloud approaches, lifts, and moves off – especially the latter. At the moment of departure a violent flash is probable. Accordingly, our immediate objective should be to try to get as far down as we could before the cloud moved.

I asked Laidlaw to take the position of honour as last man down, and went to the front to do the cutting. One hard slash with the corner of the blade made a scrape sufficient to take at least our edge-nails safely; that was good enough for an intermediate step. We went down facing sideways, and made fair speed to the ice-scoop. Here we had to go down facing in. The holds had been well spaced, so Laidlaw went first while I paid out rope and kept a wary eye aloft. To my dismay I saw that the danger area was exposed to view. This meant that the cloud was lifting. It could not possibly have begun to happen at a worse time; our position was the one spot on the whole buttress to which everything that fell would most naturally converge.

I shrugged my shoulders and turned away. There was no point in worrying any further. We had taken in advance all right precautions, gained reliable reports on the snow, risen early, and climbed as well and as fast as we could. Our own share had been done and the rest was not for us to decide. This was only the last of many occasions when events had impressed on me, both on mountains and off them, that skill, energy, foresight, and the strenuous prosecution of plans, are by themselves quite insufficient for success. One's own best efforts must always be made, but having been made they have still to be seconded by Providence: therefore let us make them, always hopefully, and resign the rest without self-concern to God's will. His energies alone must bring *all* human actions, trivial or of great moment, to their best end. That was how I felt while I waited at the scoop for the cloud to lift. There is no such thing as luck.

I told Laidlaw not to stop halfway, but to carry on to the foot. Before the hundred feet ran out I gave him a final shout of warning and began descending at the same time as himself. For the first time for several hours I felt in high spirits. I enjoyed the green ice, and wished we had had a little sun to draw out the colour. At the bottom I found myself smiling at Laidlaw instead of growling as before, and he, always an extraordinarily responsive youth, grinned delightedly at being smiled at. 'Things are going well after all,' he said. 'Even that cloud's lifting off the top.'

I hesitated – but what would be the use? So I said nothing. I turned and looked up. The cloud was right on top of the Castle, but the main body of it was leaning in a vast bulge to northwards. 'Let's get going,' I urged. 'It will be dark in no time – four o'clock already.'

Speed was of far more consequence than any security the rope might give us, so from now onwards we moved together and dispensed altogether with belays. I went first as before, at as hard a pace as I dared, cutting only when I had to as fast as inspired muscles would move. It was a most glorious sensation to feel on top of the world, and to have every and urgent need so to feel. Dusk was gathering when we reached the steep iced rocks thirty feet above the last overhang. We were so near – and yet this last part was going to take, indeed to devour, time. I looked again at the turrets. I could not see them properly in the darkness, but could distinguish the mass of the cloud towering aslant and obviously near to pulling away. The flash would be any moment now.

I did not see how we could get down that next thirty feet in less than thirty minutes if we *climbed*, down. This was the very place for my long-treasured piton: we fetched out electric torches and looked for a suitable crack into which to drive it. After a few minutes' search we had failed to find one and grew impatient. So I let Laidlaw try to climb down on the end of a tight rope. However, the acute difficulties of finding small ice-holds by torchlight from above were beyond him. I lacked a good enough stance to lower him all the way, so back he came. We searched anew and at last uncovered a suitably thin crack. I drove the piton – tied a spare loop to it – doubled the rope through. Then we roped off. I have never gone down a rope faster. I burned my hands. As my feet struck the top of the snow-cone all the nervous apprehension I had felt above the ice-scoop returned for a space.

'Don't stop to coil the rope,' I barked, as I jerked it down through the loop. 'We've to get clear while we can.'

We took to the lower snow-slopes at a run, and were several hundred feet down, and stumbling with weariness, before I would consent to halt. We coiled the rope. All remained quiet above. We walked leisurely towards the Allt a Mhuilinn and crossed to the path on the right bank. We had gone maybe a hundred yards on this path when a flash and thunder peal came from the Castle, echoing in stupendous volume from the cliffs. Before the echoes had died there was a second and much greater flash, lighting the white walls of the Castle corrie from top to bottom and side to side. The simultaneous and reverberating roar, and the long-drawn echoes, completely drowned all other noises. It was not possible to tell whether the slabs had avalanched. Latterly we heard a rattle of stones, quickly muffled. But no man could have said whence they fell.

21

An Teallach and Dundonnell Forest

By 1950 it had become one of the anomalies of my mountaineering life, a trick of fate one might say, that An Teallach, which started me climbing (a few words describing its summit-ridge having had power to flush me from my roost in the plains, and send me winging over the mountain world), should be one mountain that I had never climbed. It lurked always in the back of my mind – lurked not phantom-like, but dynamically, the ideal mountain.

Time and distance cut me off from it at first; opportunities for going to Wester Ross and the Dundonnell Forest never arose of their own accord. Nor did I make such opportunities at a later date: I feared that An Teallach in the flesh must disappoint me. I dared not expect it to live up to the original vision, which had been so powerful as to overcome an inertia as great as mine, and start body and soul into exploratory action. But in February 1950 I was forced to dismiss these fears. Three friends and I planned an expedition to the Himalaya, starting in April, and it seemed to me unthinkable that I should venture there never having known An Teallach – whose name means 'The Forge' – upon which I had been hammered these fifteen years.

On 21st February, at 5 p.m., MacAlpine, Richard Meyer, and I arrived at Dundonnell. We stopped on the roadway two and a half miles short of Little Loch Broom, at the point where a hill track runs five miles southwards to the lonely Strath na Sheallag. We had heard of a deserted cottage there called Shenavall, on the south flank of An Teallach itself. Judged by the map it would make an excellent base, if weather-proof; it stood right in among the hills at the meeting place of three deer forests, and looked across the breadth of the Strath into the east corrie of Beinn Dearg Mor, where cliffs of untouched sandstone awaited explorers. From

Dundonnell these cliffs were hopelessly inaccessible but from Shenavall almost convenient.

At 6 p.m., loaded with four days' food, we started over the seven miles' track to Shenavall. The track rose eleven hundred feet to a moorland pass, yet was neither steep nor stony, so that in little more than an hour we were crossing the watershed. Dusk had fallen. Two miles to northwards the white and crowded towers of An Teallach encircled their east corrie. The great length of the ridge augured a long day. Would it be next day? I wondered. I thought not. The sky showed starred patches, but the west wind was fetching too heavy masses of cloud up the sea-lanes from the coast. My day on An Teallach must be graced with perfect weather – or I would not go: upon that I was determined; which meant that we might have to spend some days skirmishing for position.

A long descent in well nigh total darkness brought us at last to the flats of Strath na Sheallag and to the solitary house of Achneigie. We were surprised to hear cattle in the byre and see a bright light in the house. For I would not have believed that in winter people could have been found to live here. The only links with civilization are the hill track to Dundonnell or a ten-mile track west to Gruinard Bay. There is no other occupied house in the glen.

We knocked at the door and met Mr Urquhart and his wife, their three children – and a schoolmistress; for it is the law of Scotland that all children shall be educated, and where they cannot go to school the school comes to them. They all welcomed us. Later they gave us milk and food. But they had no accommodation so on we went to Shenavall.

Shenavall at the first glance looked a very small cottage, but proved to be surprisingly commodious within. There were four rooms downstairs and three above. There were tables and chairs, spring-beds and mattresses. Even firewood. The house had been unoccupied for ten years, yet was dry inside. A heavy deposit of mice dirt lay spread over the floors, but that was a trifle. Within the hour we had a good fire in the hearth and hot soup inside us. We had settled in.

I awakened in the morning to the patter of sleet upon the

skylight window. It swirled thinly from grey cloud. This was no day for An Teallach. I turned over, rejoicing in sloth; until suddenly I remembered Beinn Dearg Mor. That north-east corrie had to be reconnoitred. All a human's difficulties about getting up in the morning are his not having sufficient incentive. Now I could rise at once and hardly notice the morning's rawness. At 10 a.m. we were off.

The approach to Beinn Dearg Mor from Shenavall is short on the map, but the flat and marshy ground presents two temper-testing hurdles in the shape of rivers feeding Loch na Sheallag – broad rivers unbridged, fast-flowing after rain, and deep. They have to be waded. One's feet are to be stung and frozen four times in one day. Beyond the second river the ground rose steeply for a thousand feet or more to the east corrie. The floor was the mountain's snow-line. I have never seen a corrie more shapely. A double summit pointed up from the centre, pillared by broad walls of sandstone. These were the central buttresses of a circle of seven, perfectly disposed in size and situation to contribute the utmost possible distinction to the main peak above them. The corrie's beauty inspires one to think big and look for a climb hard enough to honour the hill. But such aspirations had to be sternly curbed today. Grey and lowering clouds, the occasional drizzle of sleet, the raw damp wind, and the loose snow massed upon crags unsuitably weathered for winter climbing, would have made any long hard route a misery. Such a climb could have been done, but with several days in hand we were in no mood for it. Instead we climbed a gully to the left of the summit. It gave a snow-climb much like the Centre Gully of Beinn Laoigh.

In summer the buttresses would all give rock-climbs, perhaps of every order of difficulty.

We sped home by the north ridge and corrie and prepared for better things on the morrow. That night the wind got up from the north-west. It came sweeping over the shoulders of An Teallach and struck the corrugated-iron roof with a boom, like a hammer hitting a gong. Our second day was thus worse than the first and I began to fear that An Teallach was to be denied us. The sleet fell as thinly as before, but continuously, and not just in swirls. Late in the forenoon we wandered up to the east corrie of An Teallach, but could see nothing, save grey veils. The outing was a mere taking of exercise from which we returned dismally to a cold squalor at Shenavall and tried, with indifferent success, to warm ourselves up with great fires and meals. The weather was most decidedly growing colder and colder. As the night wore on it hardened to frost – even robbing us of sleep in the small hours. But this time our reward was a clear sky at dawn.

We were up at 7 a.m., unregretful of bed and eager to be off. Air and sky sparkled, and ground too, for the turf was frosted and each furred blade raised its individual spearhead. When we moved off at 9 a.m. the grass slopes above Shenavall felt like rock under the boot. We climbed leisurely, idling up with an exaggerated slowness, just waiting for the springs of energy to flow, as they would suddenly, and carry us easily up to the south-east top, Sail Liath. For our plan was to traverse the summit-ridge from south-east to north, and then descend to the east corrie. After we had climbed an hour from Shenavall the moment of flow came. We struck rhythm. The pace of ascent grew swift and painless. Until then we had climbed in a stupor: now the world came alive. Dry crisp snow lay on the frozen ground, but the sun shone with the full, refreshing warmth of an early spring morning. We were out on the rounded back of the ridge where it could reach us. Consciously we lived and moved in it and were no longer blind to the liveliness of the mountains. Boulders thrust red heads out of the snow, the slant of the sunlight fetching a glow from them, dotting the flash of the slope with colour, unexpectedly. As we gained height our speed increased; for we felt stimulated and even excited by the sharp air and sun, and our movement towards the sky, and the near approach of our great ridge.

The last slope of Sail Liath was a wind-packed snow-field, arching up to a huge silver dome. The edge of the dome had a curve like good china, a vast and flawless curve starting out against the blue behind. The blue was lucid: that early morning blue, which one associates with South Sea lagoons; and the snow-dome's edge flowed upon it. I had seen nothing on mountains more simple than this edge, and nothing more beautiful. It is a beauty that every natural thing manifested through the universe seems to exhibit by reason of its very being.

Sometimes I find it distressing on mountains to see beauty alone. I want others to see and share it too, otherwise I have a sense of vicarious frustration; beauty is meant for all men. I hovered to let Meyer catch up. He was beaming with enthusiasm.

'What a day!' he exclaimed. 'What a country!' The words convey nothing but the tone of voice satisfied even me. I grinned, and we followed our own ways to the cairn, where MacAlpine soon joined us. We rested no more than a minute, for a breeze was blowing from the north-west. A quick glimpse over the northern edge showed us where the great corrie lay, fourteen hundred feet below, its Loch Toll an Lochain hidden from us by the bulge of the precipice. Far beyond, a screen of grey-blue haze covered the full length of the Atlantic; but the mainland side stayed clear, from the distant ripple of the Cairngorms to the nearby spikes of Torridon, and between, a white innumerable mob of no outstanding character. A more individual ruggedness lay close at hand. The towers of our ridge curled like a whip-lash through the sky – flicked two miles around the corrie. An Teallach waited.

At midday we set off north-west round the ridge, which at first was broad, going easily down to a col and over a second rounded dome. Then the ridge narrowed. It was buried deep in the soft snow of the recent fall. This proved little hindrance while our course lay downwards, and our subsequent ascent to the third peak was at first aided by rock out-crops. These, we could see, were topped by a high summit-buttress, destined to give trouble. The prelude to the ridge was over. At once the crest narrowed again. We scrambled over massive blocks until halted by a fifteen-foot wall. Although steep it was snow-covered, for the weathered fracture-lines in sandstone can support a thick skin.

This last thought encouraged me. When high-angle rock is able to support much soft dry snow there must be excellent holds underneath. And so it proved. Their excavation cost time, but they were good enough to let us climb unroped to a higher crest of now Alpine narrowness. The buttress jerked out of the ridge close above. I moved to its foot and we roped up. As I turned to watch the others a golden eagle swept round the corner of the buttress immediately behind them, so close to their backs, indeed, and so fast, that collision seemed certain. But the astounded bird stood on its tail just in time, and swept back the way it had come, over the corrie.

I appropriated the lead. This, I felt, was an occasion: An Teallach ought to get the best I could give. But for quite other reasons my decision to lead was to prove doubly fortunate. The route again lay up a short wall, just to the left side of the crest. Under its thinner snow-coating I could see long wrinkles, small and dipping out. From a snow-ledge on top the buttress sprang with a renewed steepness. Meanwhile MacAlpine belayed me. I brushed over the wall with gloved hands. I scraped the wrinkles with my axe. This revealed one hold in the middle, giving a move that none of my party will forget in a hurry – a balance move on a crease. I could just get the edge-nail of my boot on to it, but it sloped out and bore a thin lichen. Being frozen, the lichen was slippery, and the question was whether my nail would hold. The upward lift from the hands had to be made with the aid of press-holds only. Thrice I half made the move – raised myself just a few inches from the holds below, and each time returned to think again. MacAlpine, watching from directly below, swore that my one-nail hold looked excessively alarming. No doubt he was thinking, as a good second should, of the best way to stop me if I fell; but I was now reasonably well satisfied that my tricouni nail (serrated cast-iron) would bite on the sandstone. So I made one quick lift, and the nail held, on the extreme outer curve of the crease. I pulled myself up.

The ledge above was good – mercifully good, for MacAlpine and Meyer were wearing Vibram rubber soles. These are excellent on Scottish snow and ice, and on clean rock, wet or dry, but on wet or frozen lichen hopelessly bad. Torridon sandstone being rough and tough, like gritstone, Vibram soles would at first sight appear to be eminently suitable; but close inspection shows much of this sandstone to be patched with lichen of delicate brand. MacAlpine's foot slipped badly on the crease and he had to come up on a tight rope. By the time that Meyer reached the fatal spot the polish had become fatally perfect. He is one of the best Alpinists in England but he had to be pulled up.

The whole passage of the third peak was a new revelation of the astonishing transformations that overtake a Scottish ridge in winter, when snow is thick and the frost hard. I have heard no one report any difficulty on the ridge of An Teallach in summer – not in the technical sense.

We had now a choice of routes: either by the right flank, up a cleft cutting the vertical face, or by a long traverse leftwards across the equally steep west face. Above that cleft or beyond this traverse we could not guess what happened. The right-hand or east face lay in shadowed frost, so we went left into sunshine. We edged carefully along a shattered ledge, then climbed a hundred feet up the flank by snow-choked scoops. On these we moved together until halted by a final chimney of fifty feet. One at a time we wormed up its snow and pressed up its iced walls, until we came out on open snows among great blocks of poised stone, and over them to the top of our third peak.

The ridge down its far side went like an aerial rail on a free flight through space. There were delightful walls, snow-crusted, down which we dropped on to narrow landings of highly inclined snow. Going down first I enjoyed these walls; while Meyer, coming last on the rope, enjoyed the ledges. The descent eased to the col. There we saw the tracks of a fox cross the ridge from west to east and traverse the face of an incipient cornice banked at sixty-five degrees above the eastern cliffs. None of us would have dared to move on such snow without a rope, but the fox had scampered quite gaily, for there was no trace of hesitation where it crossed the arête. I put my nose to the paw-prints and the musty stink made me rise in a hurry. They reeked. The fox must have crossed this forenoon. But why – and to what end?

We continued along the ridge rising towards our fourth peak, a cluster of four towers called Corrag Bhuidhe. The name means

'The Yellow Finger,' for which no reason was apparent from this angle, the ridge being barred near the top by crags standing markedly red against their background of white and blue. Intense weathering had given the sandstone the piled-block formation for which the granite of Arran is so well known. We climbed direct to the first tower of Corrag Bhuidhe, then crossed a gap to the second tower.

A new surprise met us there – the titbit of the day: a stretch of ridge like a high, dry-stone dyke running a hundred feet to the third tower. Crested with a sharp snow-edge, the flanks fell sheer, notably on the right-hand side, where a cliff dropped one thousand seven hundred feet to the loch. I had seen no comparable *arête* outside the Alps, although I have no doubt that in similar conditions its counterpart will be found in the Cuillin of Skye. We dealt easily with the soft snow; none the less we had to balance along step by step, arms half outstretched, and defy a natural inclination to sit astride. The third tower was only a knob at the end of the ridge, but cut off from the fourth by a vertical cleft, which could not be taken direct. So I returned a few feet, doubled a rope round a spike on the ridge, then roped off on the left flank. This brought me on to a slope just above the col. The others followed and flicked the rope down after them. We climbed easy crags to the fourth tower.

From this viewpoint the knife-edged dyke behind us looked extraordinarily sensational, nicked along its crest by our footsteps. The whole mountain scene around – plum-coloured isles and bays, bared teeth of the Cuillin fifty miles south-west, the clean dazzle of the highland ranges – this whole, rich panorama fell into place as a mere backcloth to the drama of An Teallach's crest. Towers and edges hung in space without visible means of support, hung over the frozen void of the east corrie, but turned to the sunny south a gay lining of snow. The edge ran stark between: it alone seemed fully real, and really true, the essential An Teallach – The Forge, which bore us.

We continued down the blade of our ridge, and up to the sharp point of the fifth peak, which bears the inappropriate name of

Lord Berkeley's Seat. The Leaning Tower of Dundonnell would be more truly descriptive, for it overhangs its base – leans right out over the corrie. Our descent by the north edge went on a wafer of rock curling out over the east face like a huge cornice. Dry snow was massed loosely on rock twice pierced by holes, through which we prospected a thousand feet of hoared cliff. This north ridge is unique in Scotland.

We lunched down on the col, then climbed the south ridge of Sgurr Fiona, 'The Peak of Wine.' It reminded me of the Second Pyramid of Gizeh, being not only shaped as such, but having its top section seemingly enclosed by an outer rock-casing. The snow at least lay smoothly in a pyramidal cap over the summit. Our ascent was a treadmill labour in dry snow – praise be to God – for it might have been wet. However long the sun may shine at this time of year in Scotland it has no melting effect on snow, for its declination is too low. Melting has to wait on warm winds. The quality of morning snow changes not at all in the afternoon. Snow conditions are thus less Alpine than arctic. We reached the top of Sgurr Fiona, point 3,474, with dry feet.

The pinnacled ridge had now ended. There followed a pure snow-ridge, falling to a col at three thousand feet, thence rising to point 3,483, called Bidein a Ghlas Thuill, 'The Peak of the Grey Hollow.' It is the summit of An Teallach. Under a heavy plaster of snow it is a great mountain. In ideal weather with few halts, but without hurry, that two miles of ridge had taken nearly six hours of our time.

The sun was sinking, but would not set, I wrongly thought, for another hour. Every horizon was in haze: smoky to the west; southward blue, with glens receding into it in successive planes; to the north-east, silver grey. Over Gruinard Bay a streak of white smoke issued from an invisible steamer. Not even the Summer Isles, close in to Loch Broom, were clear. The Hebrides loomed indistinctly as humps. I wanted to wait up on the ridge for sunset, which would be unusually spectacular, but the northerly air-stream spoke an icy no.

We turned east along the north arm of the horseshoe. Upon

leaving the cairn we observed great claw-marks in the snow-bonnet of a boulder and a still deeper imprint five yards below on the corrie-flank of the ridge, where an eagle had taken one heavy hop before launching itself over the cliff. After traversing a quarter of a mile we felt free to follow its example, and so launched ourselves down a twelve-hundred-foot snow-slope to Loch Toll an Lochain. We glissaded fast, and were halfway down when the south-eastern peaks stopped us. Creamy-coloured for the last hour or so, now they reddened, while the once blue sky above turned sea-green.

The full display to be seen only from a summit had been lost to us, but as we came to the shore of Loch Toll an Lochain constantly changing lights began to play along the full length of the easterly haze-bank. It might have been a skin, inhabited by some celestial chameleon, so rapidly did the colours react to the altering west, and blend: all shaded subtleties of red, green, blue, and yellow, bloomed and faded, renewed themselves and died, coming and going with a stealth quite imperceptible, so that always one saw them there, yet never caught the flicker of the change.

The floor of the corrie flattened at the entrance to form a mountain belvedere, from which we looked far out across the valley of Dundonnell to half-hidden and mysterious ranges.

I stopped to let the others go on. It is not the sort of place that I ever feel inclined to leave. A last pallor had taken the hills; the tops were shrouds, the skies just so much empty space, the haze-banks fog. Within five minutes of this sudden death the reawakening started. Pale blue colour flowed back into the north-east sky and the peaks whitened. Before I had realized what was happening all the haze had gone. For a while I had thought that it was simply whitening, but instead, the white solidified, stepped forward, as it were, in form of mountains, revealed to their feet for the first time this day. As the blue of the east deepened the air sharpened, grew clean, and the night's frost swept the land. A star twinkled above the corrie.

I turned to look up at An Teallach. The first of the moonlight was filtering between the pinnacles. The vast circle of their frozen walls stared down at a frozen loch – a sombre circle, but lifting high in the centre to that five-pointed crown rimmed by light.

Corrie and mountain are the natural altars of the earth to be used as such before one goes.

22

Effects of Mountaineering on Men

The effect that men have had upon mountaineering, and the record of their climbs in the club journals, constitute mountaineering history, about which much has been written.

It is a safe subject: there the records are, and no man may gainsay them. But very little has been written of the effects of mountaineering on men. For *that* subject is downright dangerous, snags and snares abounding. Yet a report true to fact may be made if a man records detachedly, and does not exceed, his own observations and experience; accordingly I make no effort to treat the subject comprehensively; for, of course, I cannot know what all the effects of mountaineering are. Nor do I set down all the effects I have seen or experienced. I choose only those that I judge to be particularly worth noting.

The men to be met on mountains are not better than other men, and I should not be greatly troubled if they were shown to be worse. The important point is that on mountains they are known in the heat of action: it is there and then that men, more frequently than in other sports, are forced back upon their real selves. I am assured by historians that man in his usual habit is an ignoble, crawling organism; but contrary to what one might infer from such a premise, it is my experience that men's behaviour is most inspired, displays a self-forgetful spirit and nobility of soul, when circumstance is most adverse. Some of the greatest changes in men occur when storm and danger and difficulty appear together on rock, snow, and ice. I have seen quite ordinary men behave then with a fearless resolution, move with unprecedented certainty and precision, as though some *deus ex machina* had descended out of the clouds to take charge of them, and so save the situation in defiance of probability. Just to have watched that performance at close quarters has been a permanent gain to me. It has filled me with a respect and admiration for man's spirit, as then giving expression to fundamental qualities far more moving than any expression of an artist's brush or a composer's music: in this sense, that these latter have aroused my enthusiasm, but have never moved me to try to alter my own character; whereas the former has inspired me with that very desire – to be firm in adversity and bold in emergency and fearless to the end. The personal virtue is the more powerful in effect, and the more lasting. The emergencies that call out such an example are, or ought to be, of rare occurrence.

The trials of mountaineering, small or great, awaken elements of character left dormant by professional life. This fact is especially obvious at the start of a man's climbing career. Some of his latent powers of personality have been given no adequate field of action in the concentrated book-work of school and office or university, or in the routine of the factory, and may be in danger of perversion if not atrophy. He has become a jailbird temporarily. Then perhaps for the first time he is given on mountains the field of free action he sorely needs to give growth and expansion to those unused elements of his character. A gradual self-fulfilment is the purpose of the individual life, and mountaineering does help in it. The beginning is modest enough.

Here I quote my own experience. For a year I hill-walked by myself. Simple work you would say? Its effect on me was considerable. I discovered that when a man has to find his own way for the first time across wide moors, and long narrow summit ridges, and over the high plateaux, the work gives him a sense of achievement which lasts all his life. Should he meet foul weather as well – as he certainly will – and have to steer through it by map and compass, he develops a confidence that grows at each repetition. Confidence in his own manhood and powers of action is one of the most valuable possessions that a man can have; it clears the way to his getting the two keys to success in more than mountaineering: knowledge of his goal and singleness of purpose.

In every branch of the craft one gets a training in self-reliance without ever looking for it. Routes have to be selected, obstacles mastered, decisions made, hard work and weather faced. The training is naturally more intense in winter. On big winter routes the climber repeatedly encounters rock and ice that cannot be climbed in the unimpassioned frame of mind sufficient unto the days of summer. They more often have to be forced. He may have to climb to his limit, and having done so, then grip the mind and stir up energy – and go still farther. His battle is fought out on small holds and icy corners, on bare slabs and frozen rock, often in discomfort, for the frequent reward of joy. The intense effort by which every step is won, and all skill employed, and the way through the difficulty resolutely engineered, brings together all the joys of the triune craft, rock-snow-ice. The mind has mastery of the body and knows it. In such moments all a man's diffidence about his own capacities is cast off; all his lack of push, due to uncertainty of his powers, is replaced by a singleness of purpose, from which springs strenuousness and real powers of initiative.

When a man is a very young man he is of necessity unsure of himself. He cannot have true confidence because he does not know what his capacities are. They are, of course, far greater than he ever dreams. But he has got to find that out. Mountains make a good testing ground – a better ground than war, which is a per-version. It is of untold benefit to him, and to us all, to be brought face to face with realities in their harshest aspect. The occasional experience of it has an educative power from which we can learn much at merciful speed – learn in a few minutes what would otherwise take years. These sharp experiences can always be turned to our good, although rarely reckoned as blessings.

In August 1949 Fred Baker and I went to the Montenvers above Chamonix, and at 4 a.m. on our first morning set out to climb the Grands Charmoz. At 6 a.m. we were moving up the Nantillons Glacier, just where the ice steepens under the Rognon. We stopped to put on crampons. Suddenly we heard a roar and looked up to see an ice-cliff collapse at the left side of the glacier and spill towards the centre. There was no time to run – apparently no way of escape – and I had just said 'By God, we've had it!' – when the first ice-block went whizzing past. At the same instant I saw a long crevasse ten feet above me. I leapt into its near end, which was only eight feet deep – in marked contrast to the far end. No sooner was I under the protection of the upper lip than the main weight of the avalanche went thundering over the top. I presumed Baker to be lost. When all was still I looked out to try to see where his body was, but could see not a sign. Then to my right-hand side a quiet voice said: 'It's all right!' And there was Baker, crouching in a mere depression, an incipient crevasse with a vertical upper wall of only three feet. The avalanche had gone shooting over his head as it had shot over mine. His was the more remarkable escape.

We continued our climb, and had an excellent day on the Grands Charmoz. But for a long time after that, if any bearer of ill-tidings had come to me reporting the total loss of everything I possessed in this world I should not have thought the news too serious. I had health and life and the ability to support myself by work. I should not, like the bankrupted financiers of Wall Street or the City, have cast myself from the top window of a skyscraper or more modestly blown out my brains. Life was seen very much in its proper perspective.

In the ordinary course of climbing similar lessons are learned, less spectacularly and more enjoyably. When a rock-climber is nearing the middle of Rosa Pinnacle on a warm day of summer, employing much skill and energy to lift himself up those next twelve inches of granite, all the other worries of life vanish, and although they most certainly do return afterwards, they return permanently shrunken: no longer do they augur the end of the world. Minor disasters are seen to be minor. In other words, the man has grown a little in stature.

Life on earth gives to a man the chance for a full development of his powers and potentialities. Their need of fulfilment arouses the spirit of exploratory adventure in all planes of his life, according to the degree of his soul's unfolding. The mountaineer, as such, is distinguished from other men only in finding some of the help that *he* needs more readily among mountains. The expression of his need is his love of them; their offering is beauty and adventure, which he accepts. The adventurous spirit is in every man. Deny him outlet for it – and there is hell to pay. Repression is evil. By that let us not mean that any lust at all should get expression; rather that all of a man's energies get a sanely directed outlet, on the human plane, not the animal.

In 1946 I assisted Kenneth Dunn in taking some youthful Glasgow gangsters on to the Glencoe and Arrochar hills. They came from the district between Anderston and the Gorbals, where street gangs abound, and were selected as giving at least some promise of an interest in climbing. We found them likeable men, aged sixteen to eighteen, with a keen sense of humour and no especial love of the gangs, of which they were members, they said, for the sake of their own protection. The larger gangs, like the San Toy with a hundred or two members and a motor-car, had armouries. A member with a feud on his hands could draw from the armoury his necessary weapon, called 'The Message,' which might be a revolver and a round or two of ammunition, a razor, or else some blunt and heavy instrument, or a motor-bicycle chain. He would wrap the chain in adhesive tape if his modest ambition was to stun the victim, but would use it bare if he desired to rip off the flesh as well.

One of our youths had a recent razor-slash on his shoulder, received on no greater provocation than his walking through a public thoroughfare, the territory of a rival gang. But a more common cause of feud, he told us, arose at a dance-hall in the Gallowgate. Men and women pay their own way in. A man may then select a partner and be getting on well with her, when someone taps him on the shoulder and says: 'Hey! Leave off. This is my moll.' If he turns a deaf ear he is waylaid in the gents' lavatory, knocked down and kicked in the face and stomach, and perhaps gets a parting razor-slash on his way home.

Well, these men had been denied an outlet for their adventurous energies. And there was hell to pay. Those whom I met I liked. Of the six whom we introduced to mountains I should guess that two would continue of their own accord – given the means and the opportunity.

The provision of a field of action is thus essential, and the beneficial use that can be made of mountains is demonstrated by one of my friends. His father died, leaving him at the age of sixteen to support his mother and sisters in London. He achieved this duty by hard work and, being untrained for any profession, by taking what he felt to be menial jobs. In the course of a year or two these gave him a sense of social inferiority and frustration, which continued after he came to Scotland. There he found mountains. *They* gave him the common rewards – beauty of scene, joy of the craft, sport and its comradeship, the health of free action through all weathers – and in addition the opportunity of working off his sense of inferiority. He took this latter opportunity in his rock-climbing, which he prosecuted with an unexampled rashness and vigour. His reputation for audacity became legendary. For example, when he went to the Right-angled Gully of the Cobbler in winter and found the wall at the direct exit too icy, it was said that he drove the pick of his axe into the frozen turf on top and climbed up the shaft. I have no idea whether that particular tale was true, but it was typical. Upon accomplishing difficult feats he would feel that after all he was not inferior to other men of his age; that indeed he was the equal of any of them. The upshot was that in a few years his sense of inferiority had been killed stone dead. My friend went on to complete his triumph by becoming one of the soundest and most skilled mountaineers in Scotland without going to the other extreme of feeling superiority on that account. To any man who is able to use mountains thus we wish good fortune. They restore him to more perfect health. And to all young men abounding in high spirits and somewhat over-bold we should not only be tolerant but give the occasional word of praise they need and deserve. The fool who sneers is in need of some dire misfortune for the cure of his soul.

Although the phrase 'working off inferiorities' has become a common idiom, containing as it does a grain of truth, none the less it is still far too shallow an interpretation. When we are dealing with man in relation to his kind any talk of his inferiority is a negative, wholly inadequate way of stating the positive truth: which is, that a man's goal in life is his self-fulfilment. To that end he acts both on mountains and off them. It is not *primarily* by belief in a creed that he is moved to act. He is in reality acting all the time. He never stops acting from birth to death. He is unable not to act. He acts daily, yearly, and all his life long in search of his self's *best* interest. His one source of all trouble is ignorance – ignorance of what his best interest is and what his 'self' is. He has to learn by experience – his own and not someone else's. At one stage he may feel well satisfied with wealth, or with a blind drunk at hogmanay, with the dictatorship of all the Russians or the first ascent of a rock climb in Glencoe, with scholarship or gipsydom. But when these in the end are found not to give lasting satisfactions, on he must go, until at the last the archetypal man is realized. To that end all men move – move now, always have moved, and always will: while they have life they will seek that which they lack, on mountains or elsewhere. In that process mountains do play a part because on them men do grow and unfold.

It is encouraging to reflect that we do that best of all when we climb mountains just to enjoy them.

But we must not be so innocent as to think that the effects of mountaineering are necessarily good. Mountaineering is like every other human activity without exception, from prayer to party politics, in this respect: that the quality of its effects upon us is determined by our purpose. We have power to choose. And the effects will shortly be very evident to our fellows and our purpose revealed. During the year that I write I have seen mountaineering used to display bounce, boast, brag, lying, vanity and deceit, and a greed for severe climbs to give a boost to a man's reputation. I have seen it bring on an unholy pomposity and the contempt for men who are beyond some predetermined pale. In all the history of mountaineering perhaps the ugliest phase was its use by the Nazis and Fascists during the late nineteen-thirties as an instrument of nationalist propaganda, breeding ill will among Alpinists on a scale not hitherto attempted. In mountaineering we have a choice. Is our best interest to be served by a self-regard or by a selfless love of the hills and men? Some men choose one and some the other.

The two results of such opposite decisions were demonstrated before me in one day in July 1947, in the Dauphine Alps.

The scene was set as follows. John Barford and Michael Ward had been climbing with me on the north-west side of the Ailefroide. We decided after a few days that next morning we should change our centre and cross the northward-running ridge from west to east by the Col de la Coste Rouge, descending thence to the Glacier Noir. We arrived at the col at 9 a.m. Our descent on the far side went by a couloir of four hundred feet, normally easy and free from stonefall. Today soft snow lay on ice, and there was a bergschrund below, so we roped up. We were halfway down the couloir when half a dozen stones fell from the wall of the Ailefroide. They came straight at us. We were all struck and fell together. I did not lose consciousness, and felt myself stopped by a wrench on the shoulders, the lower three-quarters of my body swinging in space. I realized then that my shoulders and heavy Bergan ruck-sack had jammed in the mouth of the bergschrund, but I was blinded by concussion and by blood running into my eyes so that I could do nothing at first. After several minutes' labour I dragged myself out. Barford and Ward were still in the bergschrund and still roped to me. I climbed back in and found Barford on a ledge. He was dead. Ten feet below, Ward was jammed by his shoulders and rucksack at a narrowing of the walls just as I had been. A deep chasm opened below him. His head was badly gashed, but he had regained consciousness and was beginning to struggle. Standing on the ledge I used all the strength I had to pull on the rope, and after long and desperate efforts he managed to clutch his way up. That is where the story begins.

Like myself, Ward had a fractured skull; in addition, the top of his ear was half off and his memory had gone. He did not know my name, or Barford's, or what mountain he was on, or where he was going. As quickly as I told him he repeated the questions. However, after he had taken stock of me he agreed to go with me downhill. With an unreasoning obstinacy I decided to carry my heavy rucksack, but Ward wisely left his behind. We slowly descended on to the upper glacier basin where the heat was intense. The

Glacier Noir now stretched below us seven kilometres to the Ailefroide valley. We halted and looked at it somewhat hopelessly. Just then I saw a Frenchman on the far side of the glacier making for the Col de la Temple. I sounded an SOS on my whistle and he came over to us.

He was a man of forty. Judging by his equipment, confident bearing, and good training, I have no doubt that he was a competent mountaineer. I told him what had happened – that Barford was dead in the bergschrund, and that Ward and I were doubtful of having enough strength to get down the glacier to the valley. Would he go with us, to make sure we arrived there? He surveyed us carefully. We must have made an ugly and bloody sight. He reflected. Then he explained that he had been making for the Col de la Temple in order to descend to La Berarde, where he had an engagement. If he were to go down the Glacier Noir with us that would take him in the opposite direction. Therefore, with our permission, he would continue on his own way. Meantime was there anything he could do for us? A mouthful of wine perhaps? He was most courteous. He could not possibly have cared less.

I would not argue. I felt too sick with disappointment in him. Ward and I continued alone down the glacier. There were numerous crevasses to be crossed, all narrow, of the kind one may readily jump. These delayed us greatly. We would hover on the brink, trying to summon up enough energy to make those easy jumps. In a short while I began to feel dreadfully hampered by the weight of my rucksack, and no doubt I looked troubled. Ward, following behind, offered to carry it for me.

A trivial service? But consider the position. Ward had fractured his skull, lost much blood, did not know who I was, and had been unable to lift his own rucksack off the ground. But he was now proposing to help me with mine. Selflessness is often thought of by the more grossly ignorant as a negative virtue; it is in fact so positively inspiring that on this occasion it relieved Ward of the need to call common-sense to his rescue and refuse at the last to implement an offer divinely mad, because it gave me all the energy

I required to shoulder my own burden. A curious situation then arose: in consequence of his injuries Ward was in some small measure dependent on myself for getting him down the glacier, but the energy by which I was enabled to do so was derived from him.

In seven hours we reached the valley. As soon as we saw other humans our sustaining vitality vanished, leaving us in a state of collapse. We were removed by ambulance. All the French people we met thereafter treated us with unfailing kindness, and a month or two later we were none the worse.

When we reflect upon the actions of these two men, the Frenchman and Ward, compare the choice before each and contrast the differing results, we are brought to a conclusion of importance: that when we go among mountains, although they will always produce effects on our personalities, yet whether they are good effects or bad is determined entirely by ourselves. It is our own attitude of mind that determines effects. Always the choice is ours. Like the jungle, mountains are neutral.

It would seem to be an office of mountains to present to us the two extreme aspects of reality: the tough, harsh aspect entailing battle with the elements and the ideal aspect manifesting beauty. There are those amongst us who would have us turn away from the one, or turn from the other, but any man who would have his mountains whole – and his own life whole – should turn from neither (undue risk of accident excepted); but to the contrary receive all that he may of both. From the schooling and discipline of the first we may learn much, and from its recreation renew our health. But what of the second aspect?

Beauty gets a very different reception from different men. Its manifestation through the mountain scene may be refused acceptance in one century and not another according as prejudice veils men's eyes or detachment clears them. A particular acceptance or rejection of that kind is in the long run of no great consequence; for beauty is manifest in the whole natural creation, and men will find it where they feel disposed to look. At the present more men than ever before are disposed to accept it from mountains. But how different is the degree in which they do so! I remember that when one of our young gangsters reached the top of the Cobbler on a fine day he did not proceed to enjoy the view, the like of which he had never set eyes on before. Squatting on the cairn he buried himself in a Sunday paper, the sports column of which wholly absorbed him until the time came to go down.

Assuming, however, that we have recognized beauty, then as with the other aspect of mountains it is for ourselves to choose what effect it has upon us. It is the good habit of men to draw occasional refreshment of their spirits from beauty, and a temporary pleasure; their bad habit to dismiss thought of it thereafter as being of no further use. On the other hand, there may be a sound core to the instinct that holds as ineffective and of little true value to man the perception of a beauty in art or nature that does not bring in its train right action. Ideals that are not practical are profitless. But – every true ideal may be *given* practical application in our active living. In brief, our response to beauty is inadequate if we passively receive and there stop short. Something more than that is expected of us. We can receive true values only if we are willing to give, to the raising up of our consciousness and way of life, that strenuousness (and also toughness) which on the physical plane men devote so willingly to mountaineering. The effect of beauty upon us may then be no less powerful than that of battle and no less profound.

Let us see how this may be so.

If we make a survey of mountaineering literature we can hardly fail to observe the frequency with which writers express perceptions of a beauty that baffles their powers of description. 'Beauty unutterable,' 'Beyond comprehension,' are favoured terms of reference. These perceptions are sometimes accompanied by a certainty of the universal unity or by the premonition of an ultimate reality, the spiritual ground of things seen. Even a hard-headed nineteenth-century scientist, Professor John Tyndall, an agnostic of the Victorian school, and therefore usually sure of himself, writes of the view from the Weisshorn: 'I opened my notebook to make a few observations but soon relinquished the attempt. There was something incongruous, if not profane, in allowing the scientific faculty to interfere where silent worship was the reasonable service.'

He writes here of that same beauty that we take so very much for granted while we climb through good, photographic scenery; not of something different, nor of greater power. The eye of his soul has been more clear, that is all. Every sensitive and intelligent man has similar experiences during his life, maybe at long intervals; but most assuredly, if he is an active mountaineer, his opportunities are many. For mountains throw into high relief a beauty that fairly takes the eye by storm. But the bodily eye is not the mind, and the mind not always receptive. Opportunities are more often lost than seized.

May it not be possible by some practical method to help one's mind to grow in awareness of beauty, to develop that faculty of perception, which lack of exercise frustrates and stunts? In truth, growth may be given to the spiritual consciousness as simply as growth and health are given to the body – by awakening it from slumber, by providing nourishment, and then by giving hard exercise. Effort must be expended, sacrifice must be faced; without *these* only imaginary mountains are climbed.

The awakening is a free decision to use the spiritual faculty and to seek a target. Its awakening is widest and consciousness most keenly alert when it is briefed for the highest of peaks – to bring union with ultimate reality. A lower goal will induce a correspondingly lower efficiency. The nourishment provided is that of feeling. It is a matter of experience that all feelings of disparagement, underestimation, contempt and carping criticism, anger and lust, are poisons that starve, stunt, and wither the spiritual faculty; and that feelings of compassion, reverence, and devotion are foods that nourish it and bestow energy. The exercise to be given makes use at first both of material forms and simple discursive thought or reflection. It is necessary to be very practical in arranging for this exercise. Time must be allotted and the habit made regular. Five minutes daily is not too little nor an hour too much.

Our search for beauty being conscious, our best policy is to begin with simple things, infinite in number and commonly disregarded: the touch of wind on the cheek, rocks, the smell of pines and bog-myrtle, morning dew and the song of water, snow-ridges in sun, tall trees and corries. Let us see their beauty and remember, and then take a wider sweep to embrace the greater things: a sea-loch winding among hills, cloudscape and sky, a mountain entire in its shape and setting of moorland, cloud, and atmosphere. Seeking always the underlying beauty, and proceeding from lesser forms to greater, we end with the form that displays to us greatest beauty, and dwell upon that: we allow it to evoke in our hearts devotion and reverence.

Encourage these feelings of love for the ideas of beauty. Let them grow and fill and reverberate through the consciousness. For within the soul they nourish a power that gradually opens the spiritual eye. Then truly our minds are in a state of growth, for where perception penetrates and love aspires, understanding follows, and reason may assume its role of guide.

The full action of meditation is usually made difficult or impossible on mountains by wind and weather, time and company. But our observations can be made for later and more effective use in privacy. We should then recall the forms of beauty, visualizing each until our love for its beauty is aroused, and end with the greatest beauty known to us – it may be a sunrising or sunsetting, or a night sky or mountain, the beauty for which no words can be found. Encourage unreservedly the awe and wonder to which this last gives rise. These feelings of the heart give nourishment and life to the will and mind, which all acting in unison raise consciousness to a new state of awareness.

At the beginning of such an expansion of soul a man's powers of perceiving beauty are doubled, and one danger of the ascent may become noticeable. He may fall into the habit of stopping at the pleasure received and exhausting it, continuing the work primarily for the pleasure rather than for love of the beauty. As soon as that element of self-seeking is introduced growth will automatically cease, and the immature spiritual faculty dwindle. With most surprising promptitude the mind reverts to its old lop-sided state.

In this work there is no static position: one goes on or one drops back. We need, above all, to persist.

Our remedy is not to deny the enjoyment, but likewise not to stop there. We must persist in working inwardly towards the widening of consciousness, reflecting upon beauty and the inherent principles of truth and good, its universal presence and inward significance for the individual self and mankind, and the ways and means by which we may realize its living presence within us, so that we, in turn, may manifest them in serving our fellow men. We must be very practical, and not allow either reason or the heart wholly to dominate us. When our work has continued a while, we become aware that infinitely various as the forms of beauty are, it is changeless and eternal. This beauty is increasingly known by the mind; for the more the will turns the mind as a mirror to the sun of beauty the more clear and revealing does its light become. We are fired by desire to be made one with beauty, in knowledge and love. By a natural law the mind grows like that which it loves, and knowledge grows as love grows.

The way in which beauty, the infinite One, reveals in the symbols of nature the infinite diversity of its life, allows us to glimpse the universe as the outer expression of an inner and spiritual unity: the one as the many and the all as one. Analogies invariably break down when pushed too far; remembering this, let us take one from music, where a single idea of beauty in the mind of a composer creates a complex symphony. That creative beauty orders the ideas and emotions that must be expressed, the balance and structure of each requiring a movement with themes and melodies, which in turn determine the phrases, the harmonies of which order the relation of the notes, each note determining the number of air vibrations required to produce its sound. We have finally a complex of air vibrations arrayed through time and moving in space. They impinge on our eardrums, combine to give sounds in sequence, and lead us back step by step through phrases, melodies, themes, and emotions to the full symphony and its root idea of beauty, which we at last know in its true ground beyond time and space. The creation of the world, and our upward ascent in meditation from the many to the One, would appear to follow a course singularly like that of our analogy. Our own part is to cast out every inner distraction and impurity so that our minds may be clear, unfretted – and receptive.

This casting out of distractions is a process of purification – a tough and exacting trial of our earnestness besides which the trials of mountaineering sometimes seem like play for children. It is again a most practical matter and not one to be by-passed, for only through it may the mind have hope of illumination and the soul of union. Beauty has been found at first in natural forms as an impersonal reality, but now it is found within ourselves and men and all creatures as the Being, Life, and Intelligence through which and in which we have our own being, the Light that lighteth all and our true End.

To that End men move, move now and always, for the most part blindly, not recognizing at first their true self and best interest, yet, while they have life, seeking what they lack, their power of choice free ... It is most fortunate for man that beauty, unlike mountains, is not neutral.

Mamore Forest, Lochaber. Sgor an Iubhair from the Devil's Ridge.
Photo by A.D.S. Macpherson.

The Crowberry Tower, from the south. At the righthand base is the snow-ledge by which escape can be made from the crest of Crowberry Ridge, which is hidden behind the tower. At the bottom righthand corner is the top of Curved Ridge, and the top of East Gully on its left. *Photo by Douglas Scott.*

Buachaille Etive Mor (North Face from Glencoe). The North Buttress falls directly from the summit with the Crowberry Gully on its left. To the left again is the Crowberry Ridge, its crest in the sunshine. The Crowberry Tower is prominent in the sun below and to the left of the summit. The Shelf Route runs up the north flank of Crowberry Ridge midway between Crowberry Gully and the crest. Its lower part may be seen as a dark score on the flank. *Photo by Douglas Scott.*

Garbh Bheinn of Ardgour (from Corrie an Iubhair). The Great Gully is directly under the summit. *Photo by D. McKellar.*

The plateau of Aonach Beag, Lochaber. The Moor of Rannoch is in the distance. *Photo by A.D.S. Macpherson.*

The Moor of Rannoch in winter. *Photo by Douglas Scott.*

The Carn Dearg cliffs, Ben Nevis. Castle Buttress is the tongue-shaped buttress on
the right, demarcated left and right by the South and North Castle Gullies. To its
right is the broad Castle Ridge, and to its left the main mass of the Carn Dearg Buttress.
Photo by W.S. Thomson.

On the eastern buttress, Sron na Ciche, Skye. *Photo by A.M. Smith.*

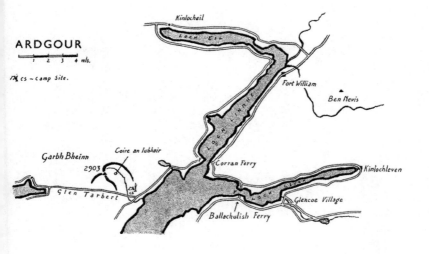

ARDGOUR

cs ~ camp site.

Kinlocheil

LOCH EIL

Fort William

Ben Nevis

Garbh Bheinn
2903

Coire an Iubhair

LOCH LINNHE

Corran Ferry

Kinlochleven

Glen Tarbert

Glencoe Village

Ballachulish Ferry

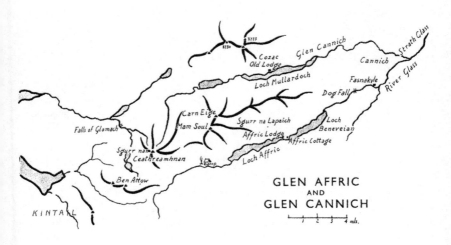

3725

3230

Cozac
Old Lodge

Glen Cannich

Cannich

Strath Glass

Loch Mullardoch

Fasnakyle

River Glass

Dog Fall

Falls of Glomach

Carn Eige

Mam Soul

Sgurr na Lapaich

Loch
Beneveian

Affric Lodge

Affric Cottage

Sgurr nan
Ceathreamhnan

Camp

Loch Affric

Ben Attow

KINTAIL

GLEN AFFRIC
AND
GLEN CANNICH

x
start

Twisting Gully, Stob Coire nan Lochan.

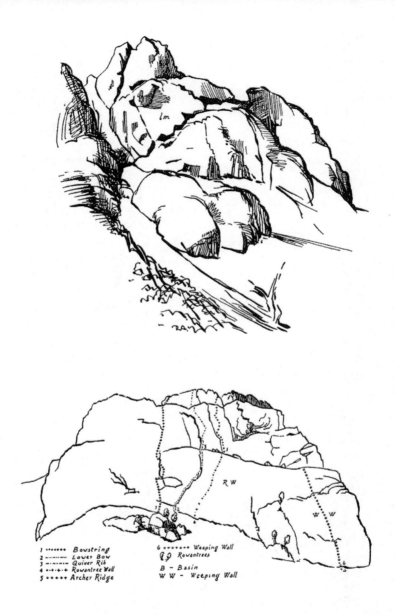

Top: Garbh Bheinn: North-East Buttress and Leac Mhor (lower middle).

Above: Aonach Dubh: east face from the bivouac.

ISLAND OF RUM

roads
paths

THE
CUILLIN
OF
SKYE

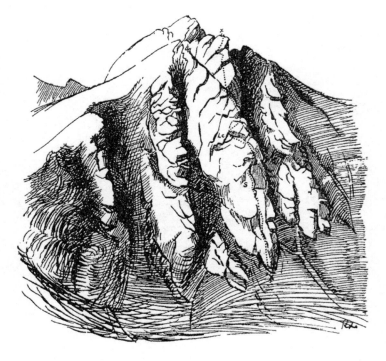

Rose Pinnacle, south face of Cir Mhor, Isle of Arran.
S = S crack. LC = Layback crack. Dotted line = route.

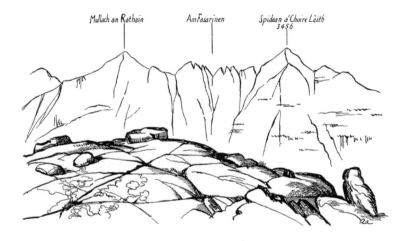

Liathach from Bealach Sgorr Ruadh-Beinn Liath Mhor.

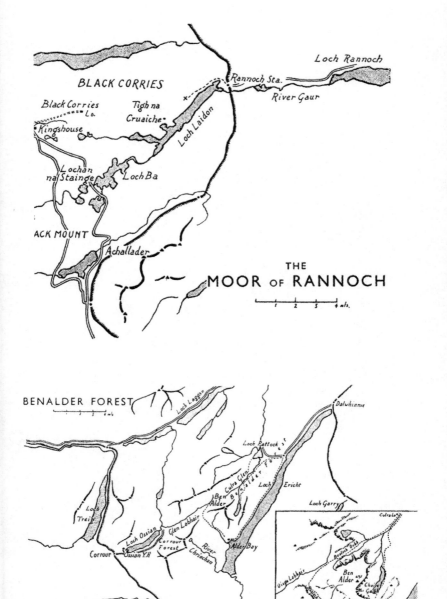

THE
MOOR OF RANNOCH

BLACK CORRIES

Black Corries Lo.

Kingshouse

Tigh na Cruaiche

Rannoch Sta.

Loch Rannoch

River Gaur

Loch Laidon

Lochan na Stainge

Loch Ba

ACK MOUNT

Achallader

BENALDER FOREST

Loch Laggan

Dalwhinnie

Loch Pattock

Culra Glen

Ben Alder

Loch Ericht

Loch Treig

Loch Garry

Culra

Loch Ossian

Corrour

Ossian Y.H.

Corrour Forest

Glen Labhair

River Chriachan

Alder Bay

Bealach Dubh

Glen Labhair

Ben Alder

Choire Gabh

Alder Burn

Benalder Cottage

Alder Bay

LOCH ERICHT

Loch Rannoch

Castle Buttress of Ben Nevis.
S = slabs.   IS = ice-scoop.   X = turning point.

Printed in Great Britain
by Amazon